CTHULHU
TALES
THE WHISPER OF MADNESS

ANDREW COSBY
ROSS RICHIE
founders

MARK WAID
editor-in-chief

ADAM FORTIER
vice president,
new business

CHIP MOSHER
marketing &
sales director

MATT GAGNON
managing editor

ED DUKESHIRE
designer

Office of publication: 6310 San Vicente Blvd, Ste 404, Los Angeles, CA 90048-5457.

First Edition: September 2008

10 9 8 7 6 5 4 3 2 1
PRINTED IN KOREA

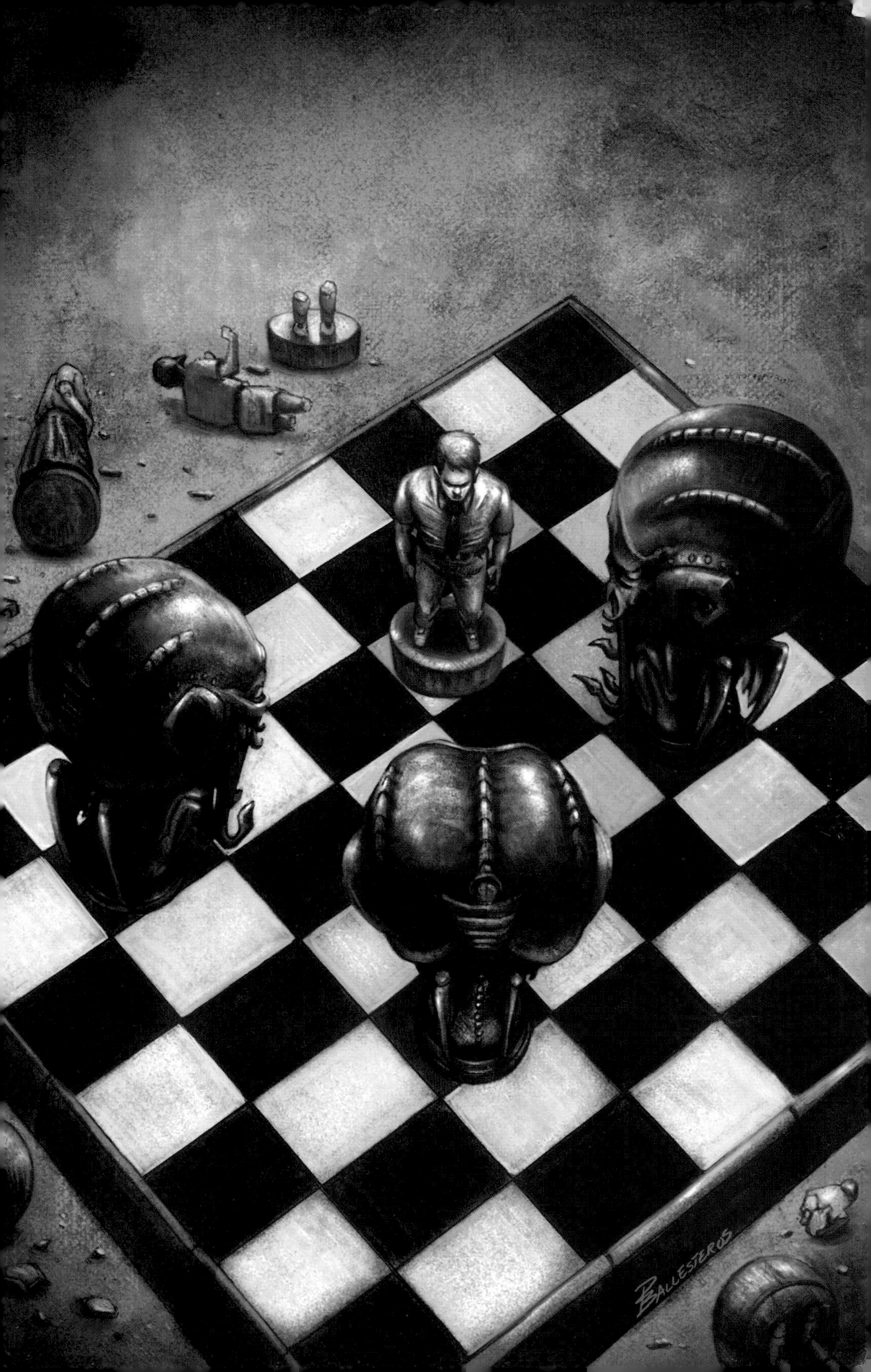
BALLESTEROS

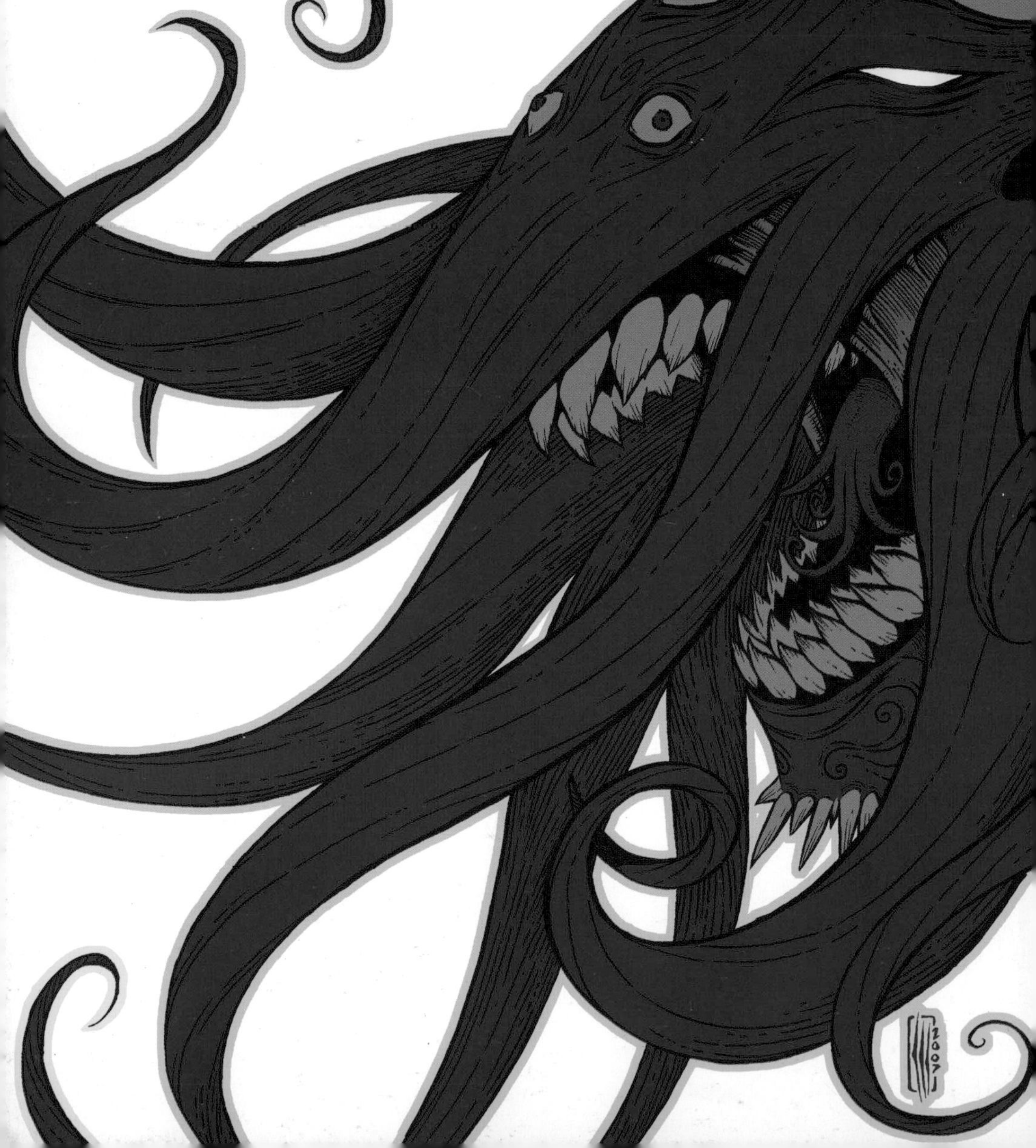

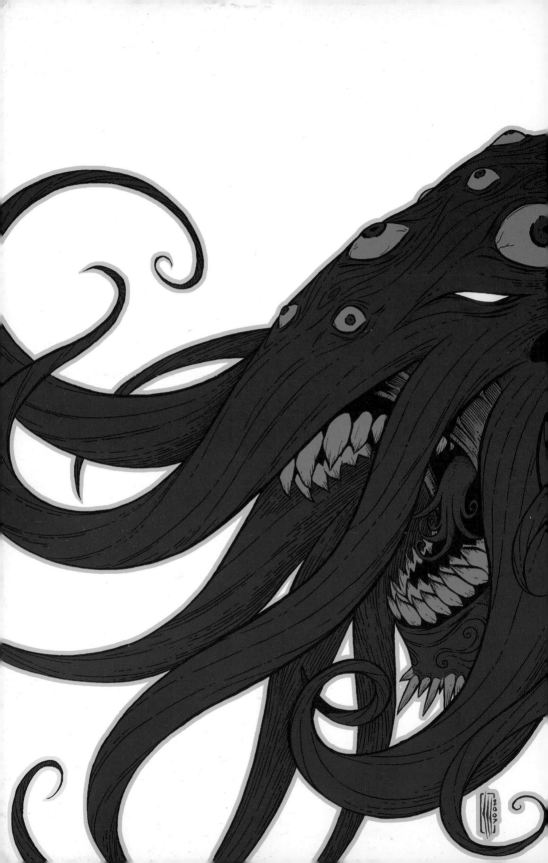

THE EYES OF MADNESS
STORY **STEVE NILES**

ART **CHEE**

THE FARM
STORY **MICHAEL ALAN NELSON**

ART **SUNDER RAJ**

EXACTLY THE RIGHT WORD
STORY **TOM PEYER**

ART **CHEE**

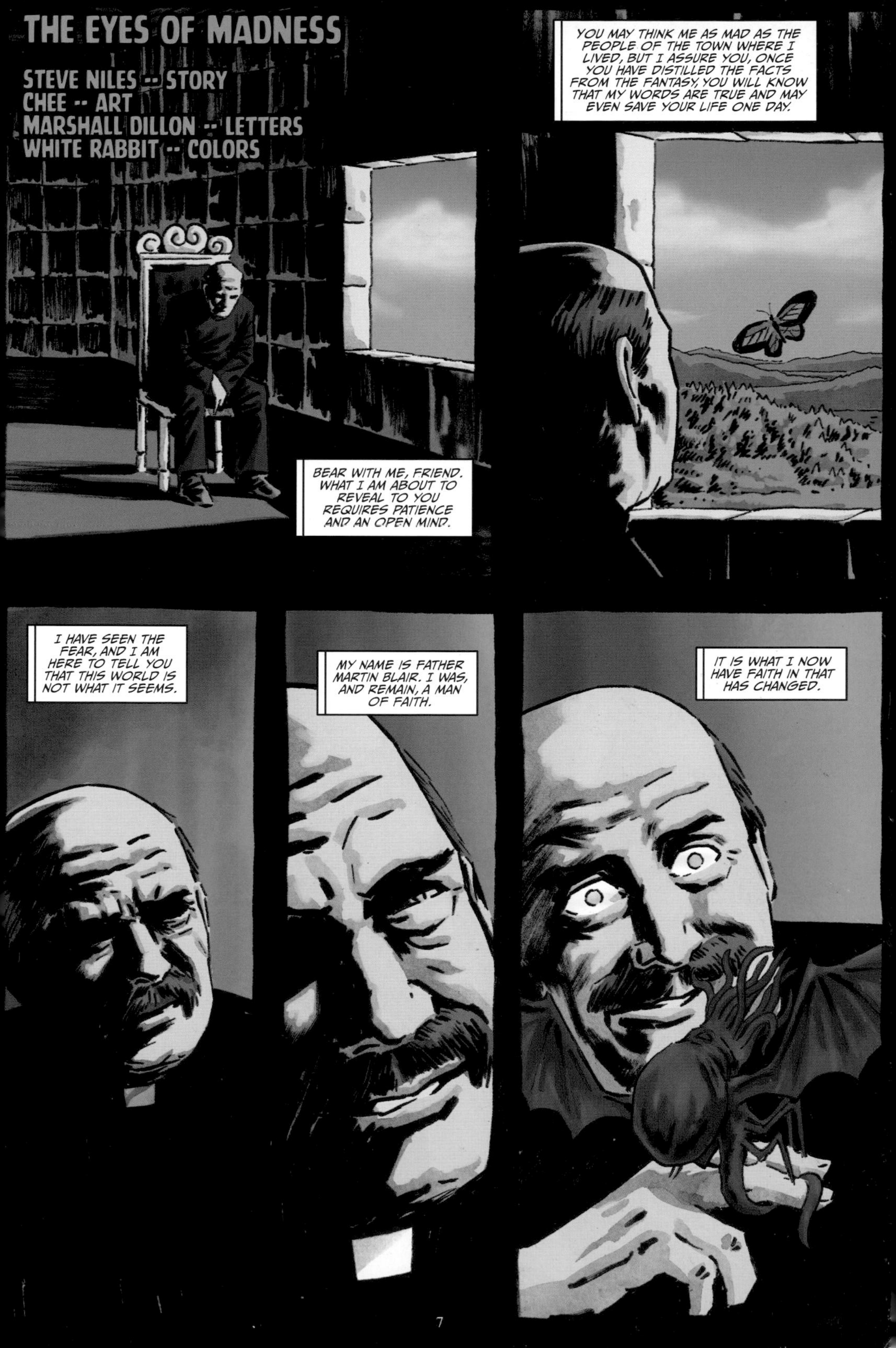
THE EYES OF MADNESS
STEVE NILES -- STORY
CHEE -- ART
MARSHALL DILLON -- LETTERS
WHITE RABBIT -- COLORS
BEAR WITH ME, FRIEND. WHAT I AM ABOUT TO REVEAL TO YOU REQUIRES PATIENCE AND AN OPEN MIND.
YOU MAY THINK ME AS MAD AS THE PEOPLE OF THE TOWN WHERE I LIVED, BUT I ASSURE YOU, ONCE YOU HAVE DISTILLED THE FACTS FROM THE FANTASY, YOU WILL KNOW THAT MY WORDS ARE TRUE AND MAY EVEN SAVE YOUR LIFE ONE DAY.
I HAVE SEEN THE FEAR, AND I AM HERE TO TELL YOU THAT THIS WORLD IS NOT WHAT IT SEEMS.
MY NAME IS FATHER MARTIN BLAIR. I WAS, AND REMAIN, A MAN OF FAITH.
IT IS WHAT I NOW HAVE FAITH IN THAT HAS CHANGED.

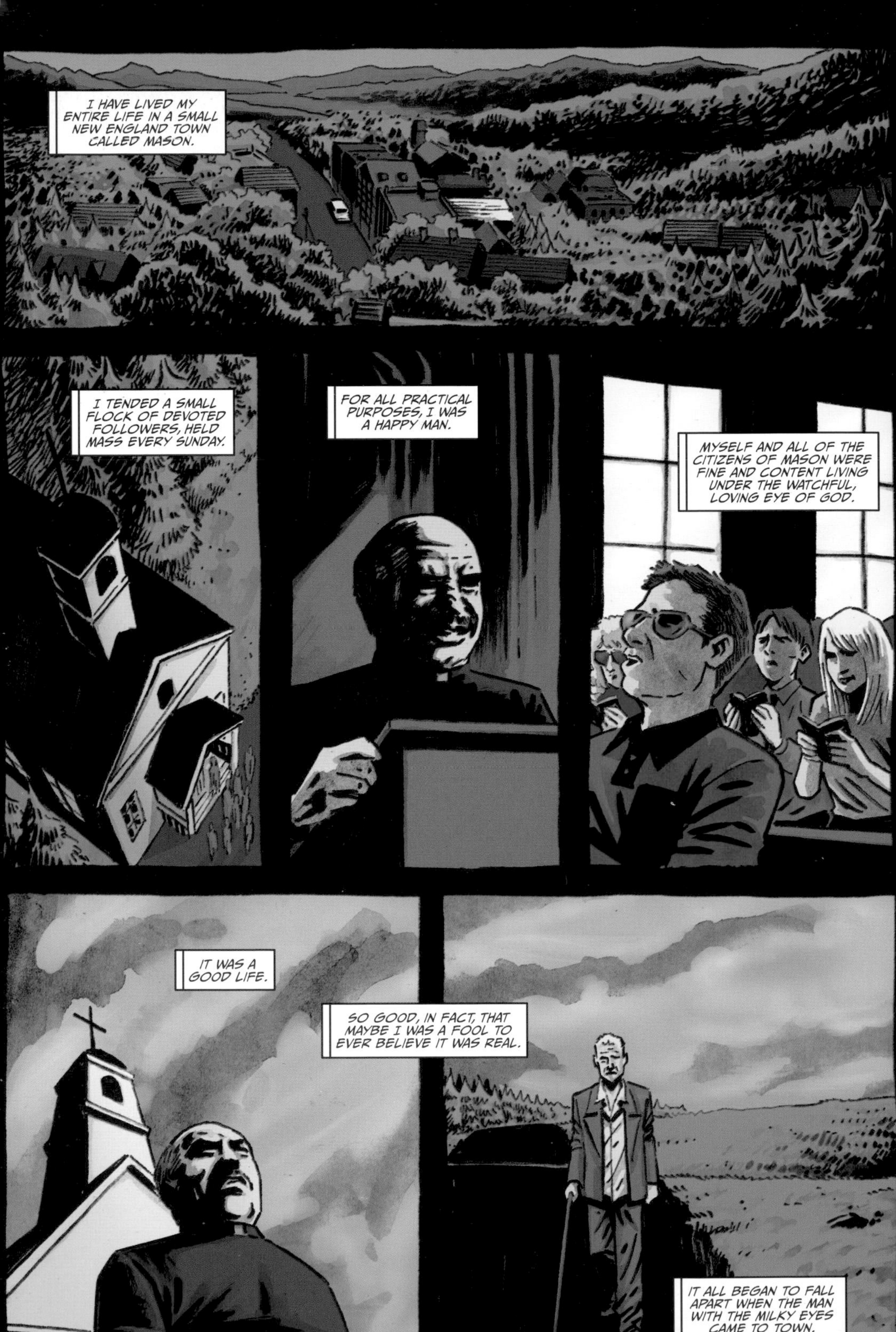
I HAVE LIVED MY ENTIRE LIFE IN A SMALL NEW ENGLAND TOWN CALLED MASON.
I TENDED A SMALL FLOCK OF DEVOTED FOLLOWERS, HELD MASS EVERY SUNDAY.
FOR ALL PRACTICAL PURPOSES, I WAS A HAPPY MAN.
MYSELF AND ALL OF THE CITIZENS OF MASON WERE FINE AND CONTENT LIVING UNDER THE WATCHFUL, LOVING EYE OF GOD.
IT WAS A GOOD LIFE.
SO GOOD, IN FACT, THAT MAYBE I WAS A FOOL TO EVER BELIEVE IT WAS REAL.
IT ALL BEGAN TO FALL APART WHEN THE MAN WITH THE MILKY EYES CAME TO TOWN.

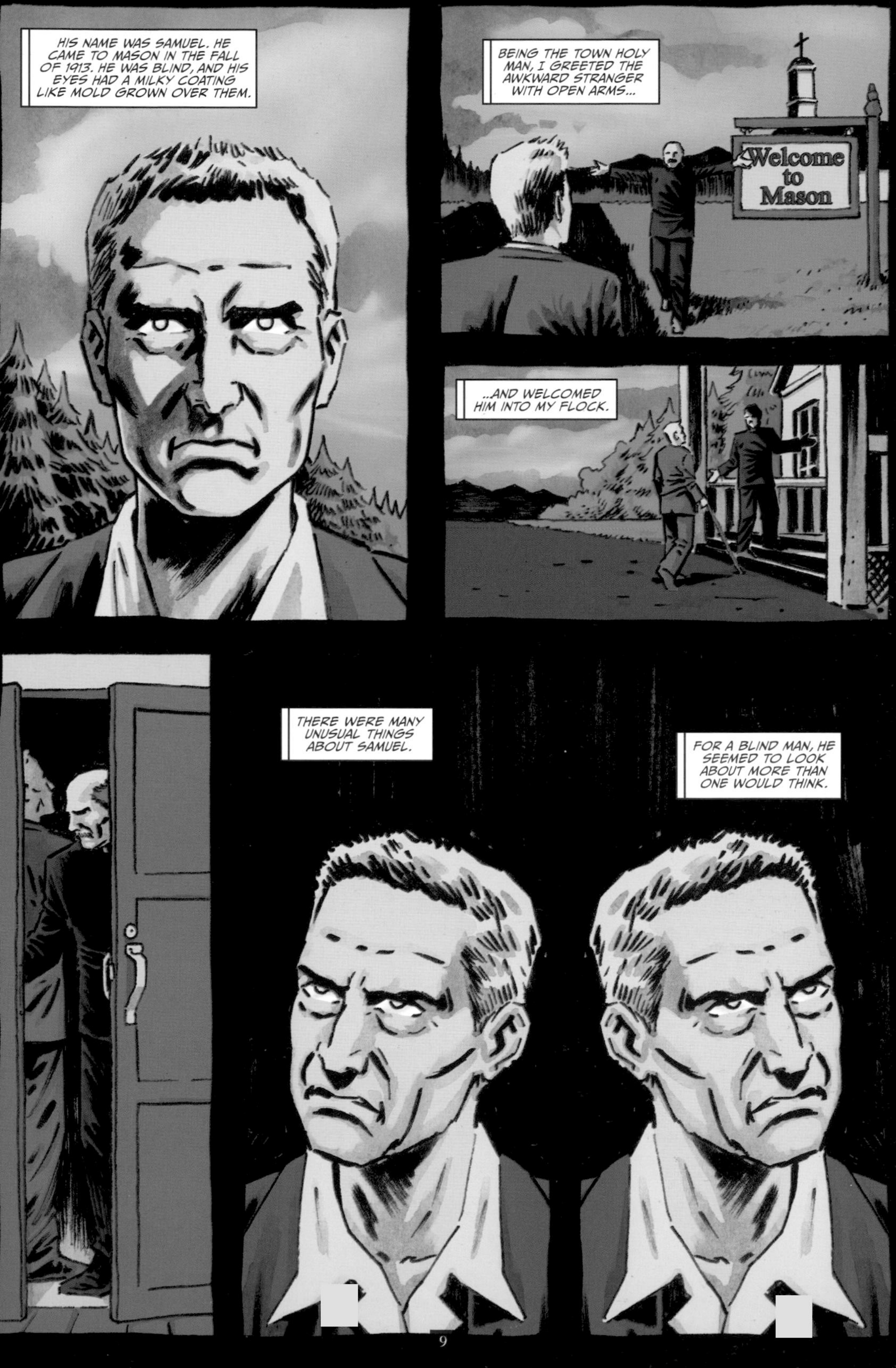
HIS NAME WAS SAMUEL. HE CAME TO MASON IN THE FALL OF 1913. HE WAS BLIND, AND HIS EYES HAD A MILKY COATING LIKE MOLD GROWN OVER THEM.
BEING THE TOWN HOLY MAN, I GREETED THE AWKWARD STRANGER WITH OPEN ARMS...
Welcome to Mason
...AND WELCOMED HIM INTO MY FLOCK.
THERE WERE MANY UNUSUAL THINGS ABOUT SAMUEL.
FOR A BLIND MAN, HE SEEMED TO LOOK ABOUT MORE THAN ONE WOULD THINK.

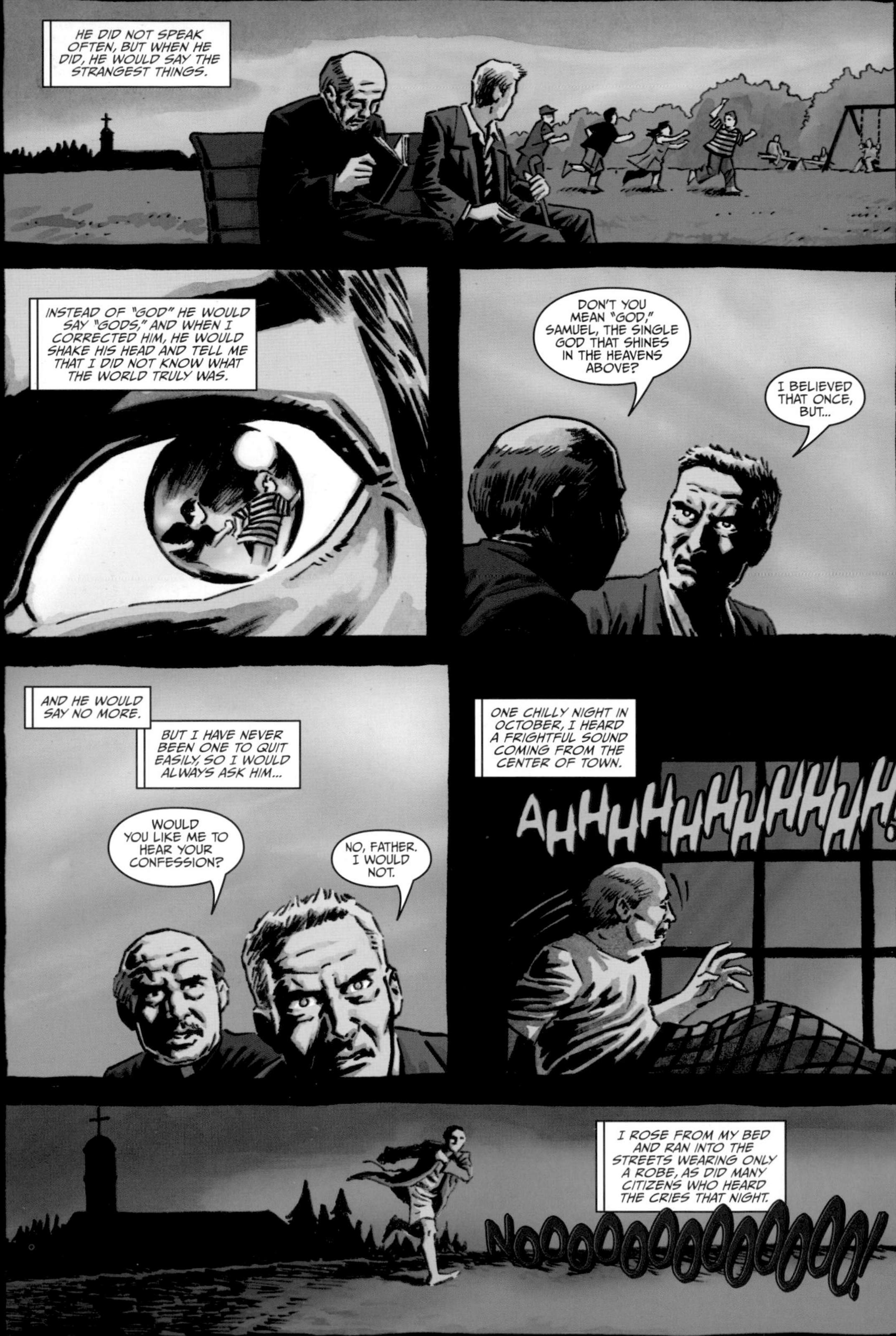
HE DID NOT SPEAK OFTEN, BUT WHEN HE DID, HE WOULD SAY THE STRANGEST THINGS.
INSTEAD OF "GOD" HE WOULD SAY "GODS," AND WHEN I CORRECTED HIM, HE WOULD SHAKE HIS HEAD AND TELL ME THAT I DID NOT KNOW WHAT THE WORLD TRULY WAS.
DON'T YOU MEAN "GOD," SAMUEL, THE SINGLE GOD THAT SHINES IN THE HEAVENS ABOVE?
I BELIEVED THAT ONCE, BUT...
AND HE WOULD SAY NO MORE.
BUT I HAVE NEVER BEEN ONE TO QUIT EASILY, SO I WOULD ALWAYS ASK HIM...
WOULD YOU LIKE ME TO HEAR YOUR CONFESSION?
NO, FATHER. I WOULD NOT.
ONE CHILLY NIGHT IN OCTOBER, I HEARD A FRIGHTFUL SOUND COMING FROM THE CENTER OF TOWN.
AHHHHHHHHHHHHHH!
I ROSE FROM MY BED AND RAN INTO THE STREETS WEARING ONLY A ROBE, AS DID MANY CITIZENS WHO HEARD THE CRIES THAT NIGHT.
NOOOOOOOOOOOOOO!

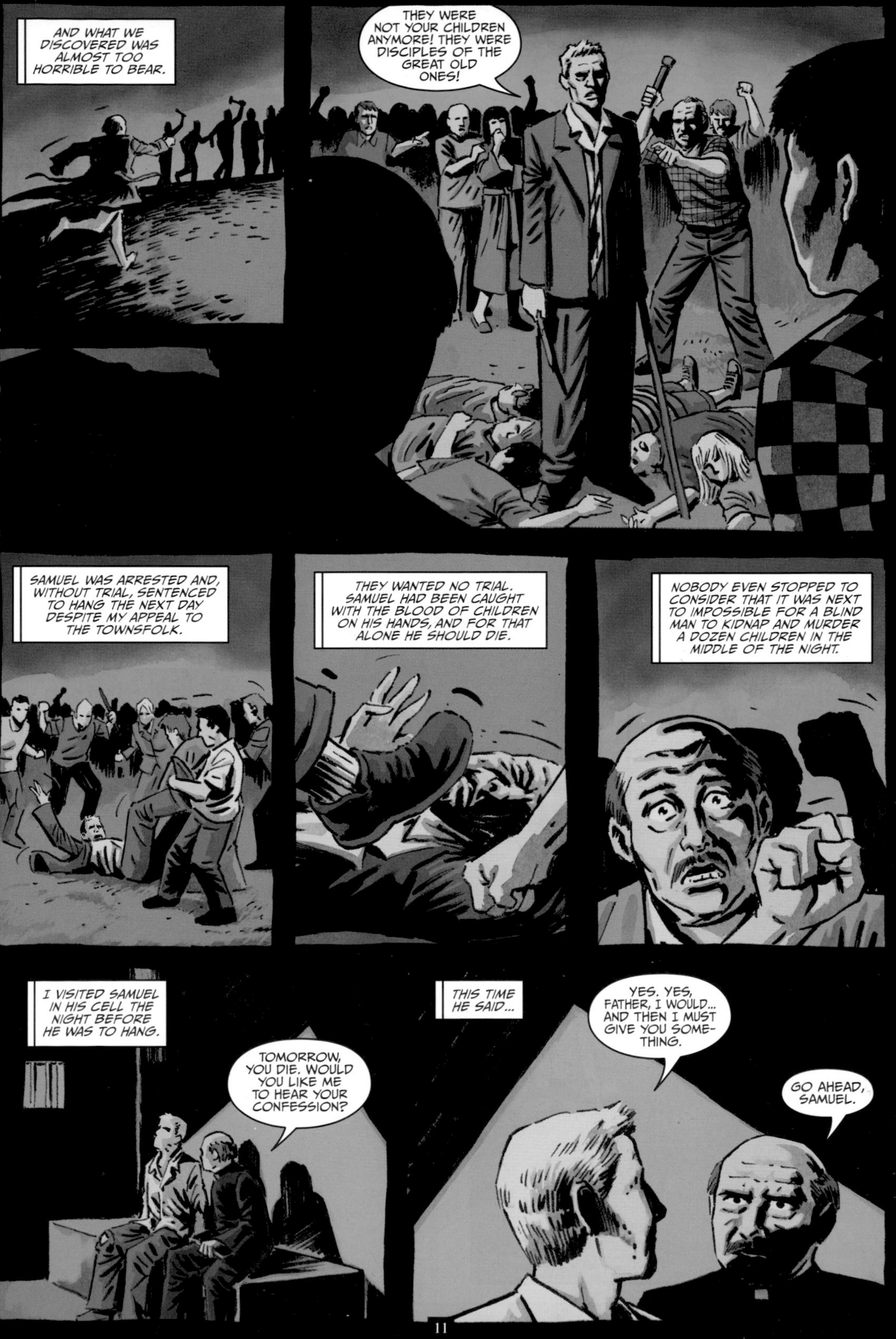
AND WHAT WE DISCOVERED WAS ALMOST TOO HORRIBLE TO BEAR.
THEY WERE NOT YOUR CHILDREN ANYMORE! THEY WERE DISCIPLES OF THE GREAT OLD ONES!
SAMUEL WAS ARRESTED AND, WITHOUT TRIAL, SENTENCED TO HANG THE NEXT DAY DESPITE MY APPEAL TO THE TOWNSFOLK.
THEY WANTED NO TRIAL. SAMUEL HAD BEEN CAUGHT WITH THE BLOOD OF CHILDREN ON HIS HANDS, AND FOR THAT ALONE HE SHOULD DIE.
NOBODY EVEN STOPPED TO CONSIDER THAT IT WAS NEXT TO IMPOSSIBLE FOR A BLIND MAN TO KIDNAP AND MURDER A DOZEN CHILDREN IN THE MIDDLE OF THE NIGHT.
I VISITED SAMUEL IN HIS CELL THE NIGHT BEFORE HE WAS TO HANG.
TOMORROW, YOU DIE. WOULD YOU LIKE ME TO HEAR YOUR CONFESSION?
THIS TIME HE SAID...
YES. YES, FATHER, I WOULD... AND THEN I MUST GIVE YOU SOMETHING.
GO AHEAD, SAMUEL.

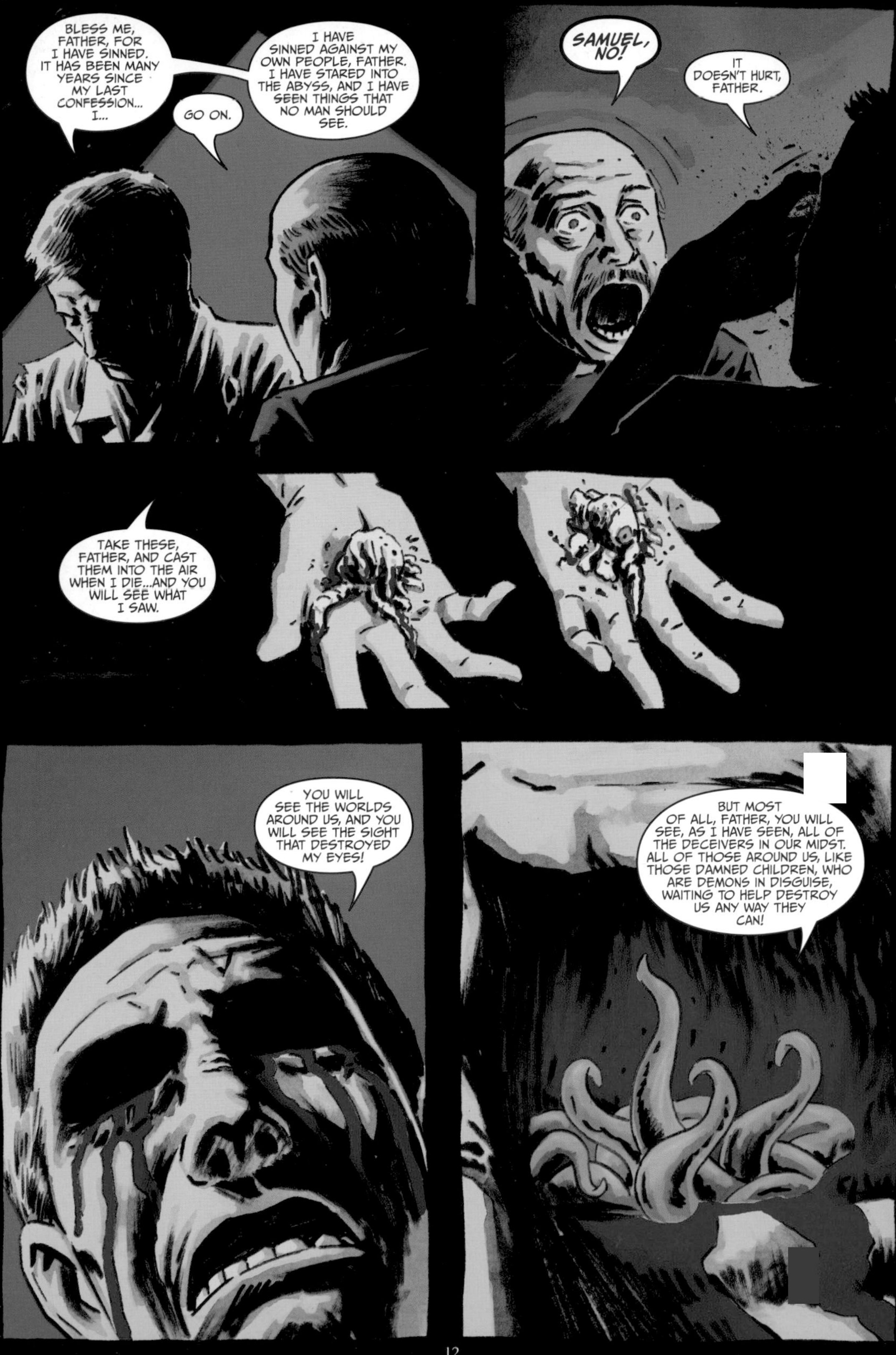

BLESS ME, FATHER, FOR I HAVE SINNED. IT HAS BEEN MANY YEARS SINCE MY LAST CONFESSION... I...
GO ON.
I HAVE SINNED AGAINST MY OWN PEOPLE, FATHER. I HAVE STARED INTO THE ABYSS, AND I HAVE SEEN THINGS THAT NO MAN SHOULD SEE.
SAMUEL, NO!
IT DOESN'T HURT, FATHER.
TAKE THESE, FATHER, AND CAST THEM INTO THE AIR WHEN I DIE...AND YOU WILL SEE WHAT I SAW.
YOU WILL SEE THE WORLDS AROUND US, AND YOU WILL SEE THE SIGHT THAT DESTROYED MY EYES!
BUT MOST OF ALL, FATHER, YOU WILL SEE, AS I HAVE SEEN, ALL OF THE DECEIVERS IN OUR MIDST. ALL OF THOSE AROUND US, LIKE THOSE DAMNED CHILDREN, WHO ARE DEMONS IN DISGUISE, WAITING TO HELP DESTROY US ANY WAY THEY CAN!

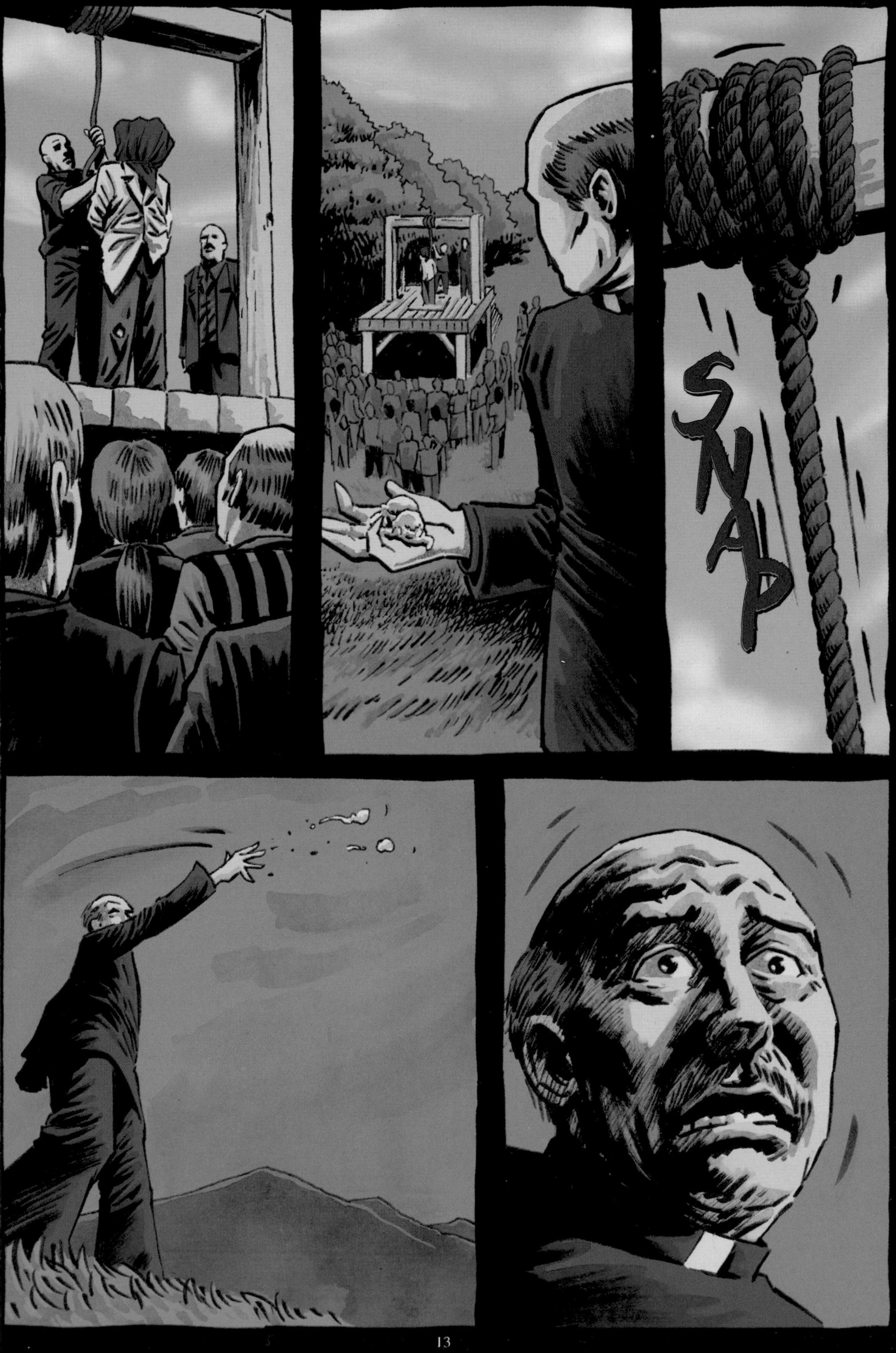
SNAP

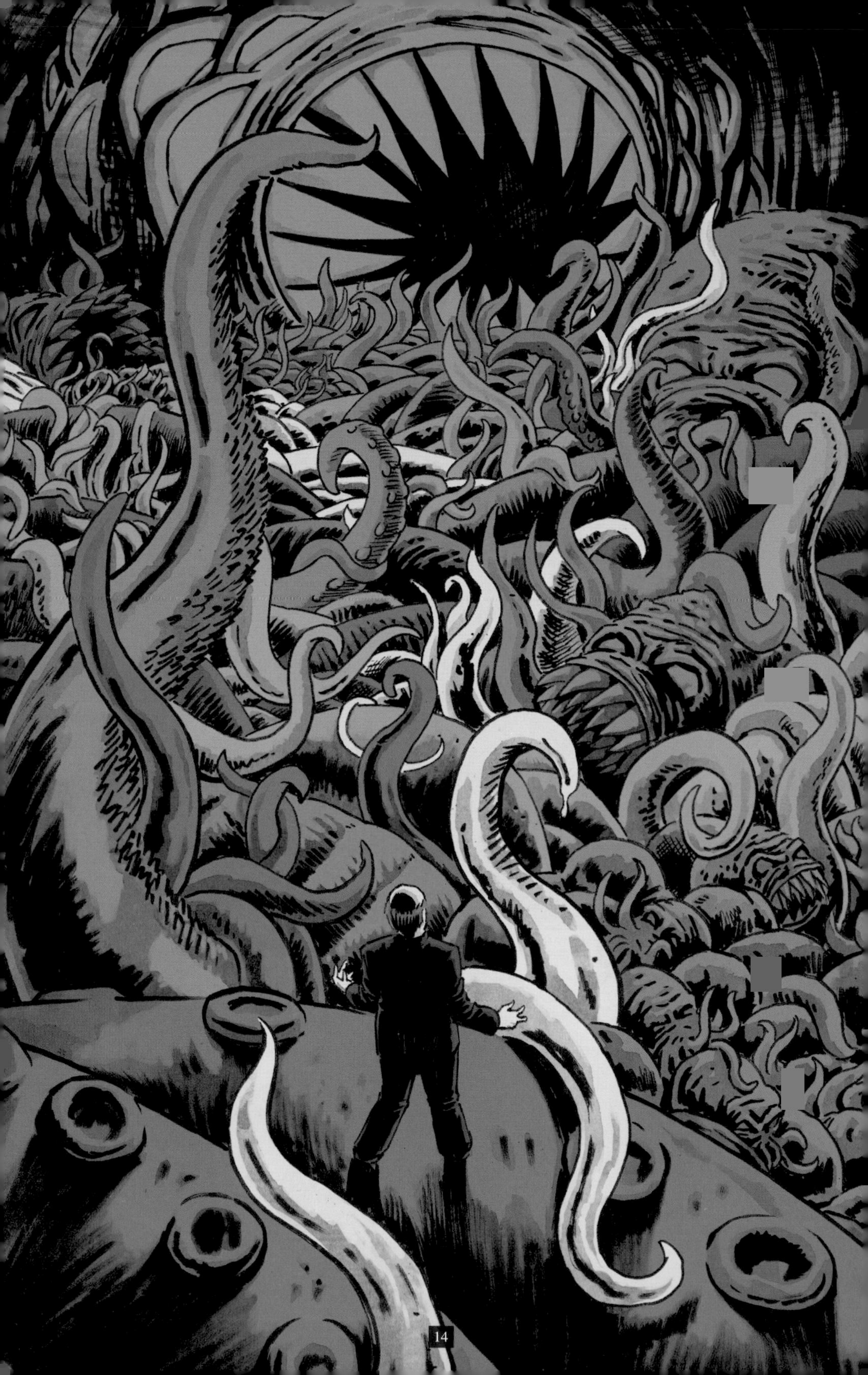

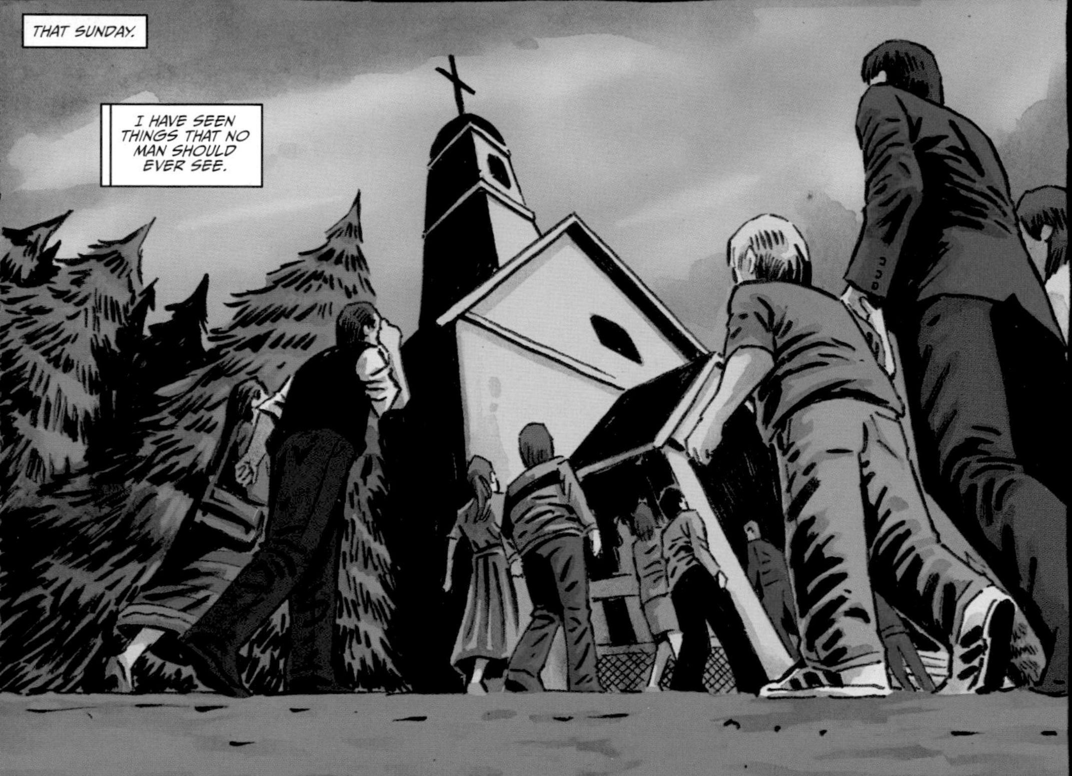
THAT SUNDAY.
I HAVE SEEN THINGS THAT NO MAN SHOULD EVER SEE.

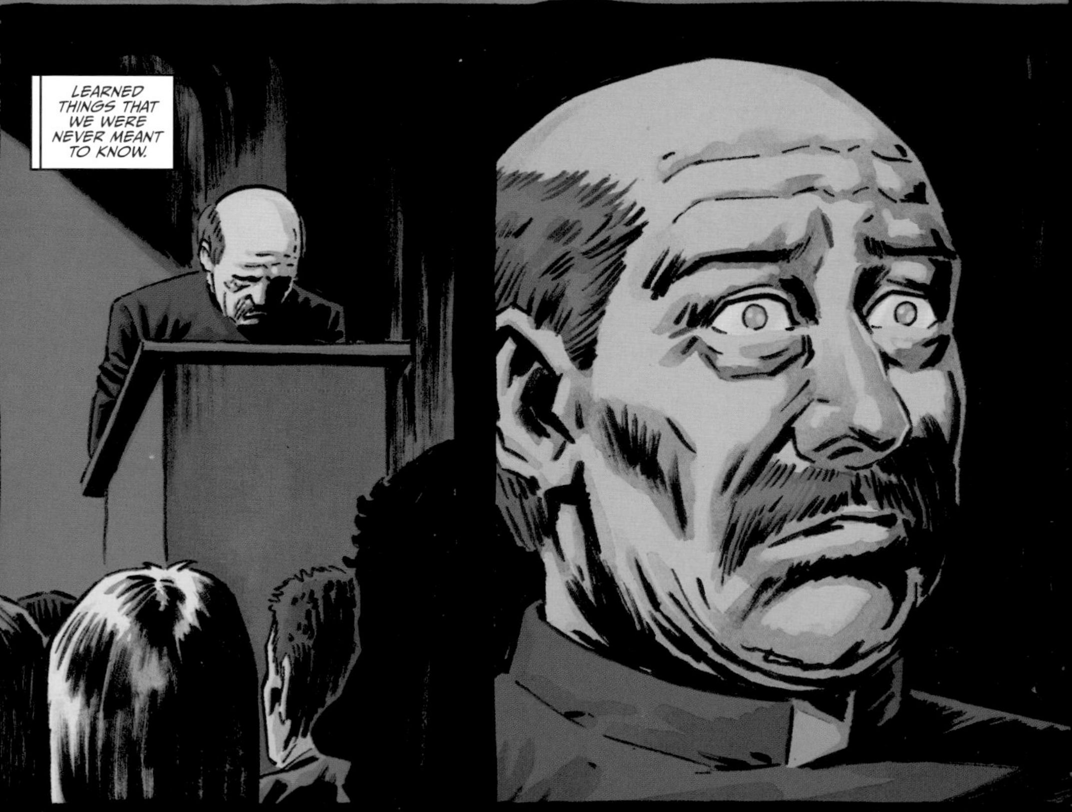
LEARNED THINGS THAT WE WERE NEVER MEANT TO KNOW.

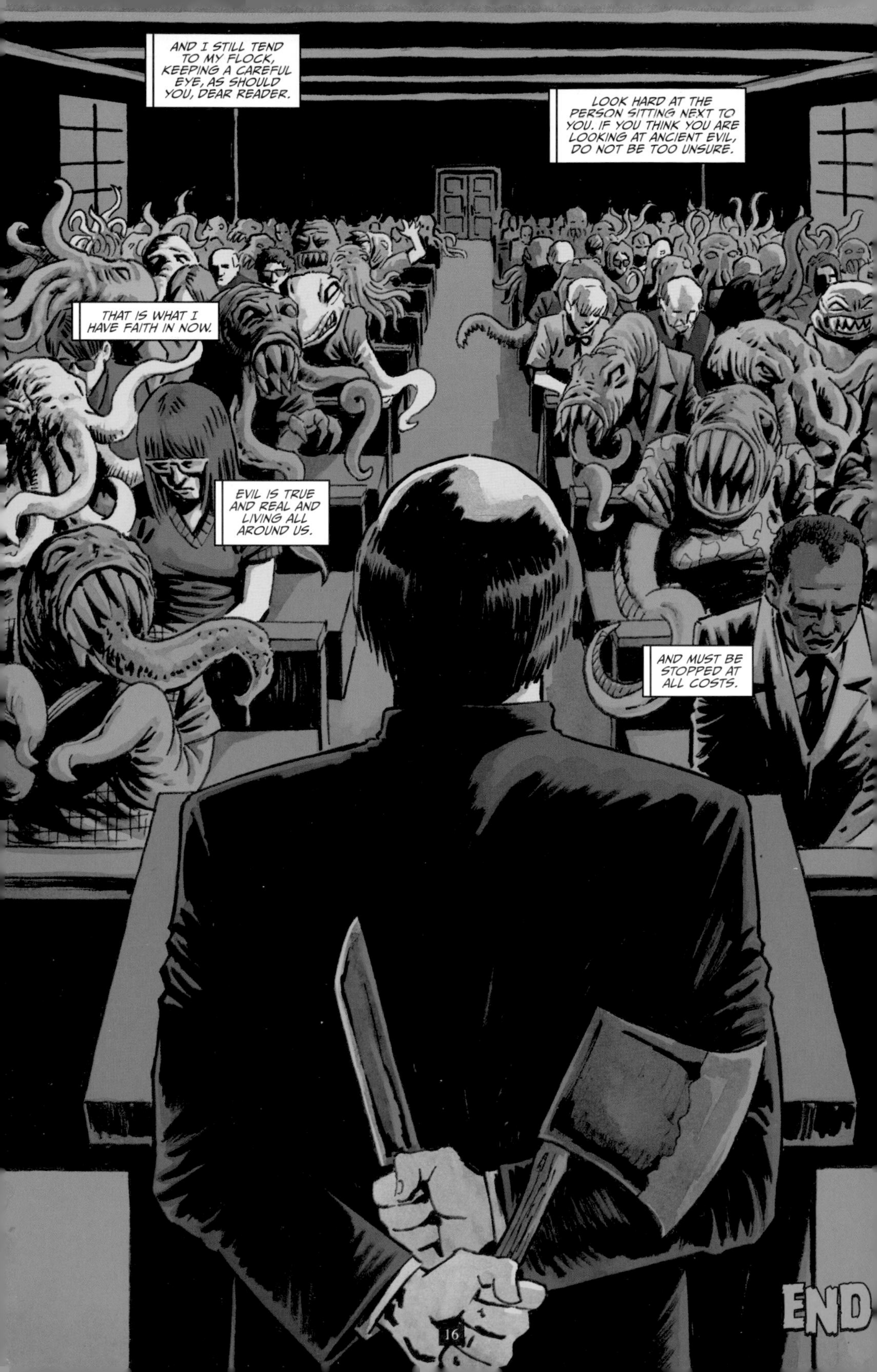
AND I STILL TEND TO MY FLOCK, KEEPING A CAREFUL EYE, AS SHOULD YOU, DEAR READER.
LOOK HARD AT THE PERSON SITTING NEXT TO YOU. IF YOU THINK YOU ARE LOOKING AT ANCIENT EVIL, DO NOT BE TOO UNSURE.
THAT IS WHAT I HAVE FAITH IN NOW.
EVIL IS TRUE AND REAL AND LIVING ALL AROUND US.
AND MUST BE STOPPED AT ALL COSTS.
END

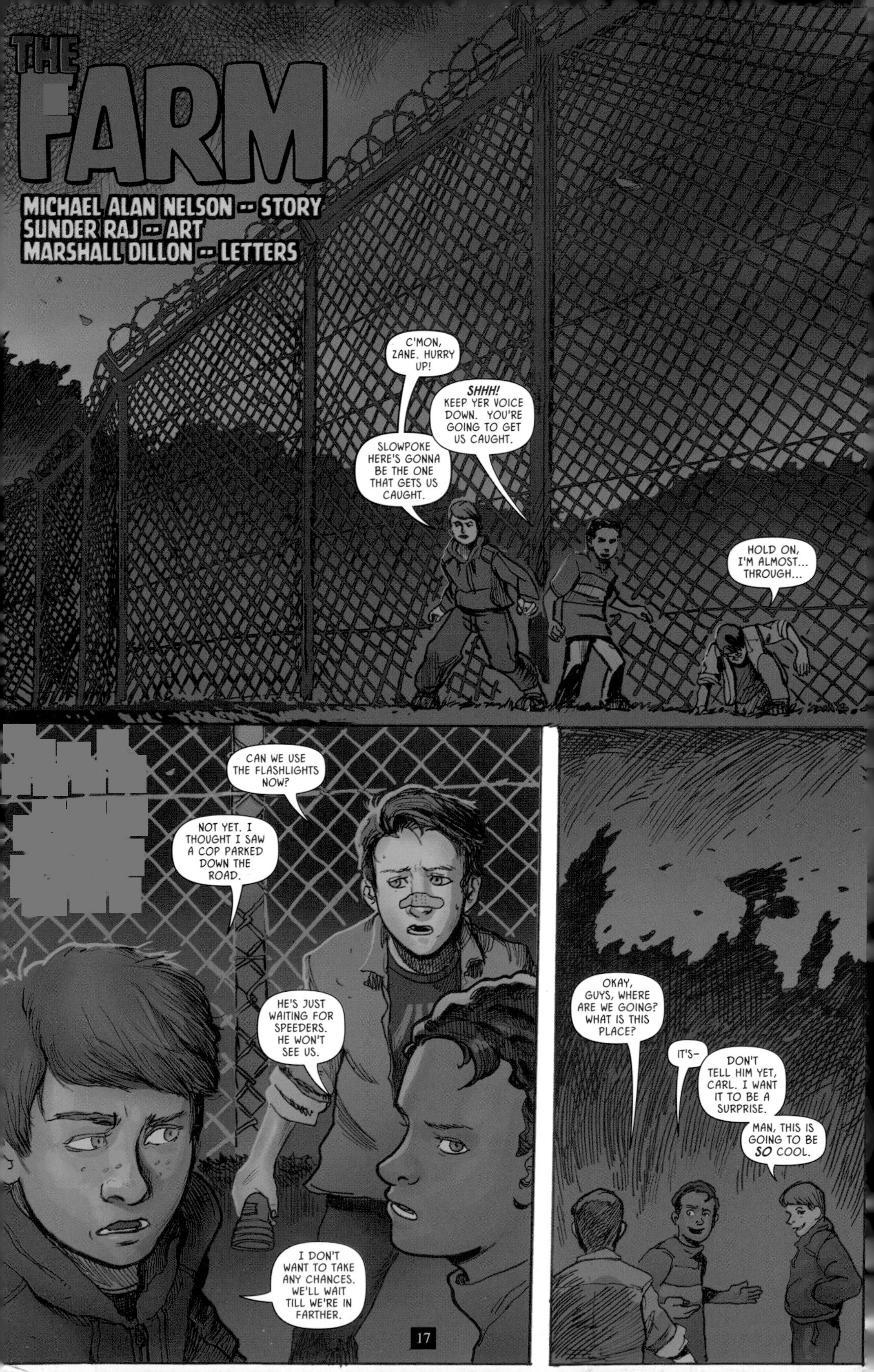
THE FARM
MICHAEL ALAN NELSON -- STORY
SUNDER RAJ -- ART
MARSHALL DILLON -- LETTERS
C'MON, ZANE. HURRY UP!
SLOWPOKE HERE'S GONNA BE THE ONE THAT GETS US CAUGHT.
SHHH! KEEP YER VOICE DOWN. YOU'RE GOING TO GET US CAUGHT.
HOLD ON, I'M ALMOST... THROUGH...
CAN WE USE THE FLASHLIGHTS NOW?
NOT YET. I THOUGHT I SAW A COP PARKED DOWN THE ROAD.
HE'S JUST WAITING FOR SPEEDERS. HE WON'T SEE US.
I DON'T WANT TO TAKE ANY CHANCES. WE'LL WAIT TILL WE'RE IN FARTHER.
OKAY, GUYS, WHERE ARE WE GOING? WHAT IS THIS PLACE?
IT'S—
DON'T TELL HIM YET, CARL. I WANT IT TO BE A SURPRISE.
MAN, THIS IS GOING TO BE SO COOL.

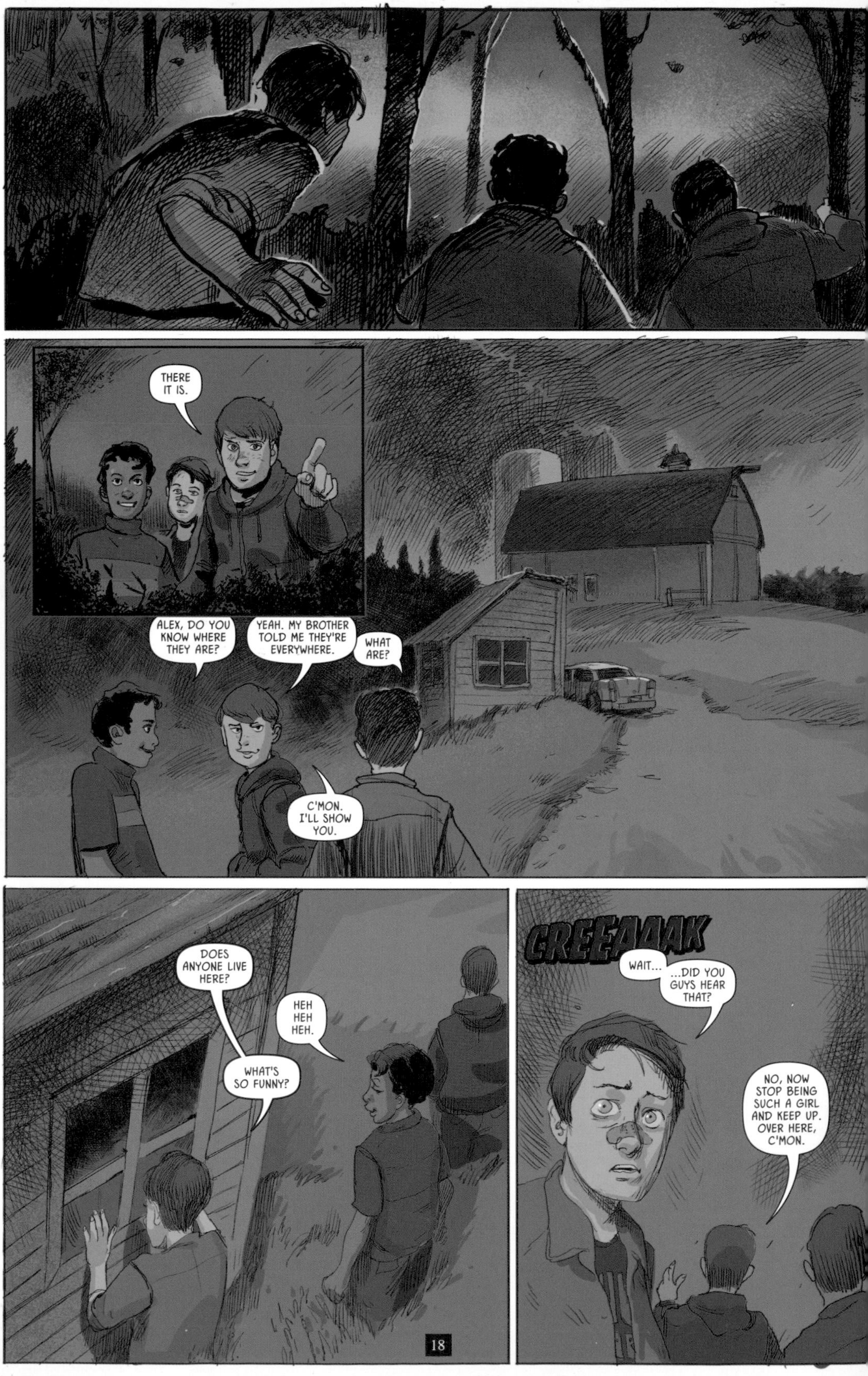
THERE IT IS.
ALEX, DO YOU KNOW WHERE THEY ARE?
YEAH. MY BROTHER TOLD ME THEY'RE EVERYWHERE.
WHAT ARE?
C'MON. I'LL SHOW YOU.
DOES ANYONE LIVE HERE?
HEH HEH HEH.
WHAT'S SO FUNNY?
CREEAAAK
WAIT...
...DID YOU GUYS HEAR THAT?
NO, NOW STOP BEING SUCH A GIRL AND KEEP UP. OVER HERE, C'MON.

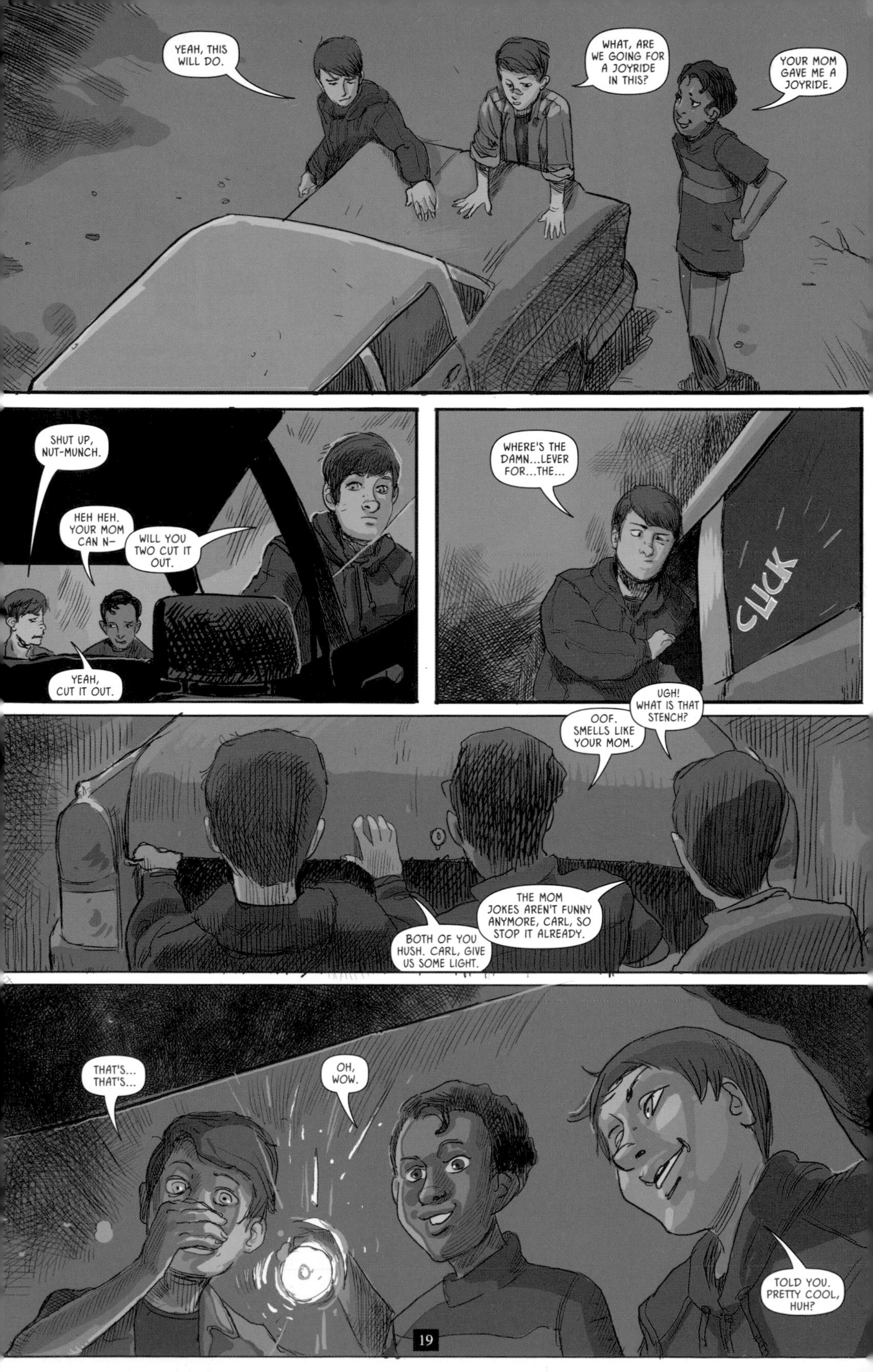
YEAH, THIS WILL DO.
WHAT, ARE WE GOING FOR A JOYRIDE IN THIS?
YOUR MOM GAVE ME A JOYRIDE.
SHUT UP, NUT-MUNCH.
HEH HEH. YOUR MOM CAN N–
WILL YOU TWO CUT IT OUT.
YEAH, CUT IT OUT.
WHERE'S THE DAMN...LEVER FOR...THE...
CLICK
OOF. SMELLS LIKE YOUR MOM.
UGH! WHAT IS THAT STENCH?
THE MOM JOKES AREN'T FUNNY ANYMORE, CARL, SO STOP IT ALREADY.
BOTH OF YOU HUSH. CARL, GIVE US SOME LIGHT.
THAT'S... THAT'S...
OH, WOW.
TOLD YOU. PRETTY COOL, HUH?

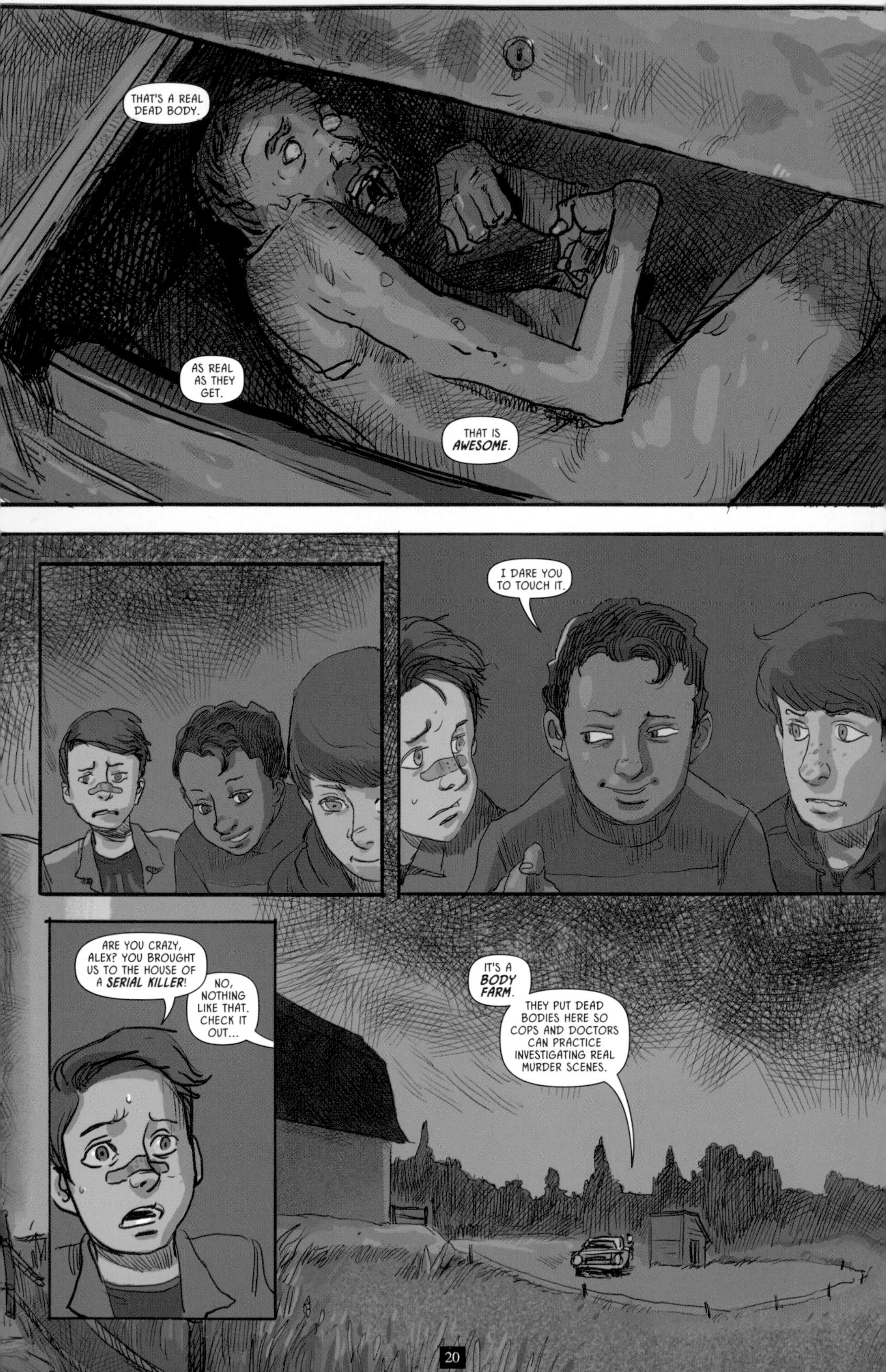
THAT'S A REAL DEAD BODY.
AS REAL AS THEY GET.
THAT IS **AWESOME**.
I DARE YOU TO TOUCH IT.
ARE YOU CRAZY, ALEX? YOU BROUGHT US TO THE HOUSE OF A **SERIAL KILLER**!
NO, NOTHING LIKE THAT. CHECK IT OUT...
IT'S A **BODY FARM**.
THEY PUT DEAD BODIES HERE SO COPS AND DOCTORS CAN PRACTICE INVESTIGATING REAL MURDER SCENES.

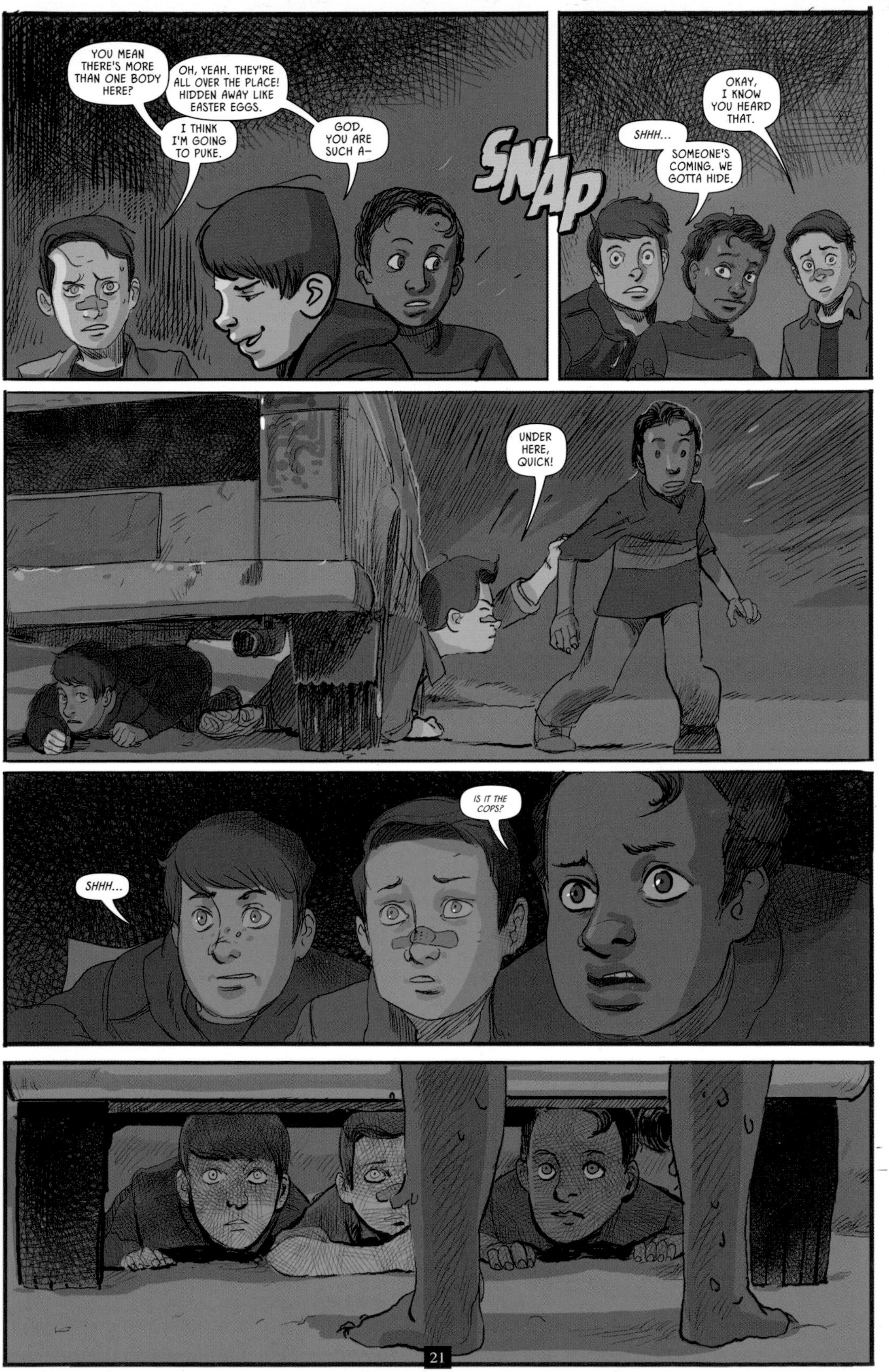
YOU MEAN THERE'S MORE THAN ONE BODY HERE?
OH, YEAH. THEY'RE ALL OVER THE PLACE! HIDDEN AWAY LIKE EASTER EGGS.
I THINK I'M GOING TO PUKE.
GOD, YOU ARE SUCH A–
SNAP
SHHH...
SOMEONE'S COMING. WE GOTTA HIDE.
OKAY, I KNOW YOU HEARD THAT.
UNDER HERE, QUICK!
SHHH...
IS IT THE COPS?

RIIIP!
GGRRRRGHHH...
WHAT'S IT DO-MMPH!
RARGGGHHH!
AAAAHHHH!!!

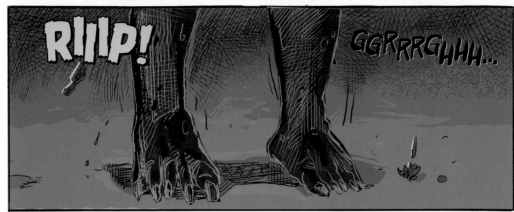

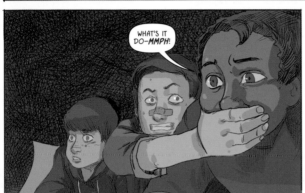

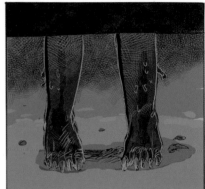

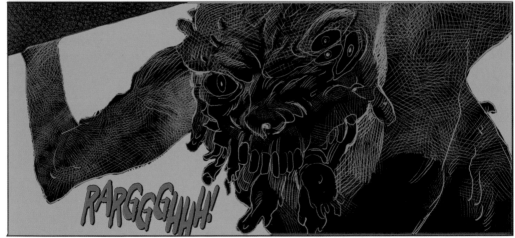

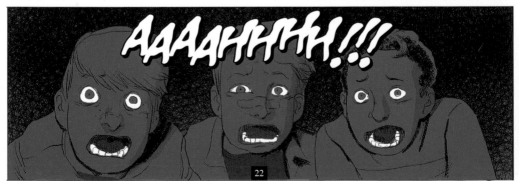

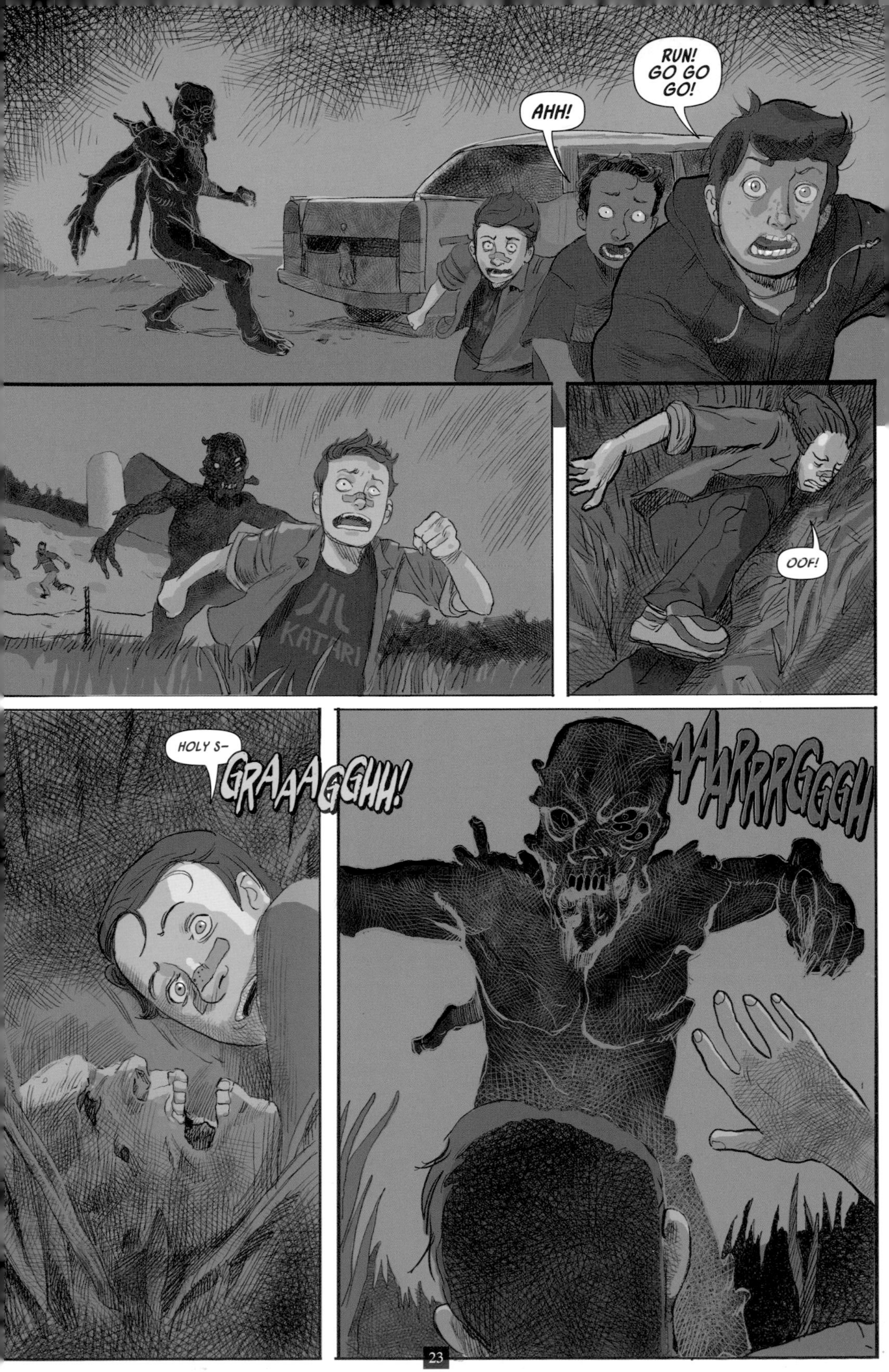
RUN! GO GO GO!
AHH!
KATARI
OOF!
HOLY S–
GRAAAGGHH!
AAARRRGGGH

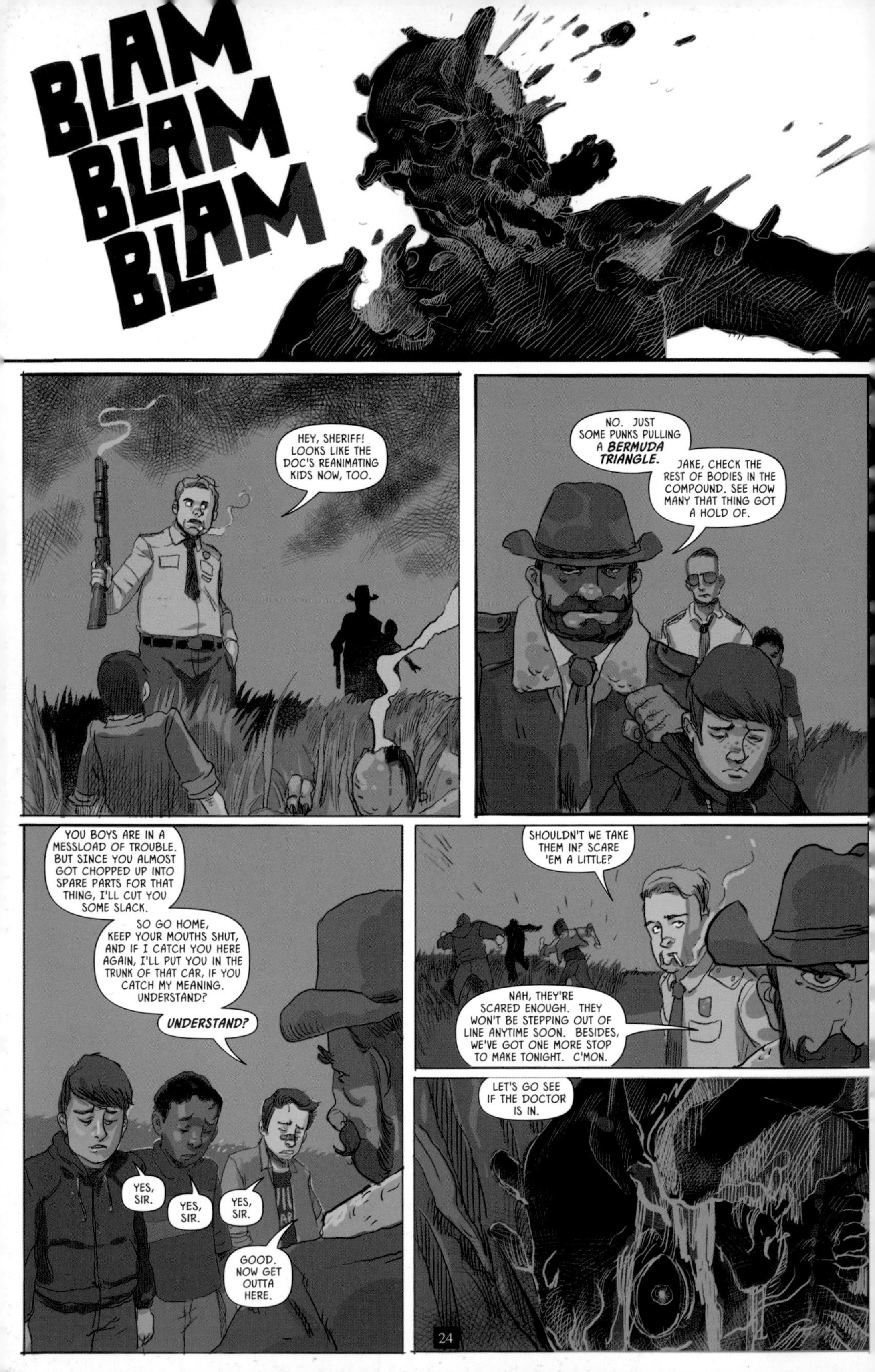
BLAM BLAM BLAM BLAM
HEY, SHERIFF! LOOKS LIKE THE DOC'S REANIMATING KIDS NOW, TOO.
NO. JUST SOME PUNKS PULLING A BERMUDA TRIANGLE.
JAKE, CHECK THE REST OF BODIES IN THE COMPOUND. SEE HOW MANY THAT THING GOT A HOLD OF.
YOU BOYS ARE IN A MESSLOAD OF TROUBLE. BUT SINCE YOU ALMOST GOT CHOPPED UP INTO SPARE PARTS FOR THAT THING, I'LL CUT YOU SOME SLACK.
SO GO HOME, KEEP YOUR MOUTHS SHUT, AND IF I CATCH YOU HERE AGAIN, I'LL PUT YOU IN THE TRUNK OF THAT CAR, IF YOU CATCH MY MEANING. UNDERSTAND?
UNDERSTAND?
YES, SIR.
YES, SIR.
YES, SIR.
GOOD. NOW GET OUTTA HERE.
SHOULDN'T WE TAKE THEM IN? SCARE 'EM A LITTLE?
NAH, THEY'RE SCARED ENOUGH. THEY WON'T BE STEPPING OUT OF LINE ANYTIME SOON. BESIDES, WE'VE GOT ONE MORE STOP TO MAKE TONIGHT. C'MON.
LET'S GO SEE IF THE DOCTOR IS IN.

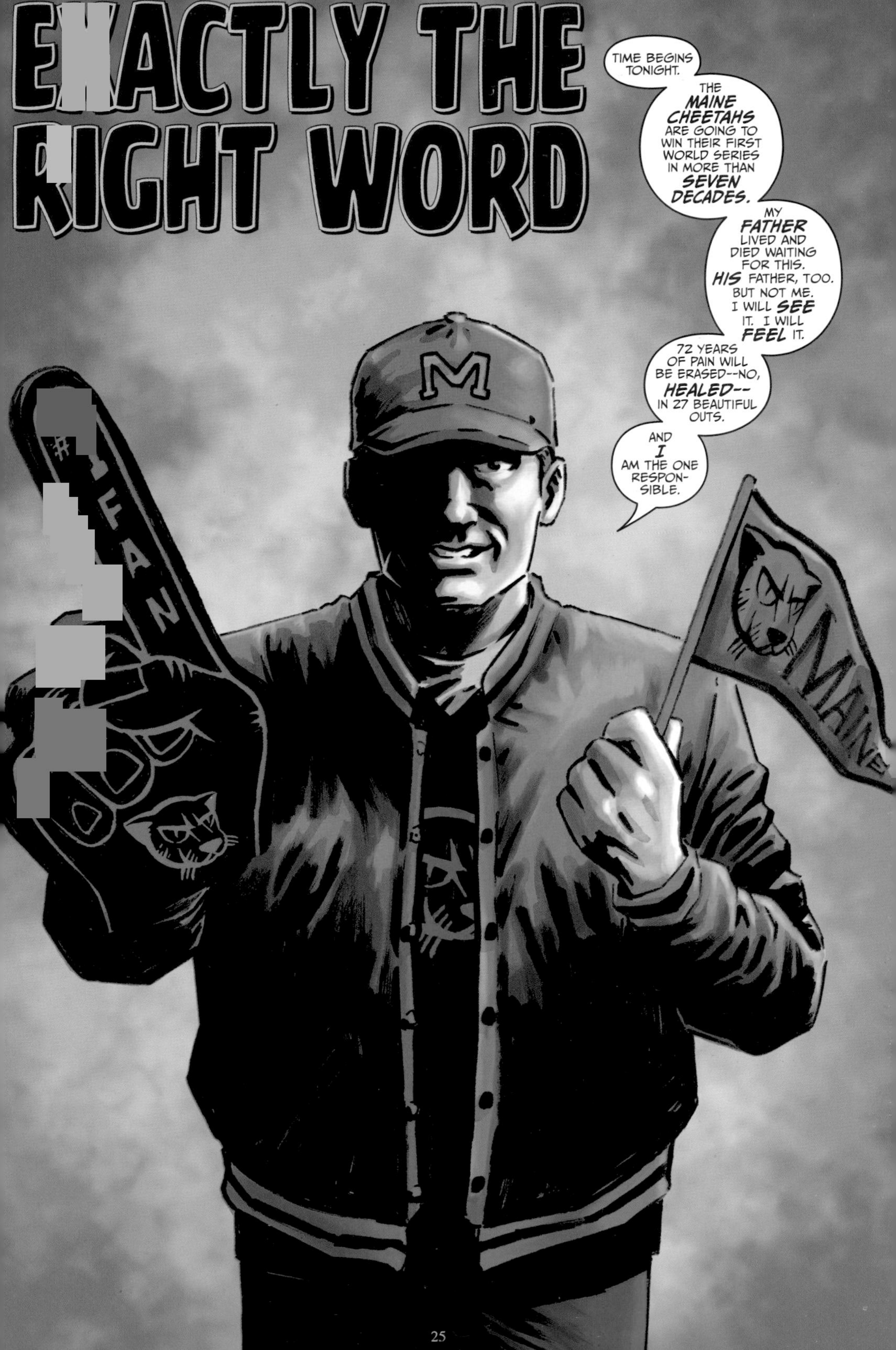
EXACTLY THE RIGHT WORD
TIME BEGINS TONIGHT.
THE MAINE CHEETAHS ARE GOING TO WIN THEIR FIRST WORLD SERIES IN MORE THAN SEVEN DECADES.
MY FATHER LIVED AND DIED WAITING FOR THIS. HIS FATHER, TOO. BUT NOT ME. I WILL SEE IT. I WILL FEEL IT.
72 YEARS OF PAIN WILL BE ERASED--NO, HEALED-- IN 27 BEAUTIFUL OUTS.
AND I AM THE ONE RESPONSIBLE.
M
#
FAN
MAINE

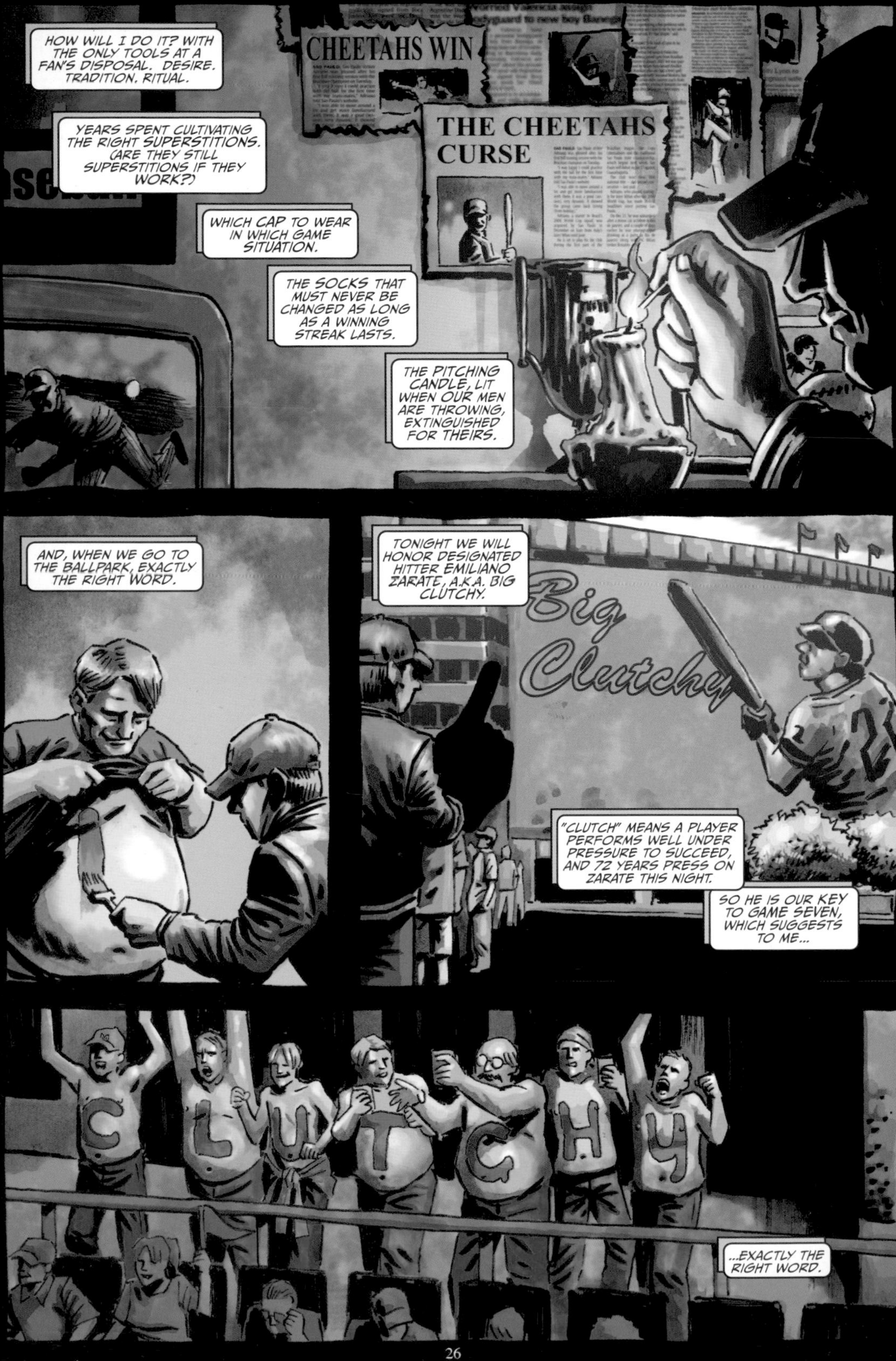

HOW WILL I DO IT? WITH THE ONLY TOOLS AT A FAN'S DISPOSAL. DESIRE. TRADITION. RITUAL.
CHEETAHS WIN
THE CHEETAHS CURSE
YEARS SPENT CULTIVATING THE RIGHT SUPERSTITIONS. (ARE THEY STILL SUPERSTITIONS IF THEY WORK?)
WHICH CAP TO WEAR IN WHICH GAME SITUATION.
THE SOCKS THAT MUST NEVER BE CHANGED AS LONG AS A WINNING STREAK LASTS.
THE PITCHING CANDLE, LIT WHEN OUR MEN ARE THROWING, EXTINGUISHED FOR THEIRS.
AND, WHEN WE GO TO THE BALLPARK, EXACTLY THE RIGHT WORD.
TONIGHT WE WILL HONOR DESIGNATED HITTER EMILIANO ZARATE, A.K.A. BIG CLUTCHY.
Big Clutchy
"CLUTCH" MEANS A PLAYER PERFORMS WELL UNDER PRESSURE TO SUCCEED, AND 72 YEARS PRESS ON ZARATE THIS NIGHT.
SO HE IS OUR KEY TO GAME SEVEN, WHICH SUGGESTS TO ME...
C L U T C H Y
...EXACTLY THE RIGHT WORD.

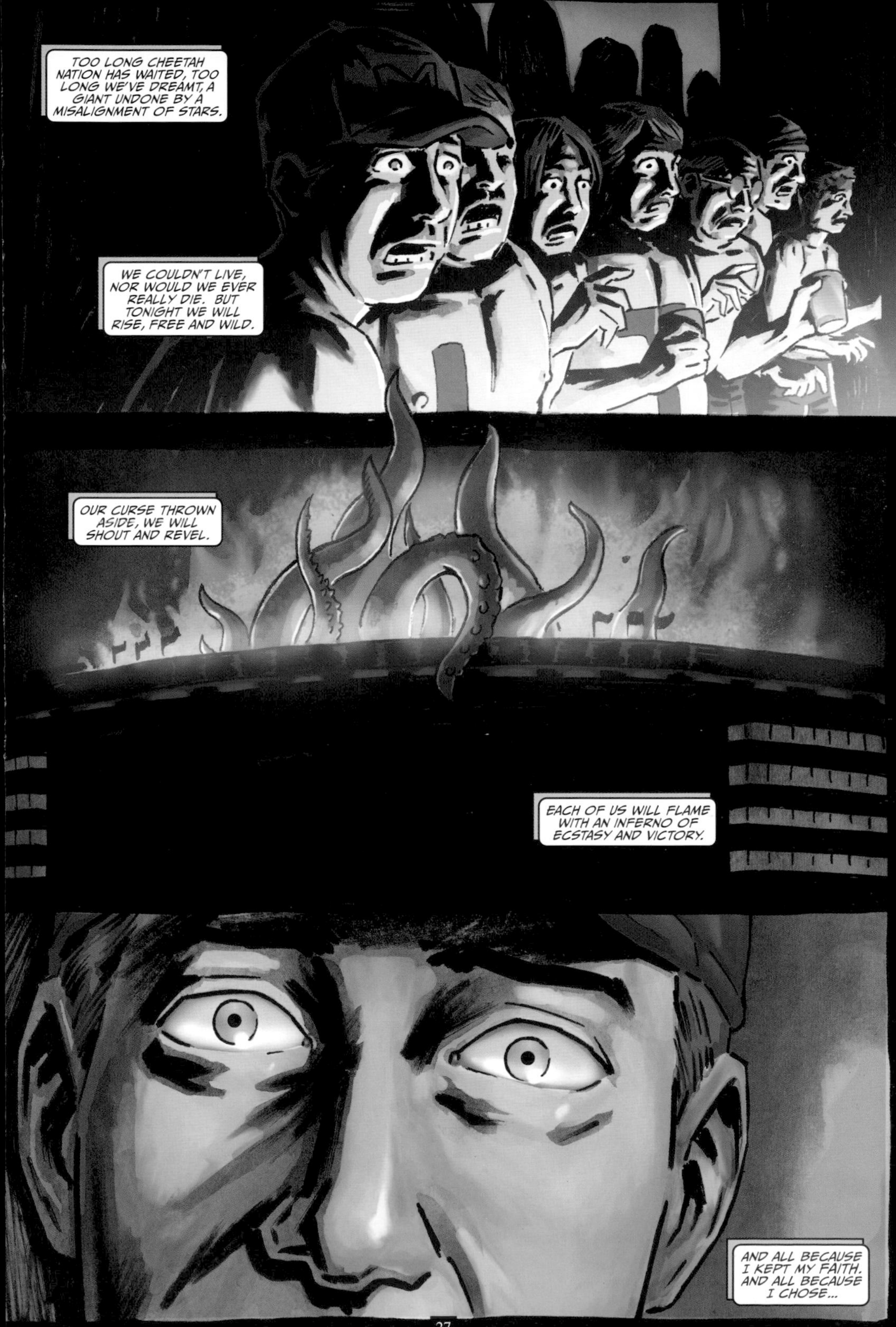
TOO LONG CHEETAH NATION HAS WAITED, TOO LONG WE'VE DREAMT, A GIANT UNDONE BY A MISALIGNMENT OF STARS.
WE COULDN'T LIVE, NOR WOULD WE EVER REALLY DIE. BUT TONIGHT WE WILL RISE, FREE AND WILD.
OUR CURSE THROWN ASIDE, WE WILL SHOUT AND REVEL.
EACH OF US WILL FLAME WITH AN INFERNO OF ECSTASY AND VICTORY.
AND ALL BECAUSE I KEPT MY FAITH. AND ALL BECAUSE I CHOSE...

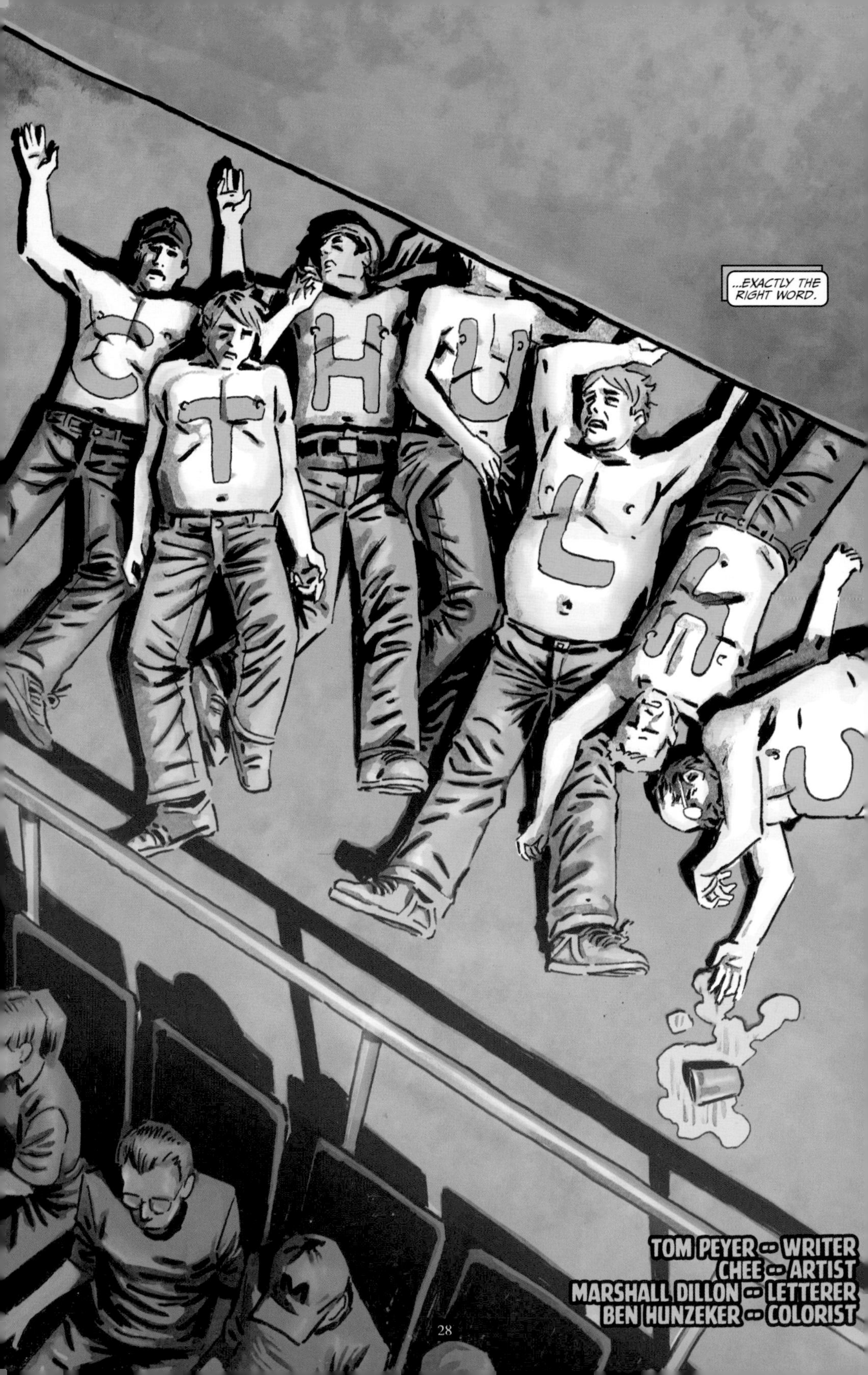
...EXACTLY THE RIGHT WORD.
C T H U L H U
TOM PEYER -- WRITER
CHEE -- ARTIST
MARSHALL DILLON -- LETTERER
BEN HUNZEKER -- COLORIST

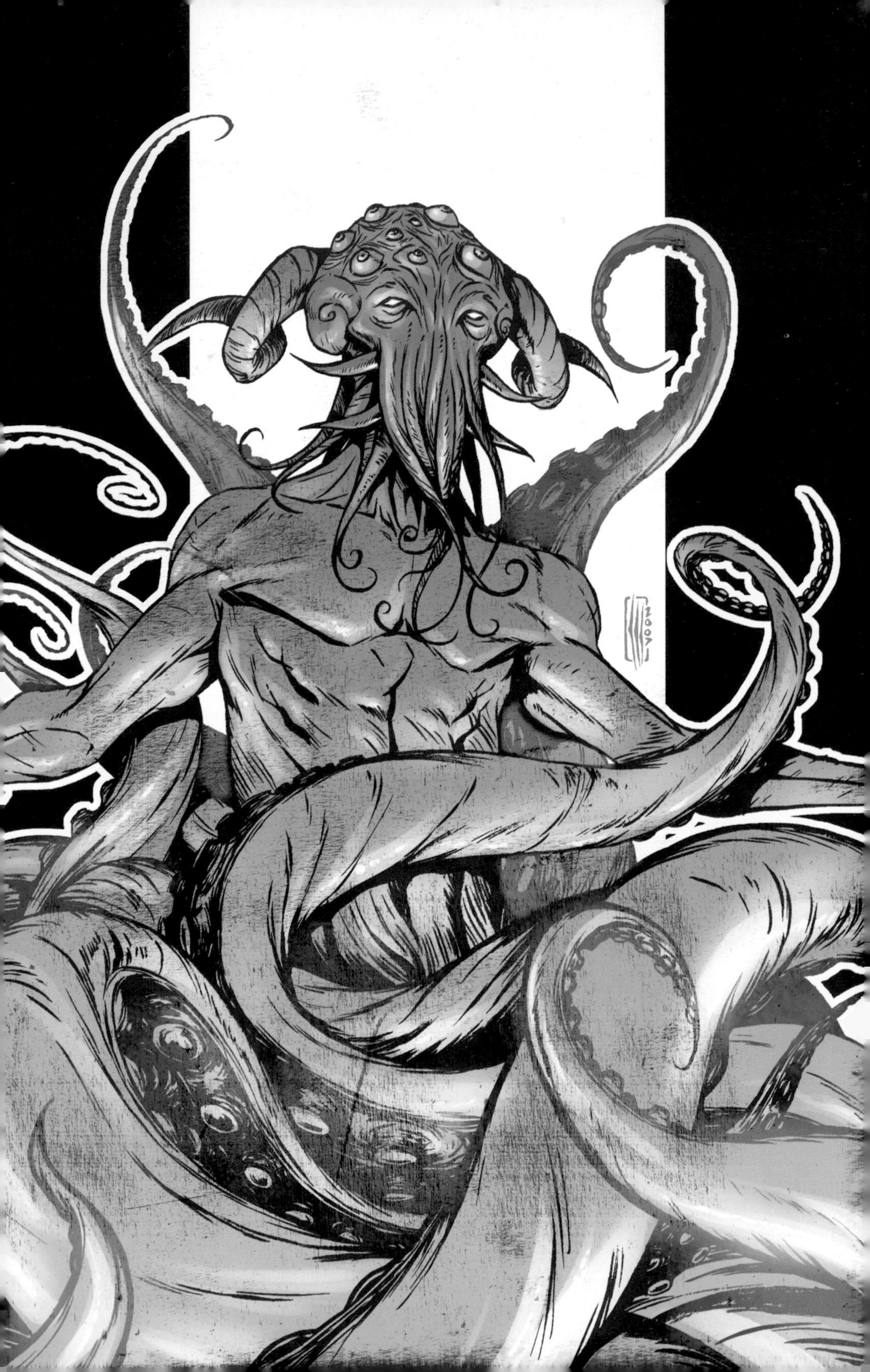

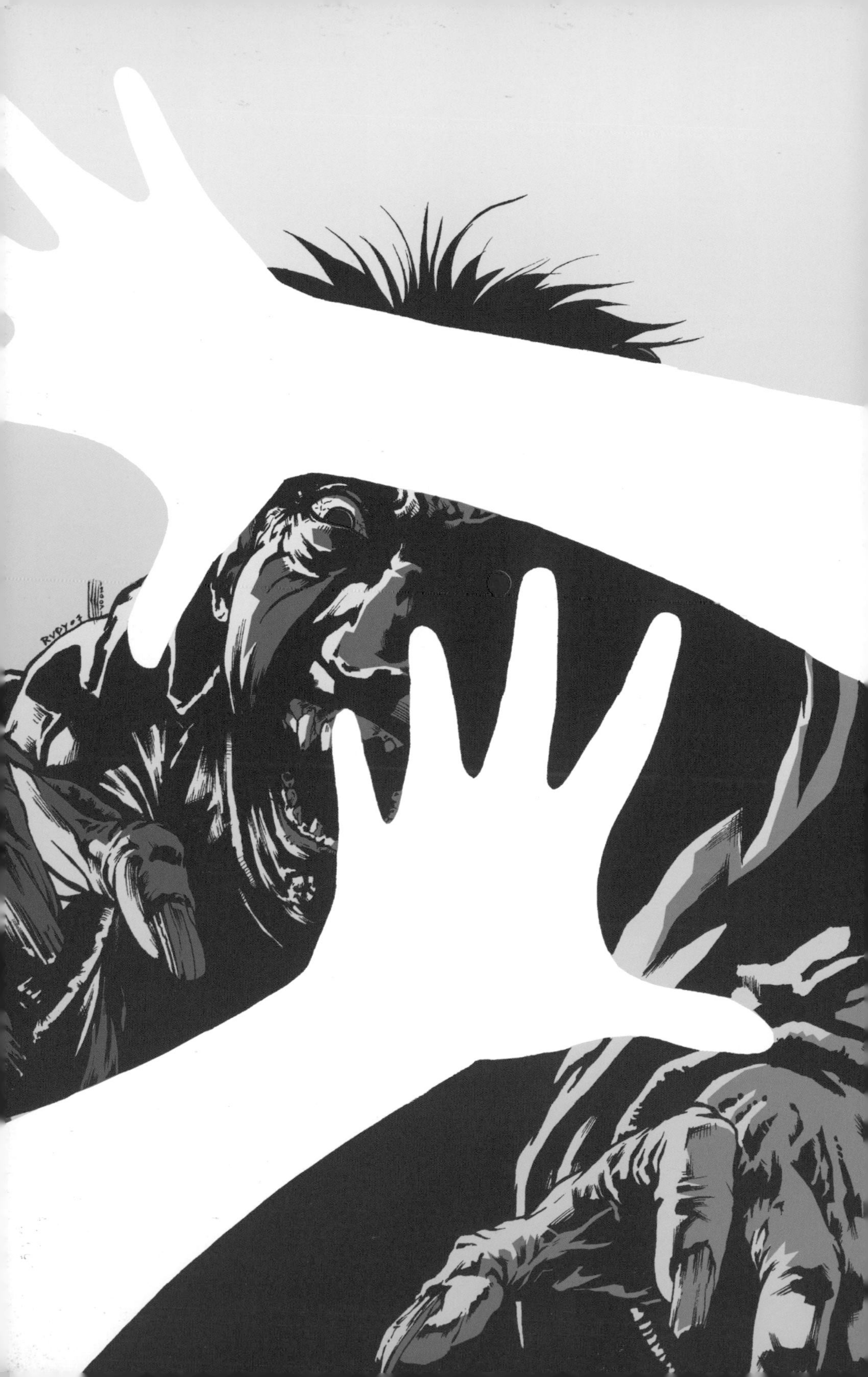

THE HIDING PLACE
STORY **STEVE NILES**
ART **SHANE OAKLEY**

KATRINA
STORY **ERIC CALDERON**
ART **JON SCHNEPP**

HOW TO GET AHEAD
IN THE OCCULT
STORY **CHRISTINE BOYLAN**
ART **CHEE**

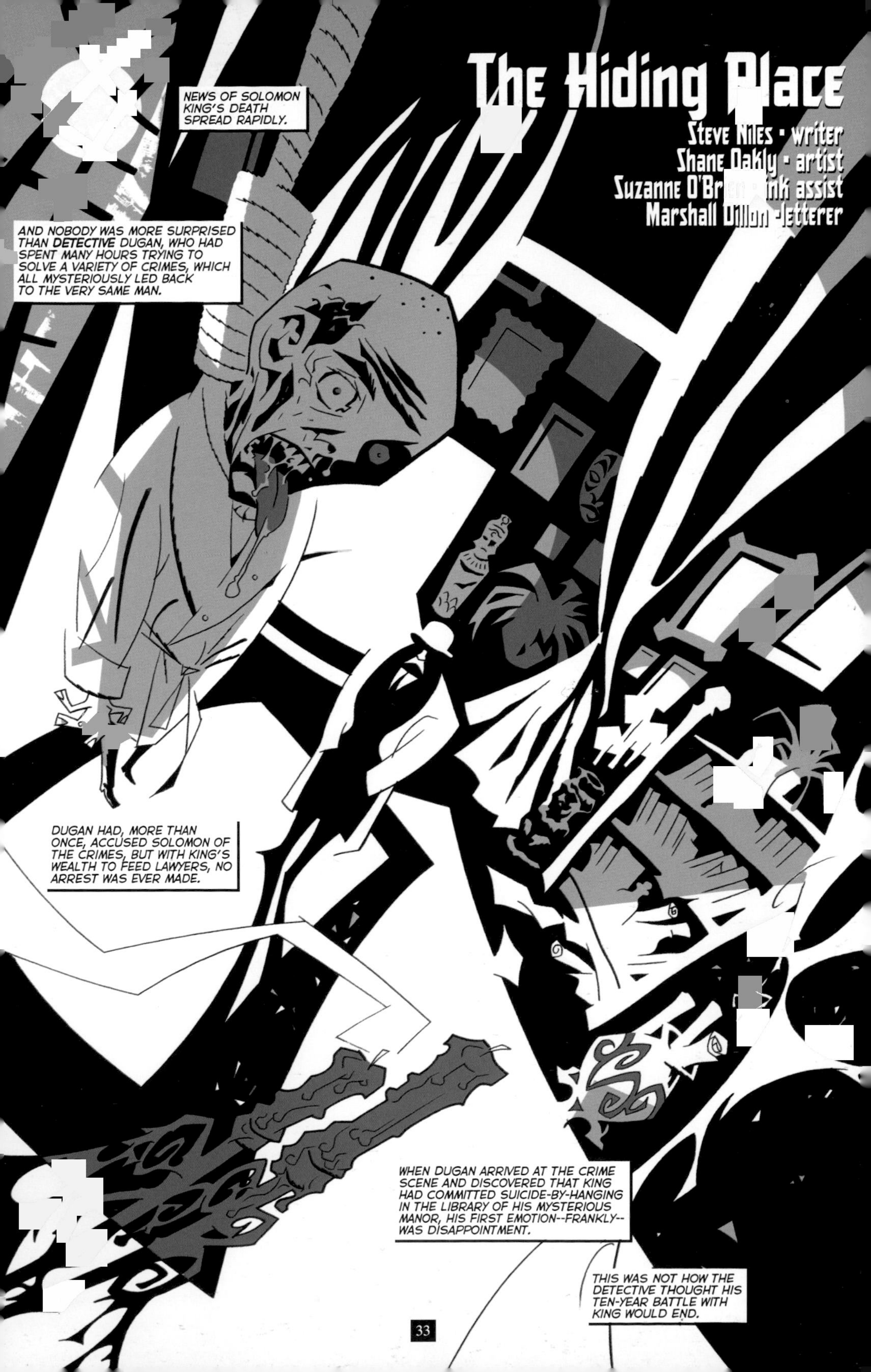
The Hiding Place
Steve Niles - writer
Shane Oakly - artist
Suzanne O'Brien - ink assist
Marshall Dillon - letterer
NEWS OF SOLOMON KING'S DEATH SPREAD RAPIDLY.
AND NOBODY WAS MORE SURPRISED THAN DETECTIVE DUGAN, WHO HAD SPENT MANY HOURS TRYING TO SOLVE A VARIETY OF CRIMES, WHICH ALL MYSTERIOUSLY LED BACK TO THE VERY SAME MAN.
DUGAN HAD, MORE THAN ONCE, ACCUSED SOLOMON OF THE CRIMES, BUT WITH KING'S WEALTH TO FEED LAWYERS, NO ARREST WAS EVER MADE.
WHEN DUGAN ARRIVED AT THE CRIME SCENE AND DISCOVERED THAT KING HAD COMMITTED SUICIDE-BY-HANGING IN THE LIBRARY OF HIS MYSTERIOUS MANOR, HIS FIRST EMOTION--FRANKLY--WAS DISAPPOINTMENT.
THIS WAS NOT HOW THE DETECTIVE THOUGHT HIS TEN-YEAR BATTLE WITH KING WOULD END.

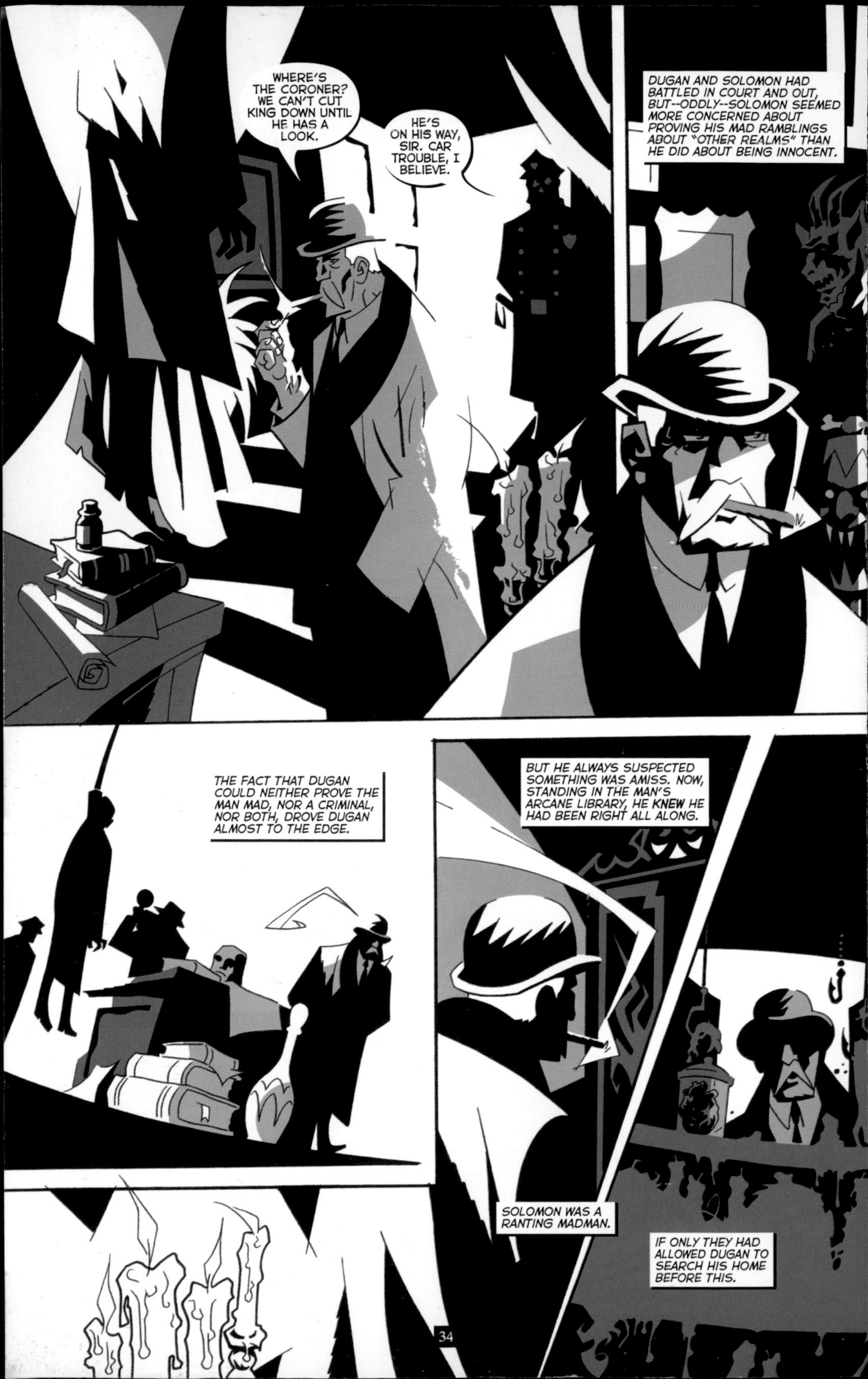
WHERE'S THE CORONER? WE CAN'T CUT KING DOWN UNTIL HE HAS A LOOK.
HE'S ON HIS WAY, SIR. CAR TROUBLE, I BELIEVE.
DUGAN AND SOLOMON HAD BATTLED IN COURT AND OUT, BUT--ODDLY--SOLOMON SEEMED MORE CONCERNED ABOUT PROVING HIS MAD RAMBLINGS ABOUT "OTHER REALMS" THAN HE DID ABOUT BEING INNOCENT.
THE FACT THAT DUGAN COULD NEITHER PROVE THE MAN MAD, NOR A CRIMINAL, NOR BOTH, DROVE DUGAN ALMOST TO THE EDGE.
BUT HE ALWAYS SUSPECTED SOMETHING WAS AMISS. NOW, STANDING IN THE MAN'S ARCANE LIBRARY, HE KNEW HE HAD BEEN RIGHT ALL ALONG.
SOLOMON WAS A RANTING MADMAN.
IF ONLY THEY HAD ALLOWED DUGAN TO SEARCH HIS HOME BEFORE THIS.

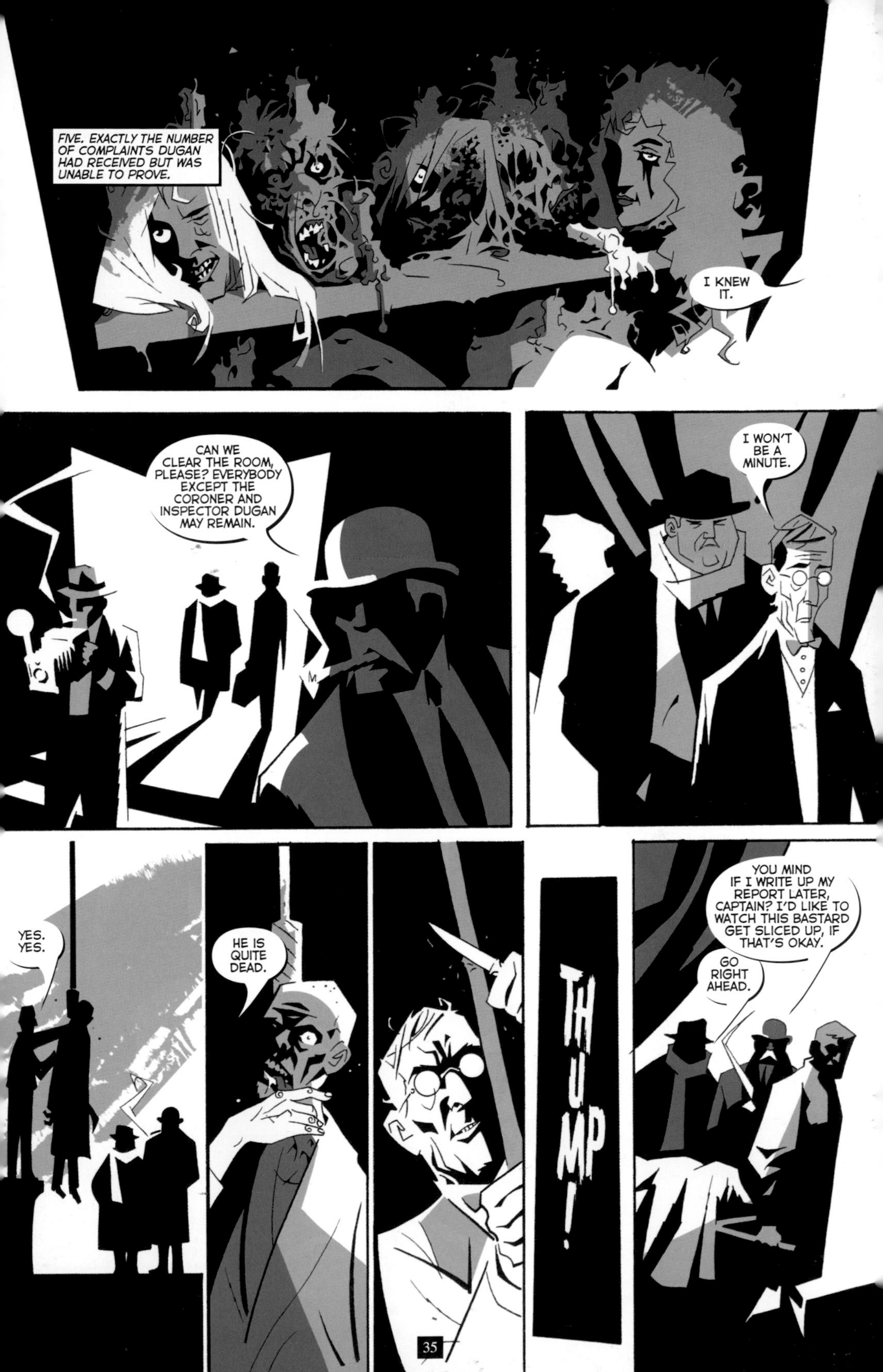

FIVE. EXACTLY THE NUMBER OF COMPLAINTS DUGAN HAD RECEIVED BUT WAS UNABLE TO PROVE.
I KNEW IT.
CAN WE CLEAR THE ROOM, PLEASE? EVERYBODY EXCEPT THE CORONER AND INSPECTOR DUGAN MAY REMAIN.
I WON'T BE A MINUTE.
YES. YES.
HE IS QUITE DEAD.
THUMP!
YOU MIND IF I WRITE UP MY REPORT LATER, CAPTAIN? I'D LIKE TO WATCH THIS BASTARD GET SLICED UP, IF THAT'S OKAY.
GO RIGHT AHEAD.

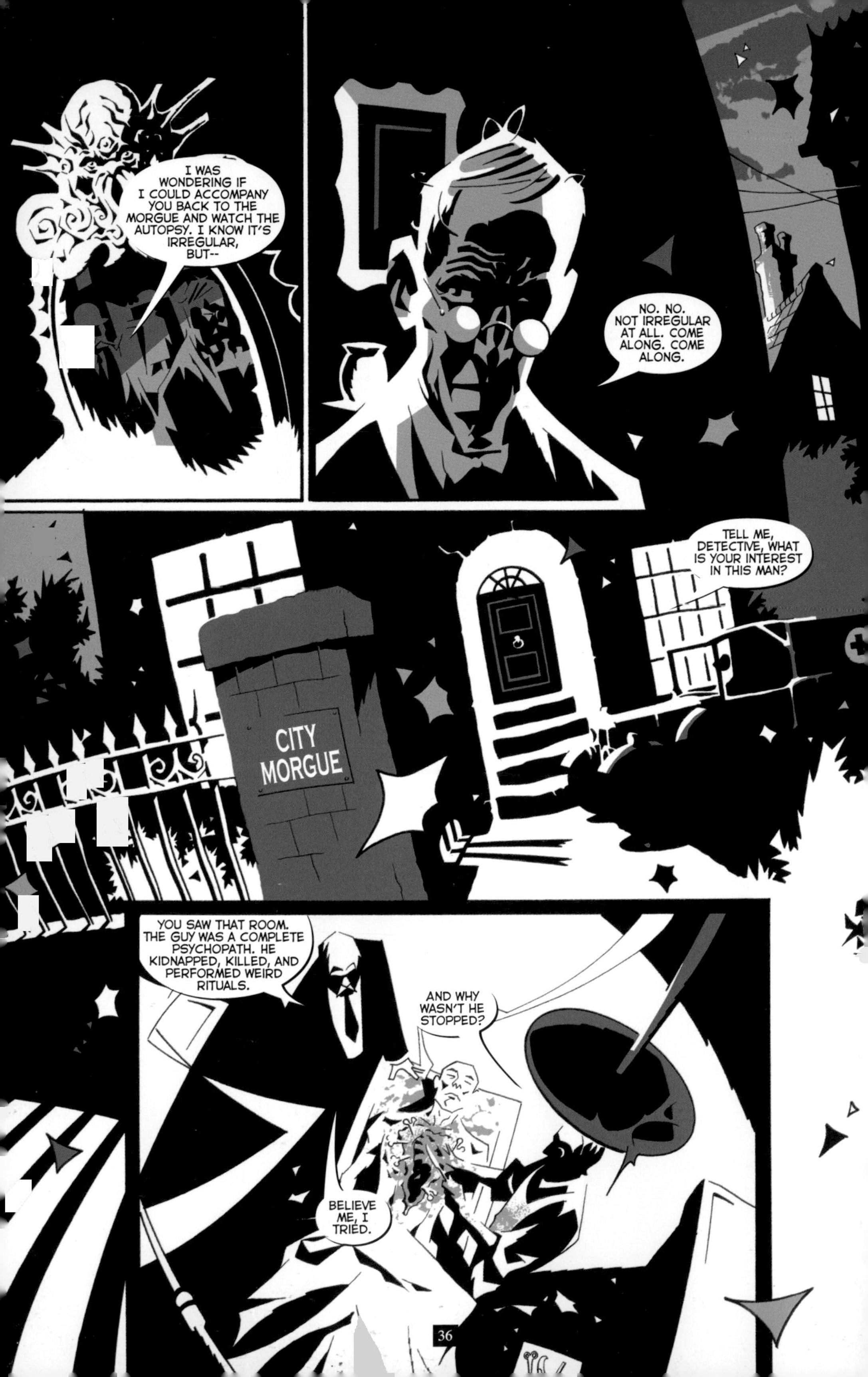
I WAS WONDERING IF I COULD ACCOMPANY YOU BACK TO THE MORGUE AND WATCH THE AUTOPSY. I KNOW IT'S IRREGULAR, BUT--
NO. NO. NOT IRREGULAR AT ALL. COME ALONG. COME ALONG.
TELL ME, DETECTIVE, WHAT IS YOUR INTEREST IN THIS MAN?
CITY MORGUE
YOU SAW THAT ROOM. THE GUY WAS A COMPLETE PSYCHOPATH. HE KIDNAPPED, KILLED, AND PERFORMED WEIRD RITUALS.
AND WHY WASN'T HE STOPPED?
BELIEVE ME, I TRIED.

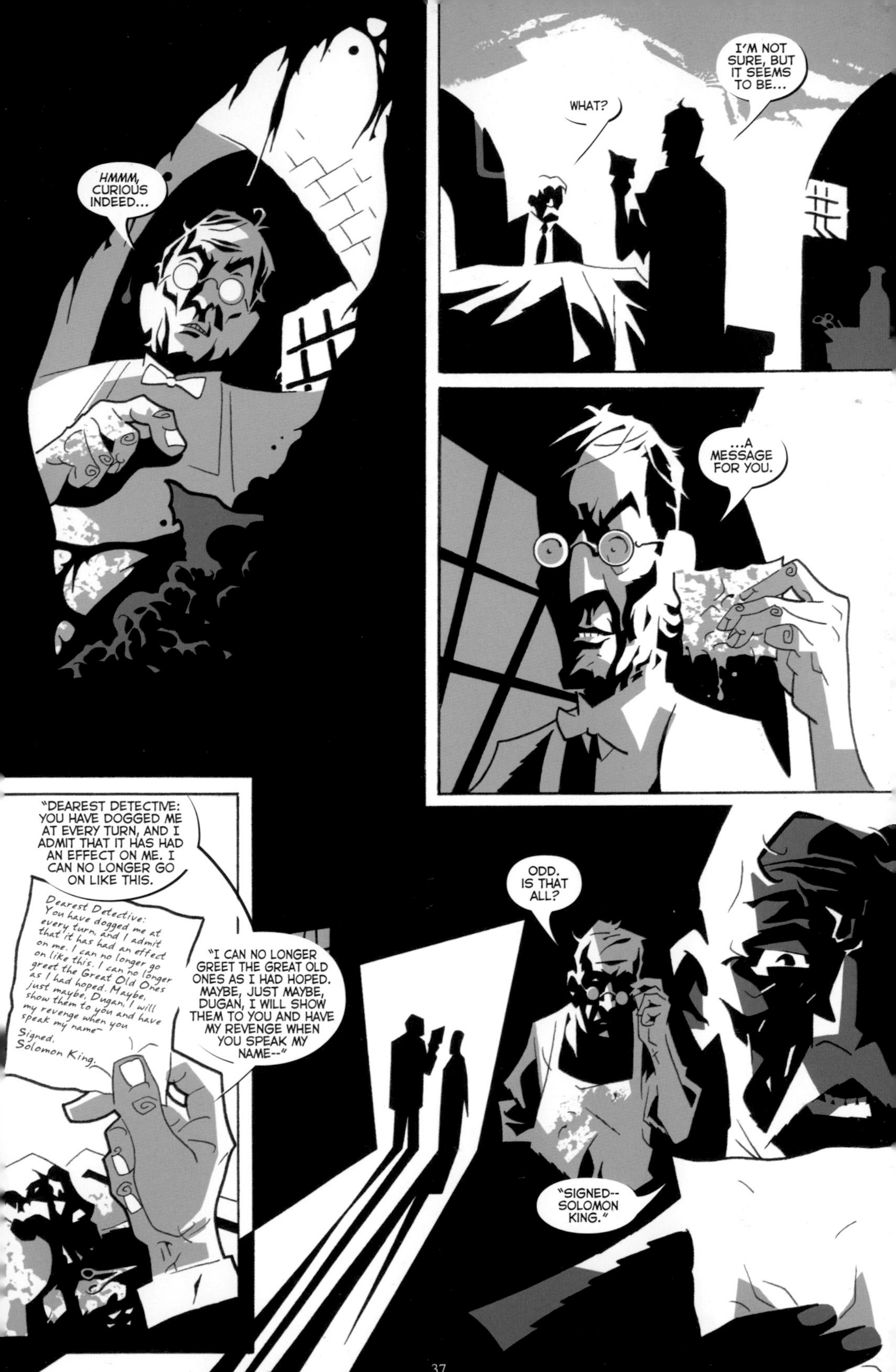
HMMM, CURIOUS INDEED...
WHAT?
I'M NOT SURE, BUT IT SEEMS TO BE...
...A MESSAGE FOR YOU.
"DEAREST DETECTIVE: YOU HAVE DOGGED ME AT EVERY TURN, AND I ADMIT THAT IT HAS HAD AN EFFECT ON ME. I CAN NO LONGER GO ON LIKE THIS.
Dearest Detective: You have dogged me at every turn, and I admit that it has had an effect on me. I can no longer go on like this. I can no longer greet the Great Old Ones as I had hoped. Maybe, just maybe, Dugan, I will show them to you and have my revenge when you speak my name
Signed, Solomon King.
"I CAN NO LONGER GREET THE GREAT OLD ONES AS I HAD HOPED. MAYBE, JUST MAYBE, DUGAN, I WILL SHOW THEM TO YOU AND HAVE MY REVENGE WHEN YOU SPEAK MY NAME--"
ODD. IS THAT ALL?
"SIGNED-- SOLOMON KING."

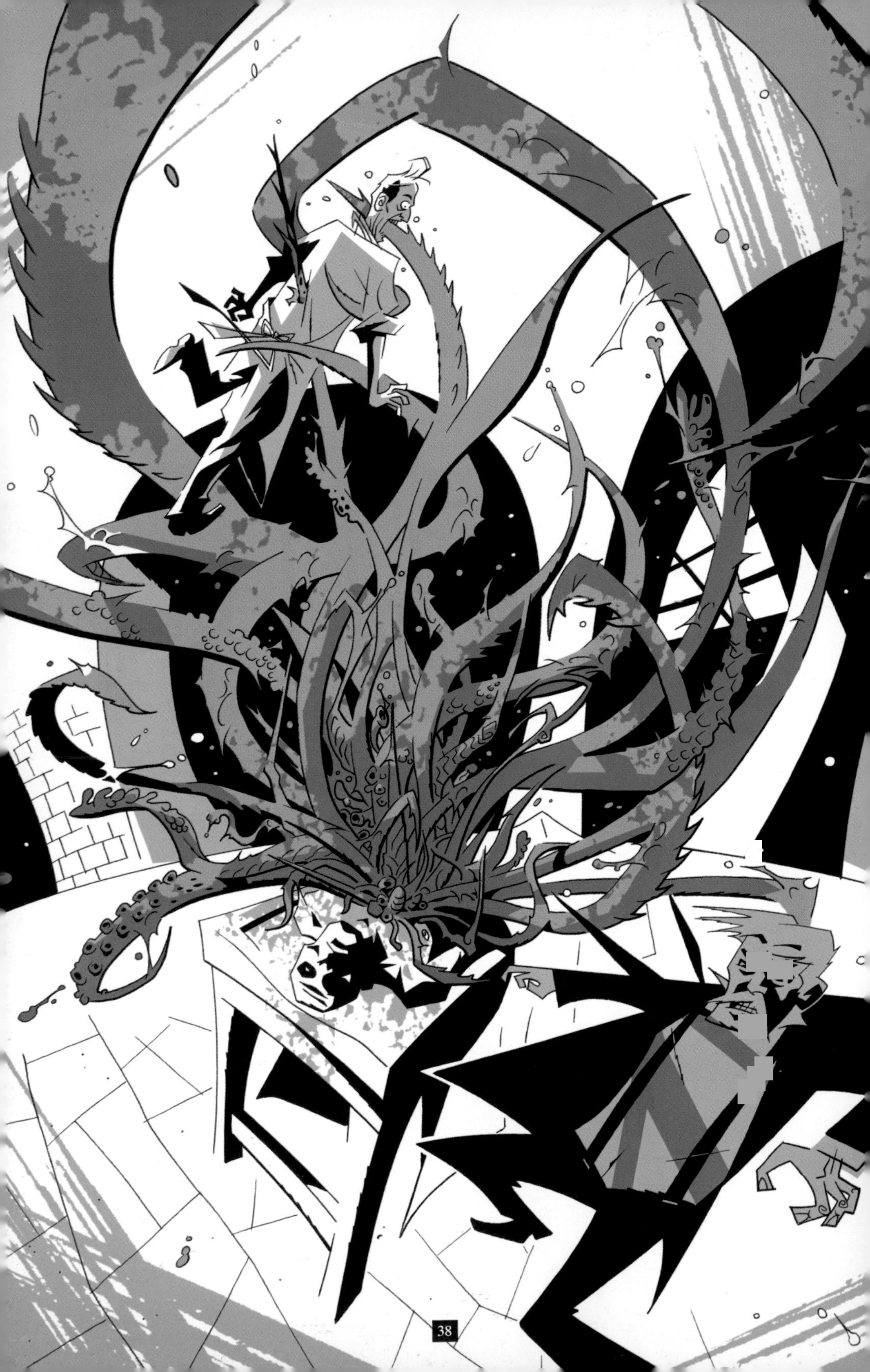

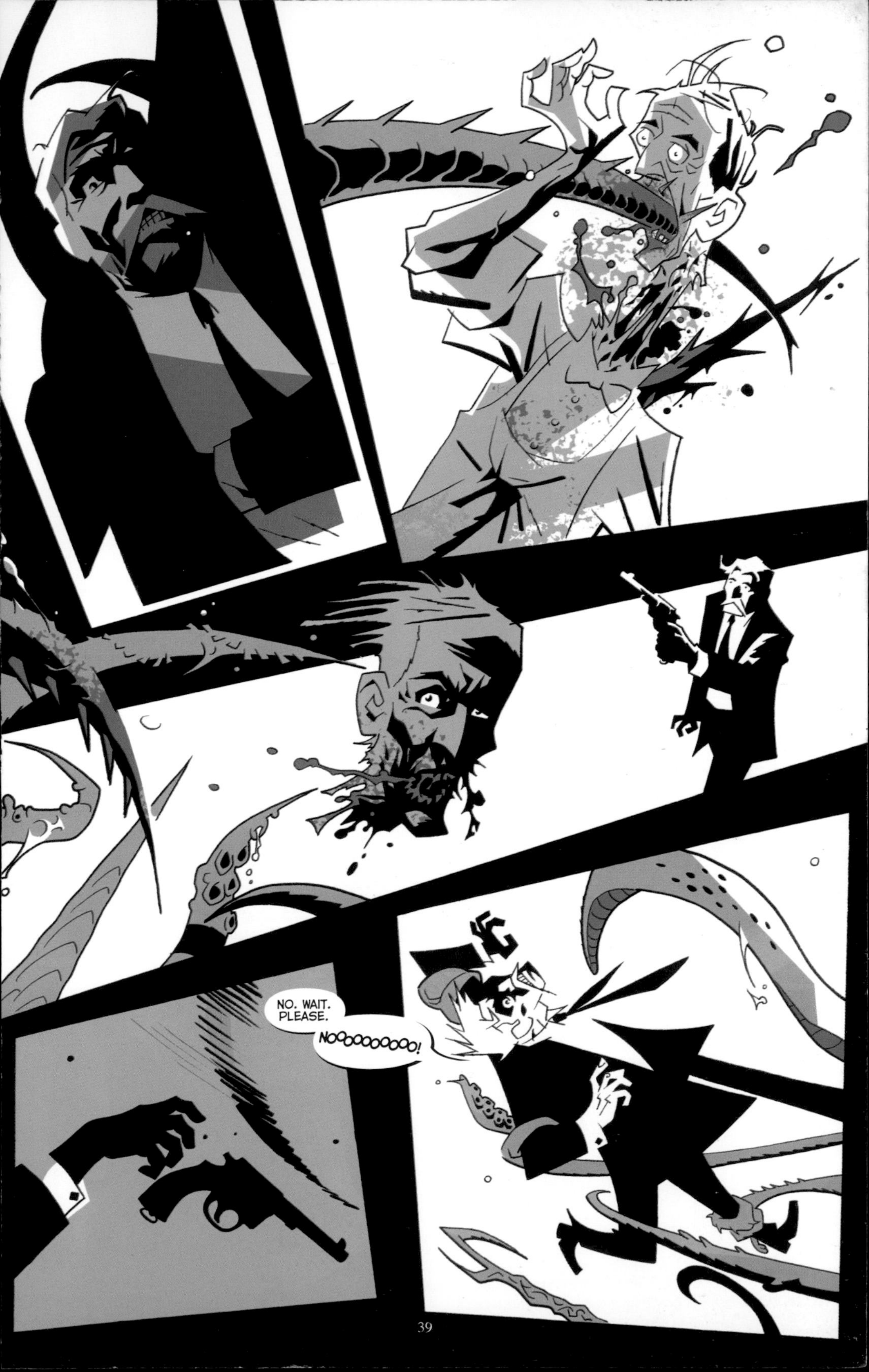
NO. WAIT. PLEASE.
NOOOOOOOOOO!

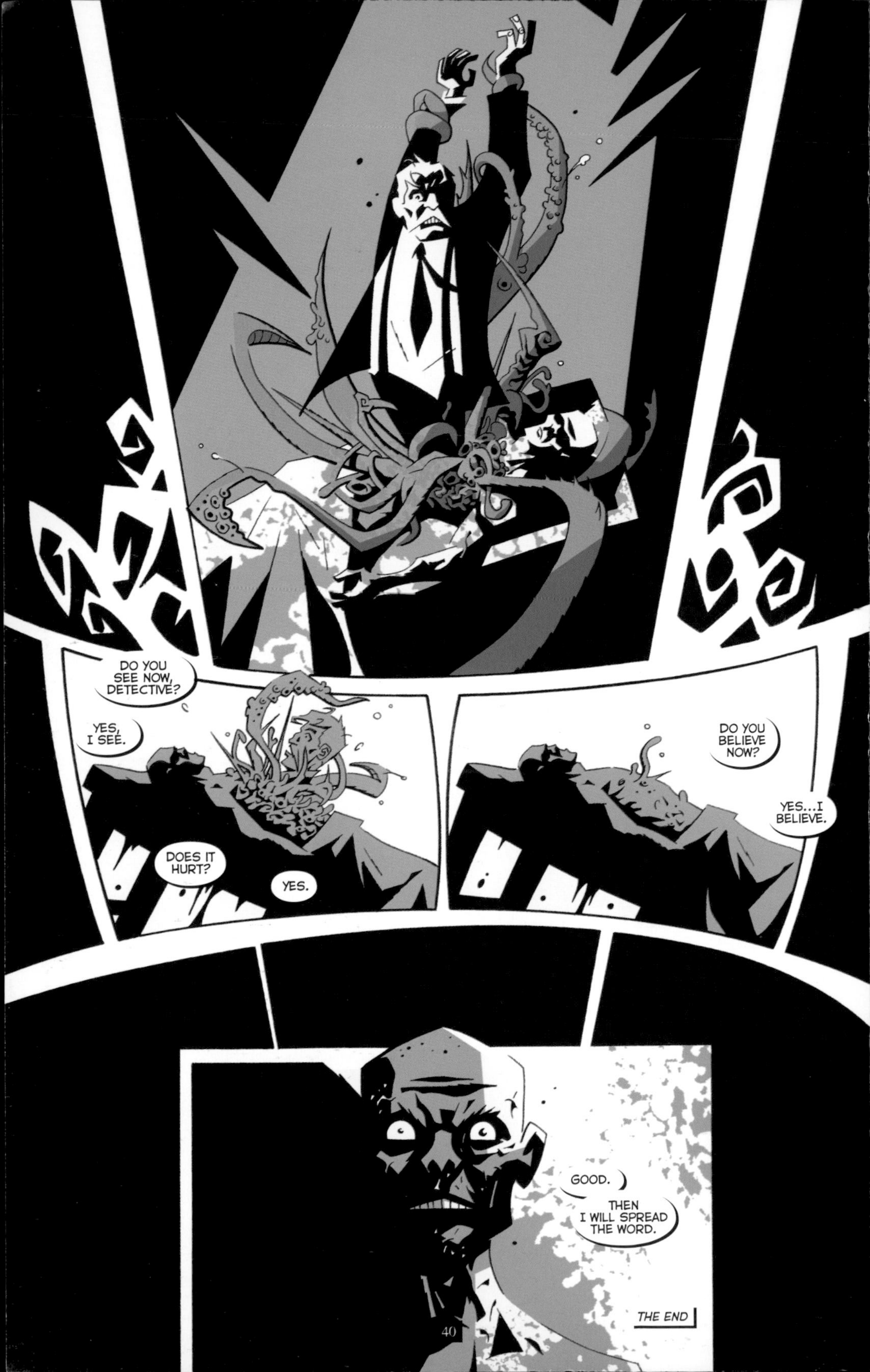
DO YOU SEE NOW, DETECTIVE?
YES, I SEE.
DOES IT HURT?
YES.
DO YOU BELIEVE NOW?
YES...I BELIEVE.
GOOD.
THEN I WILL SPREAD THE WORD.
THE END

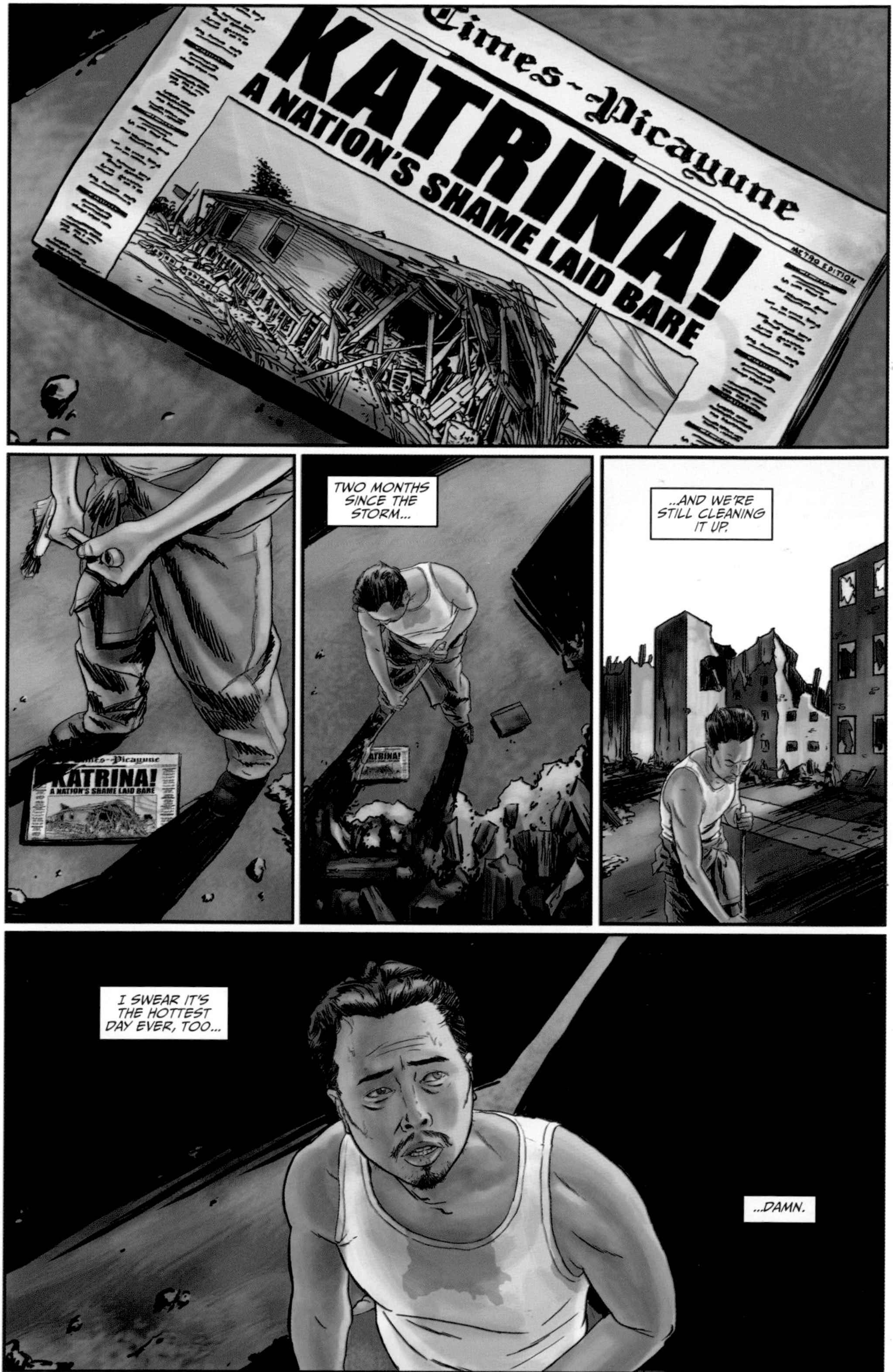
Times-Picayune
KATRINA!
A NATION'S SHAME LAID BARE
METRO EDITION
TWO MONTHS SINCE THE STORM...
...AND WE'RE STILL CLEANING IT UP.
I SWEAR IT'S THE HOTTEST DAY EVER, TOO...
...DAMN.

story: Eric Calderon visuals: Jon Schnepp
inks: Dik Pose colors: Dan Bigelow letters: Marshall Dillon

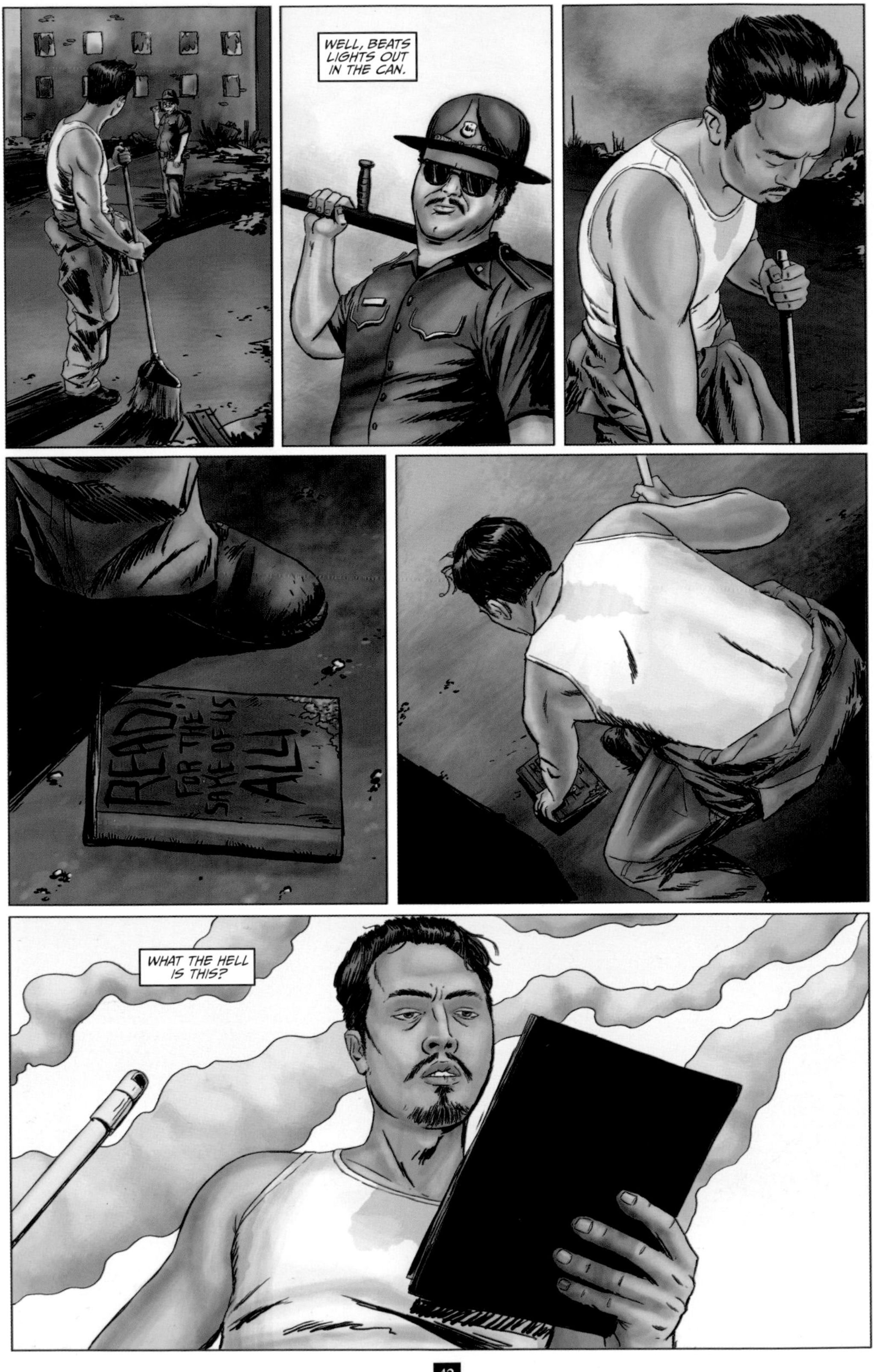
WELL, BEATS LIGHTS OUT IN THE CAN.
READ! FOR THE SAKE OF US ALL!
WHAT THE HELL IS THIS?

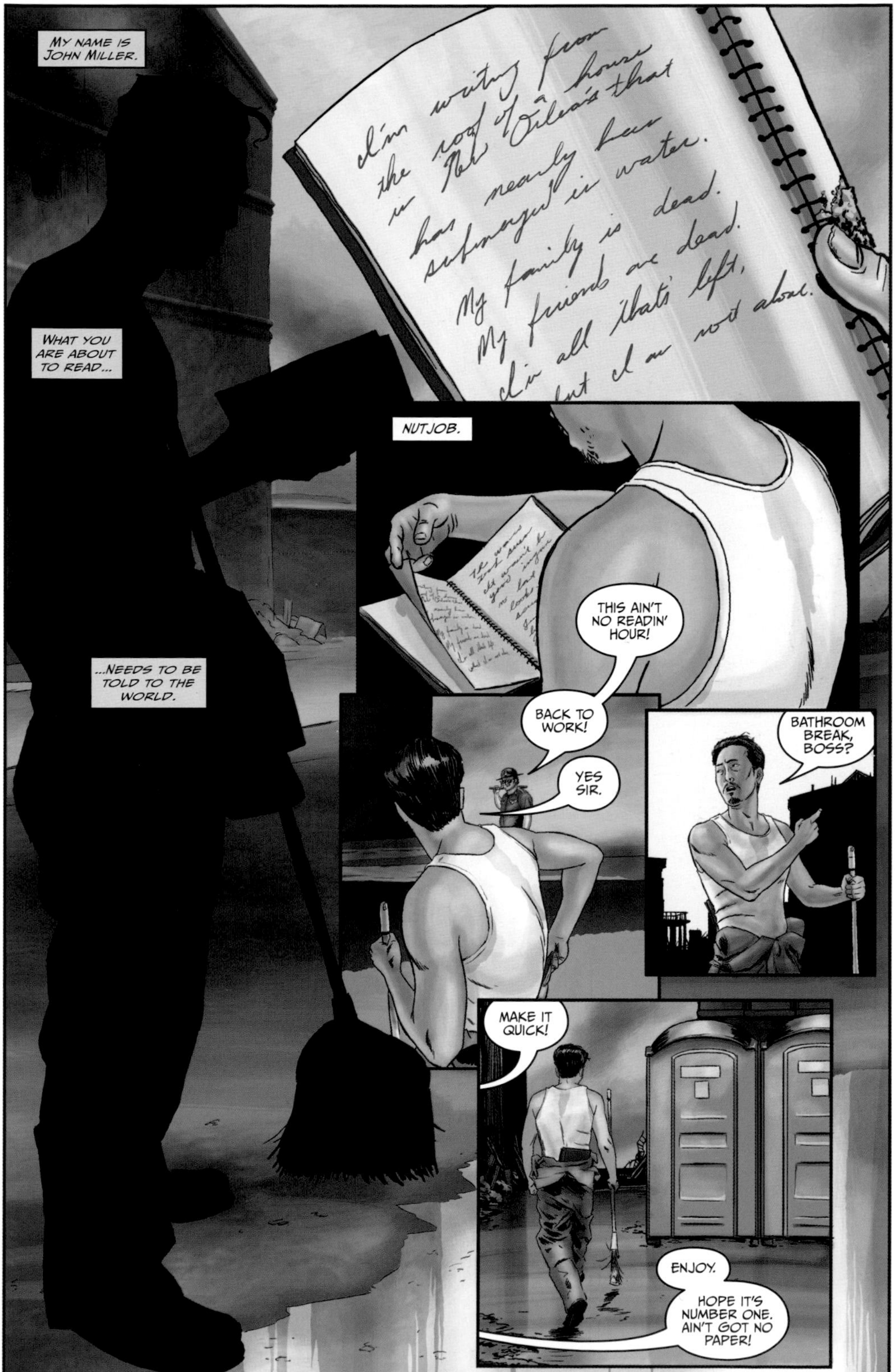

MY NAME IS JOHN MILLER.
I'm writing from the roof of a house in New Orleans that has nearly been submerged in water.
My family is dead.
My friends are dead.
I'm all that's left,
WHAT YOU ARE ABOUT TO READ...
NUTJOB.
THIS AIN'T NO READIN' HOUR!
BACK TO WORK!
...NEEDS TO BE TOLD TO THE WORLD.
YES SIR.
BATHROOM BREAK, BOSS?
MAKE IT QUICK!
ENJOY.
HOPE IT'S NUMBER ONE. AIN'T GOT NO PAPER!

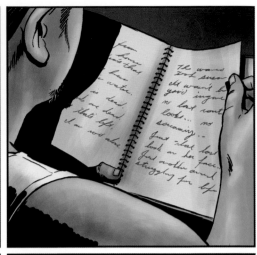

THE WAVES TOOK SUSAN. IT WASN'T LIKE YOU'D IMAGINE.

NO LAST ROMANTIC LOOKS.

NO SCREAMING.

JUST THAT LAST LOOK ON HER FACE.

JUST ANOTHER ANIMAL STRUGGLING FOR LIFE.

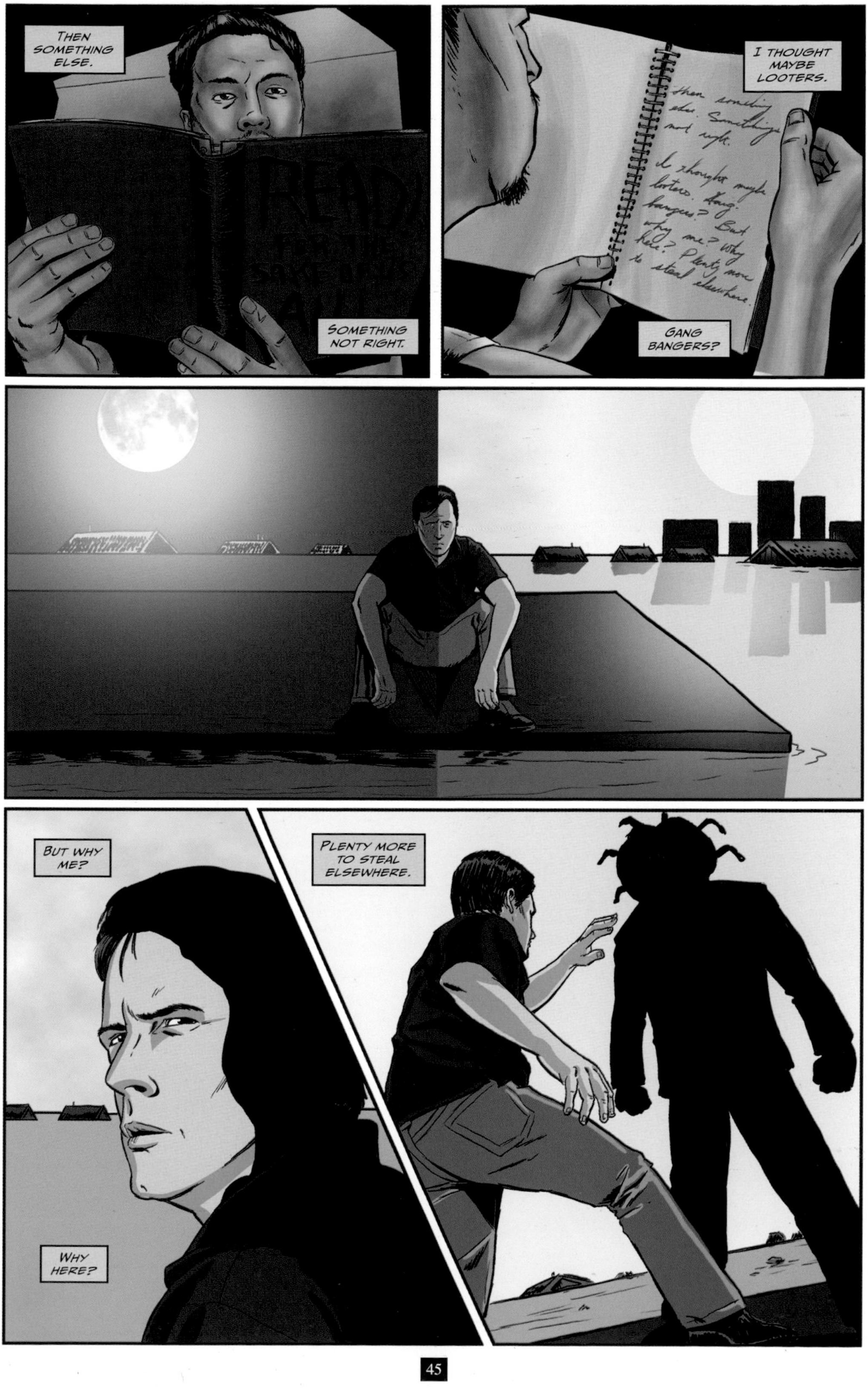
THEN SOMETHING ELSE.
SOMETHING NOT RIGHT.
I THOUGHT MAYBE LOOTERS.
GANG BANGERS?
BUT WHY ME?
WHY HERE?
PLENTY MORE TO STEAL ELSEWHERE.

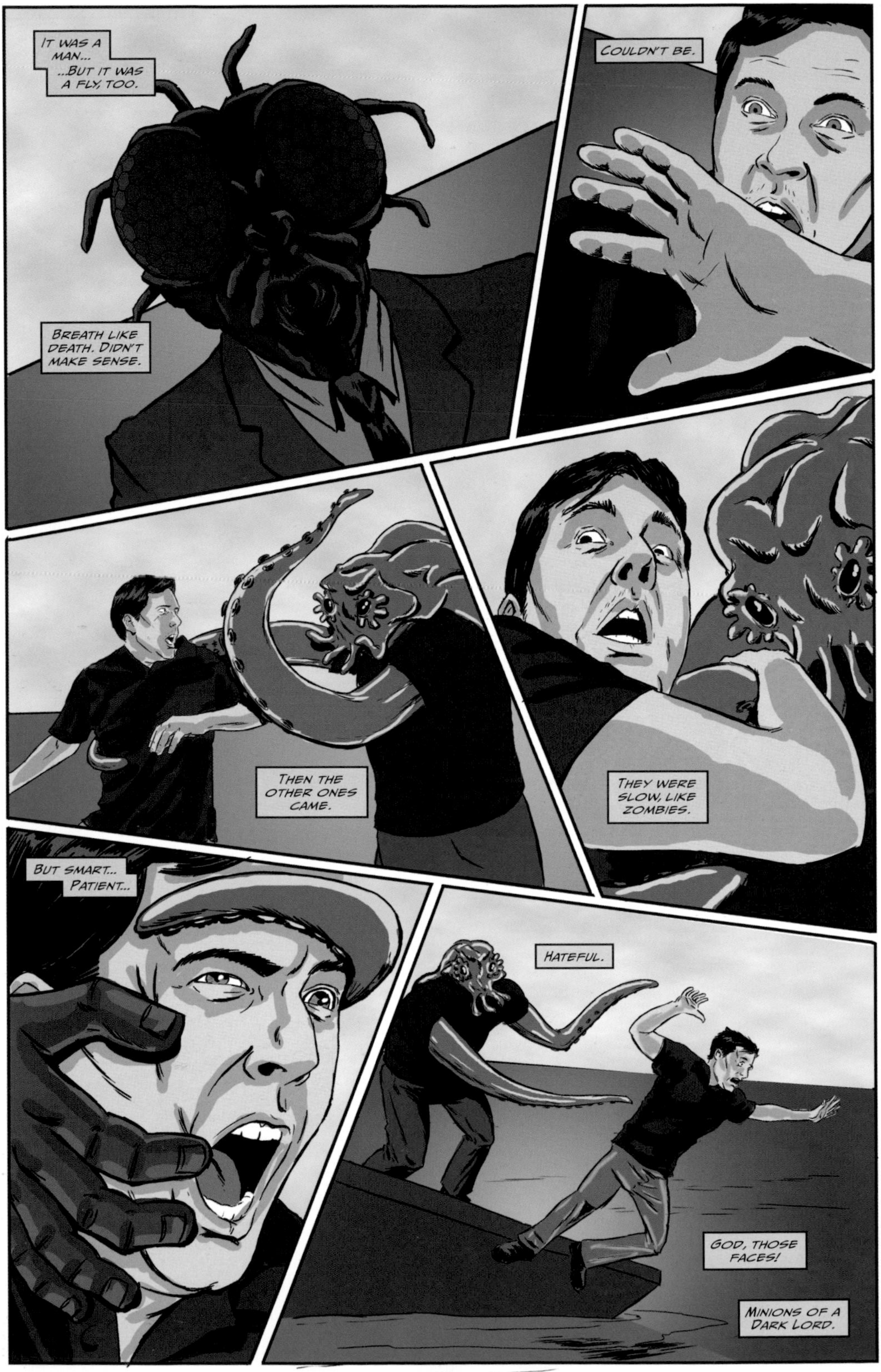
IT WAS A MAN...
...BUT IT WAS A FLY, TOO.
BREATH LIKE DEATH. DIDN'T MAKE SENSE.
COULDN'T BE.
THEN THE OTHER ONES CAME.
THEY WERE SLOW, LIKE ZOMBIES.
BUT SMART... PATIENT...
HATEFUL.
GOD, THOSE FACES!
MINIONS OF A DARK LORD.

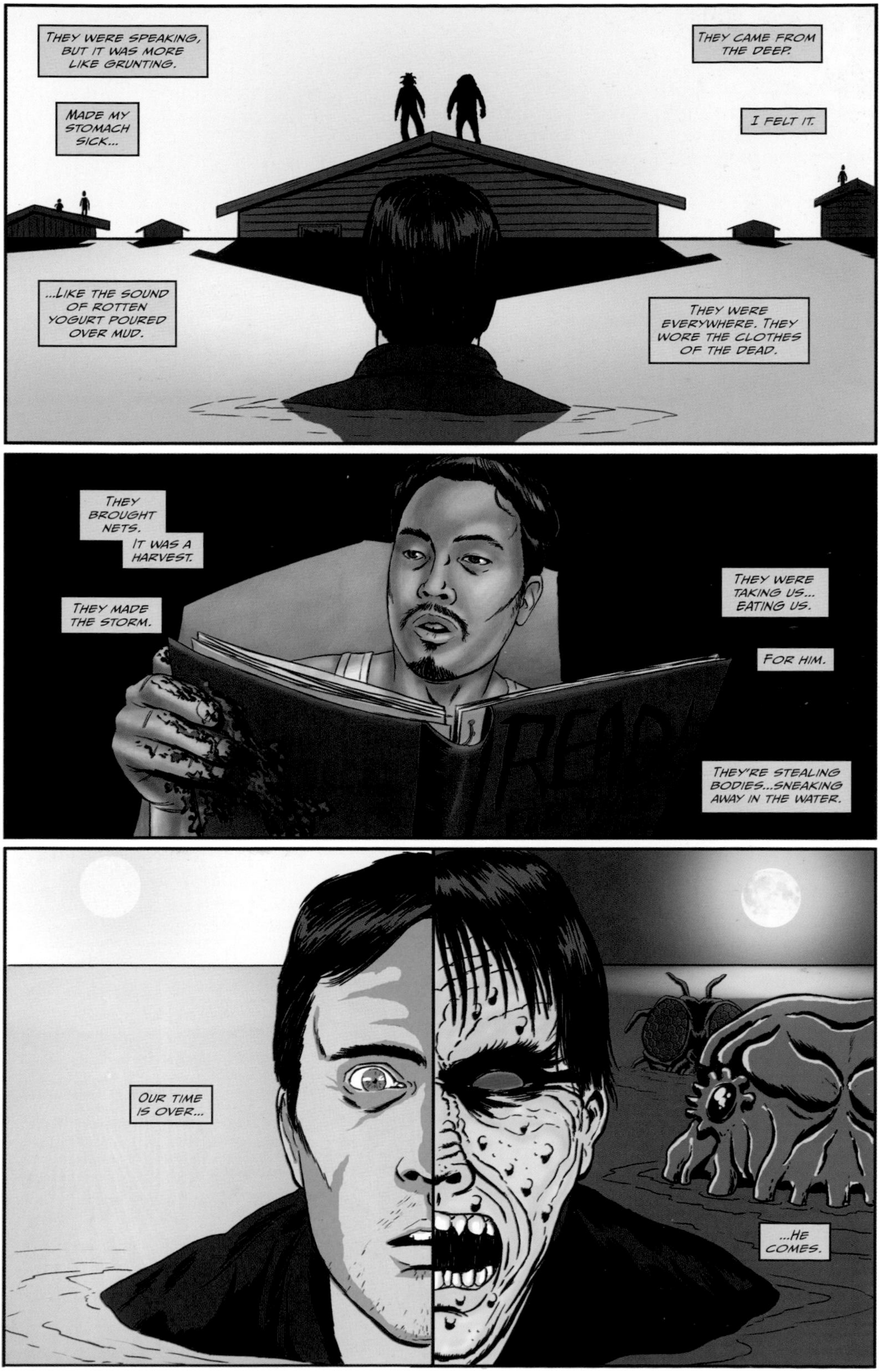
THEY WERE SPEAKING, BUT IT WAS MORE LIKE GRUNTING.
MADE MY STOMACH SICK...
...LIKE THE SOUND OF ROTTEN YOGURT POURED OVER MUD.
THEY CAME FROM THE DEEP.
I FELT IT.
THEY WERE EVERYWHERE. THEY WORE THE CLOTHES OF THE DEAD.
THEY BROUGHT NETS.
IT WAS A HARVEST.
THEY MADE THE STORM.
THEY WERE TAKING US... EATING US.
FOR HIM.
THEY'RE STEALING BODIES...SNEAKING AWAY IN THE WATER.
OUR TIME IS OVER...
...HE COMES.

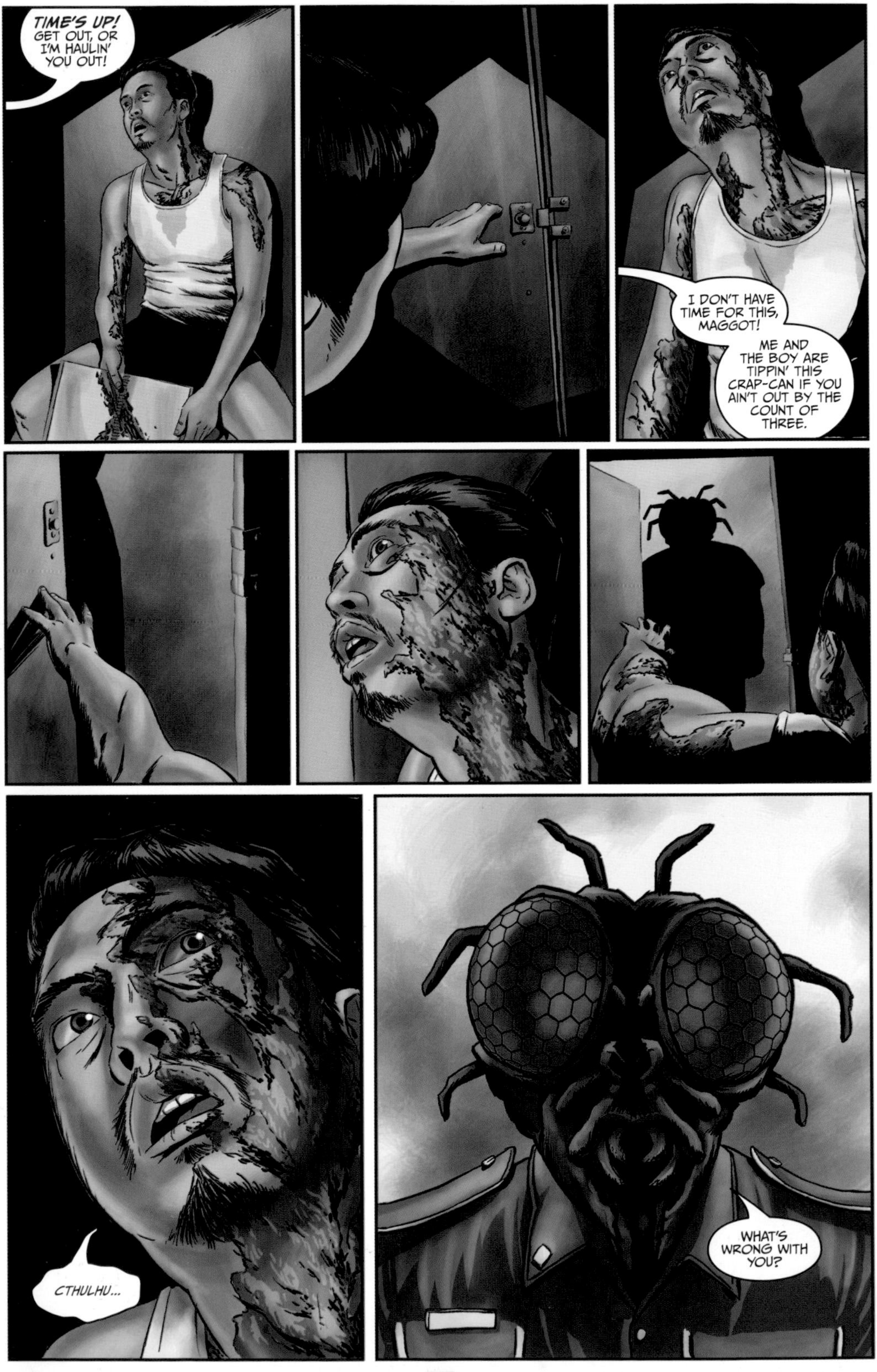
TIME'S UP! GET OUT, OR I'M HAULIN' YOU OUT!
I DON'T HAVE TIME FOR THIS, MAGGOT!
ME AND THE BOY ARE TIPPIN' THIS CRAP-CAN IF YOU AIN'T OUT BY THE COUNT OF THREE.
CTHULHU...
WHAT'S WRONG WITH YOU?

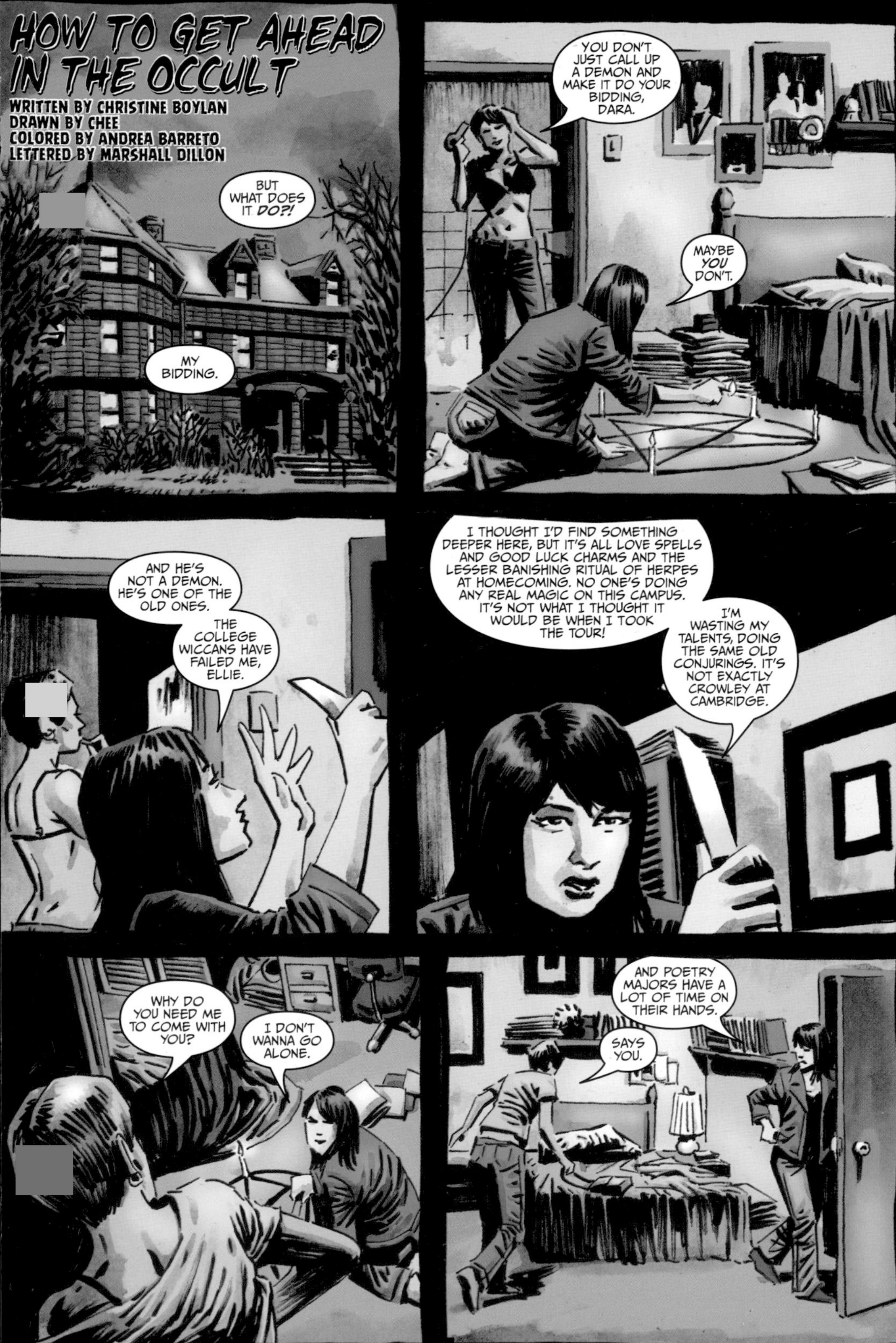
HOW TO GET AHEAD IN THE OCCULT
WRITTEN BY CHRISTINE BOYLAN
DRAWN BY CHEE
COLORED BY ANDREA BARRETO
LETTERED BY MARSHALL DILLON
BUT WHAT DOES IT DO?!
MY BIDDING.
YOU DON'T JUST CALL UP A DEMON AND MAKE IT DO YOUR BIDDING, DARA.
MAYBE YOU DON'T.
AND HE'S NOT A DEMON. HE'S ONE OF THE OLD ONES.
THE COLLEGE WICCANS HAVE FAILED ME, ELLIE.
I THOUGHT I'D FIND SOMETHING DEEPER HERE, BUT IT'S ALL LOVE SPELLS AND GOOD LUCK CHARMS AND THE LESSER BANISHING RITUAL OF HERPES AT HOMECOMING. NO ONE'S DOING ANY REAL MAGIC ON THIS CAMPUS. IT'S NOT WHAT I THOUGHT IT WOULD BE WHEN I TOOK THE TOUR!
I'M WASTING MY TALENTS, DOING THE SAME OLD CONJURINGS. IT'S NOT EXACTLY CROWLEY AT CAMBRIDGE.
WHY DO YOU NEED ME TO COME WITH YOU?
I DON'T WANNA GO ALONE.
AND POETRY MAJORS HAVE A LOT OF TIME ON THEIR HANDS.
SAYS YOU.

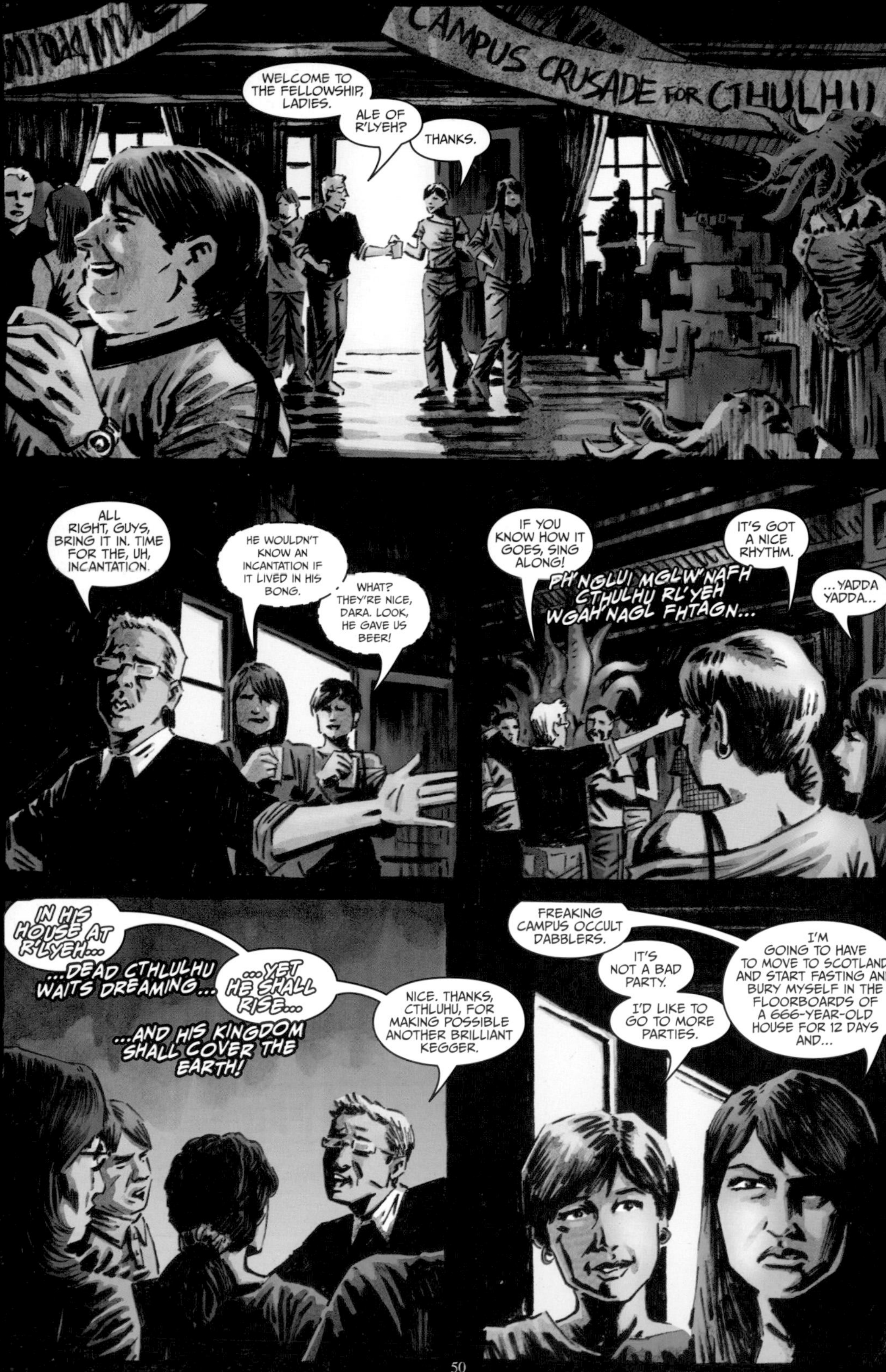
CAMPUS CRUSADE FOR CTHULHU
WELCOME TO THE FELLOWSHIP, LADIES.
ALE OF R'LYEH?
THANKS.
ALL RIGHT, GUYS, BRING IT IN. TIME FOR THE, UH, INCANTATION.
HE WOULDN'T KNOW AN INCANTATION IF IT LIVED IN HIS BONG.
WHAT? THEY'RE NICE, DARA. LOOK, HE GAVE US BEER!
IF YOU KNOW HOW IT GOES, SING ALONG!
PH'NGLUI MGLW'NAFH CTHULHU RL'YEH WGAH'NAGL FHTAGN...
IT'S GOT A NICE RHYTHM.
...YADDA YADDA...
IN HIS HOUSE AT R'LYEH...
...DEAD CTHLULHU WAITS DREAMING...
...YET HE SHALL RISE...
...AND HIS KINGDOM SHALL COVER THE EARTH!
NICE. THANKS, CTHLUHU, FOR MAKING POSSIBLE ANOTHER BRILLIANT KEGGER.
FREAKING CAMPUS OCCULT DABBLERS.
IT'S NOT A BAD PARTY.
I'D LIKE TO GO TO MORE PARTIES.
I'M GOING TO HAVE TO MOVE TO SCOTLAND AND START FASTING AND BURY MYSELF IN THE FLOORBOARDS OF A 666-YEAR-OLD HOUSE FOR 12 DAYS AND...

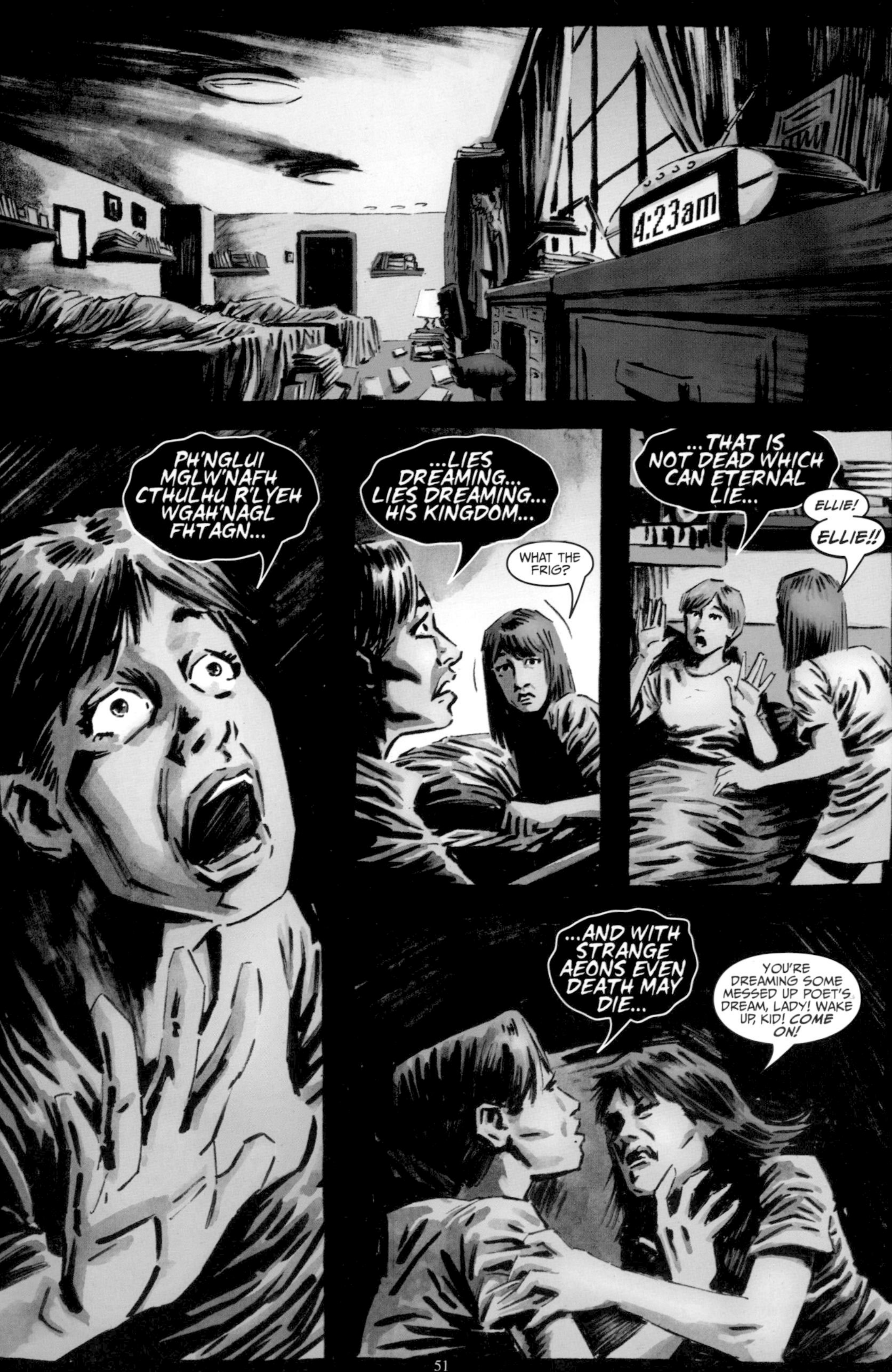
4:23am
PH'NGLUI MGLW'NAFH CTHULHU R'LYEH WGAH'NAGL FHTAGN...
...LIES DREAMING... LIES DREAMING... HIS KINGDOM...
WHAT THE FRIG?
...THAT IS NOT DEAD WHICH CAN ETERNAL LIE...
ELLIE!
ELLIE!!
...AND WITH STRANGE AEONS EVEN DEATH MAY DIE...
YOU'RE DREAMING SOME MESSED UP POET'S DREAM, LADY! WAKE UP, KID! COME ON!

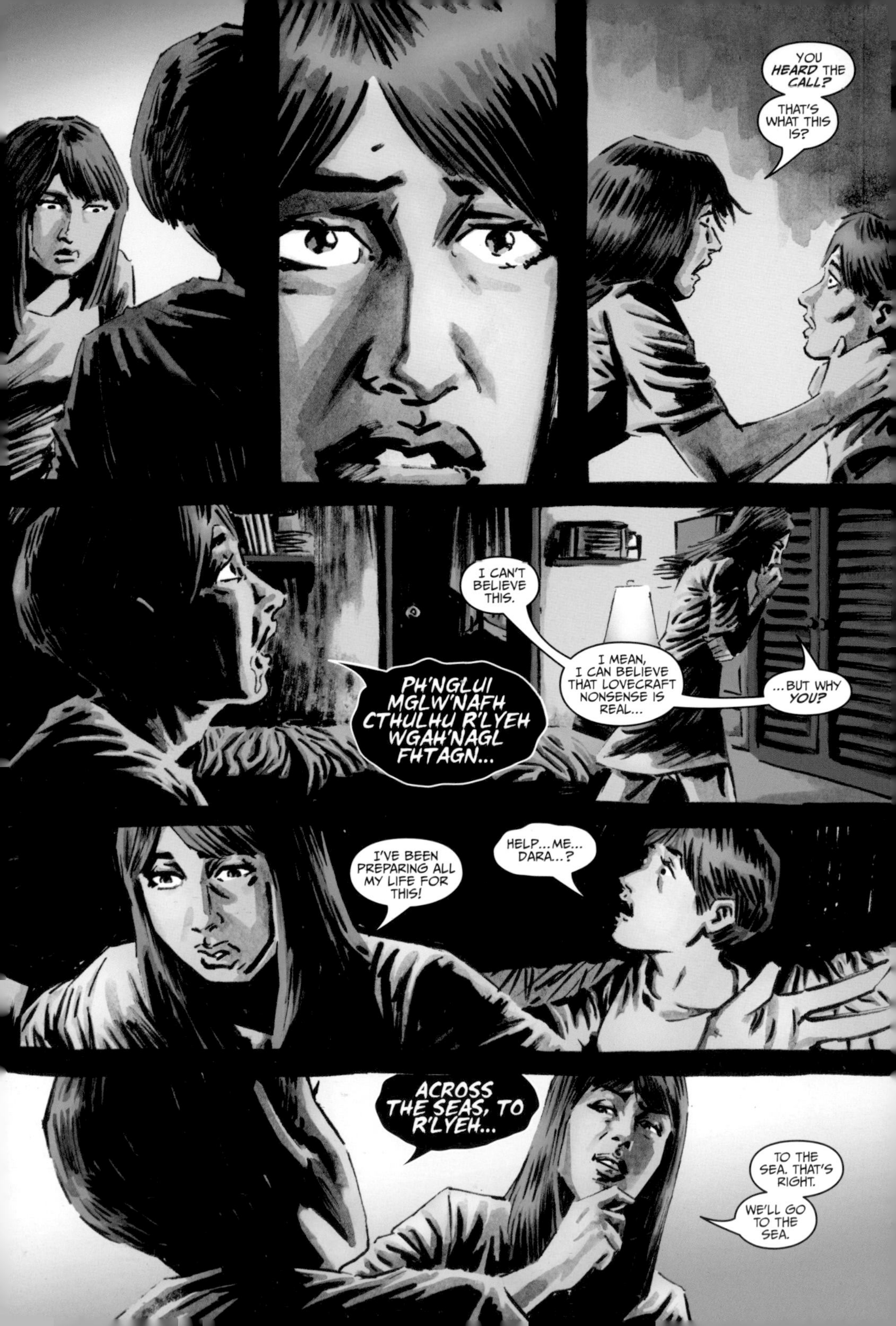
YOU HEARD THE CALL?
THAT'S WHAT THIS IS?
I CAN'T BELIEVE THIS.
I MEAN, I CAN BELIEVE THAT LOVECRAFT NONSENSE IS REAL...
...BUT WHY YOU?
PH'NGLUI MGLW'NAFH CTHULHU R'LYEH WGAH'NAGL FHTAGN...
I'VE BEEN PREPARING ALL MY LIFE FOR THIS!
HELP...ME... DARA...?
ACROSS THE SEAS, TO R'LYEH...
TO THE SEA. THAT'S RIGHT.
WE'LL GO TO THE SEA.

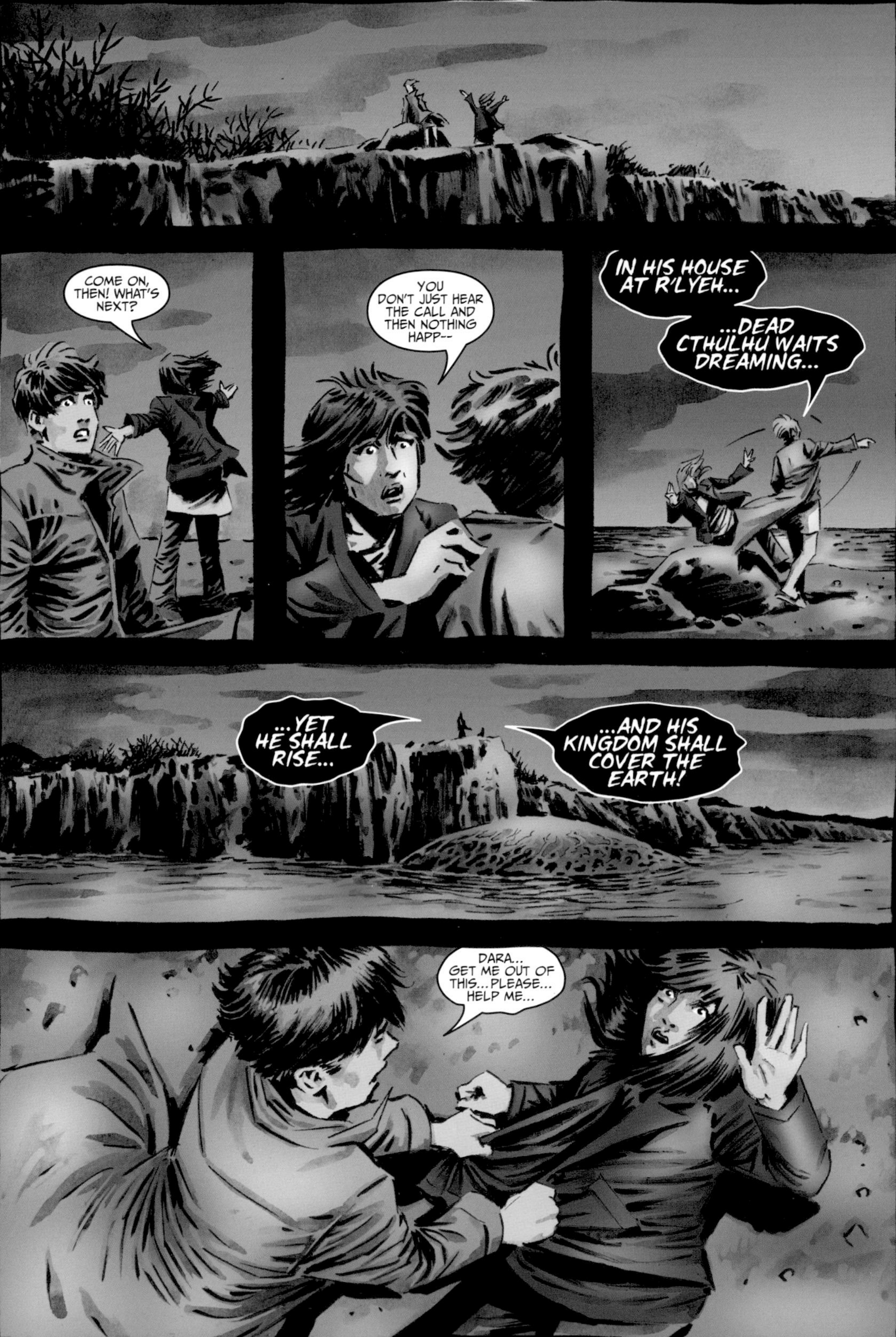
COME ON, THEN! WHAT'S NEXT?
YOU DON'T JUST HEAR THE CALL AND THEN NOTHING HAPP--
IN HIS HOUSE AT R'LYEH...
...DEAD CTHULHU WAITS DREAMING...
...YET HE SHALL RISE...
...AND HIS KINGDOM SHALL COVER THE EARTH!
DARA... GET ME OUT OF THIS...PLEASE... HELP ME...

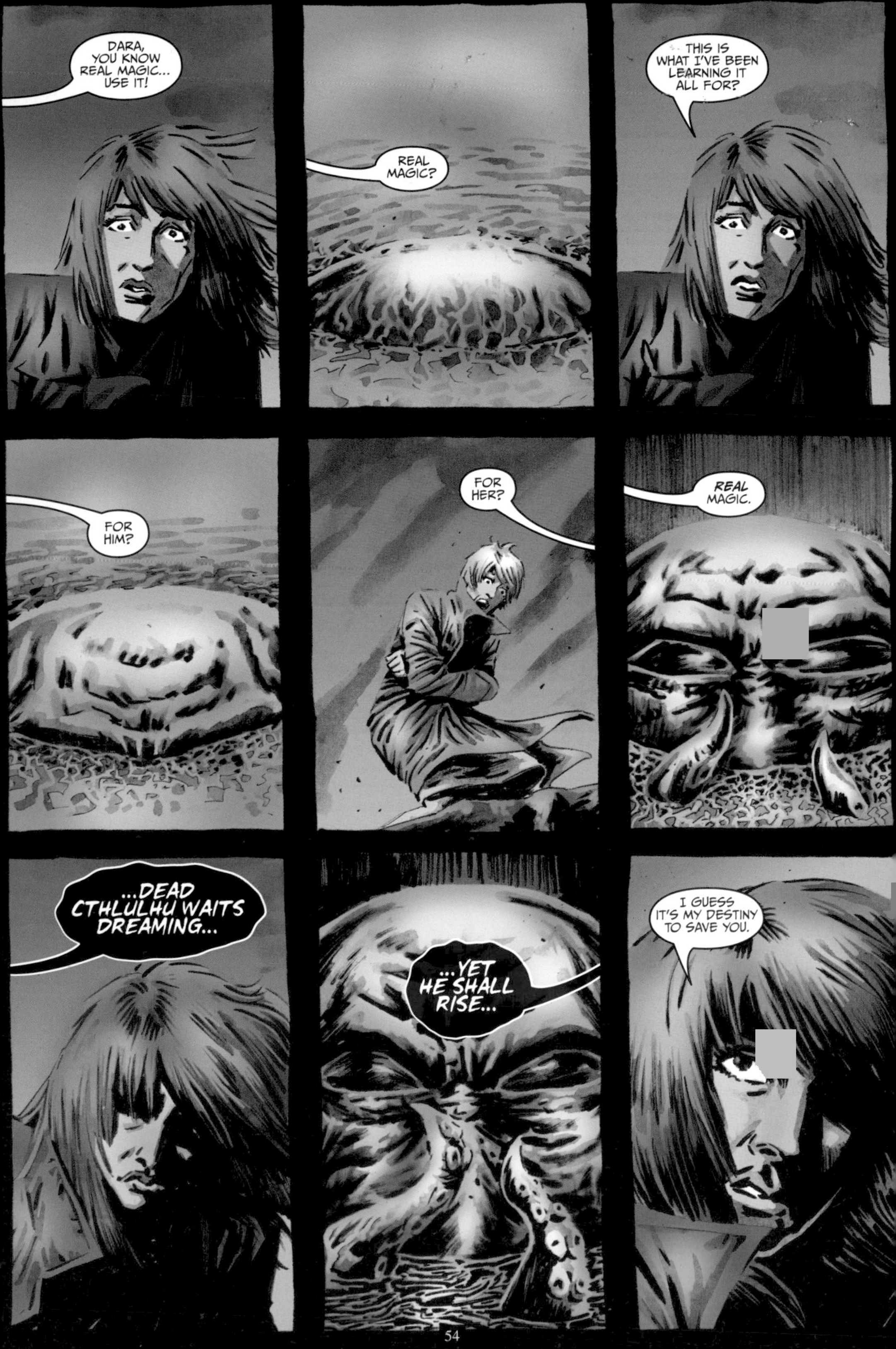
DARA, YOU KNOW REAL MAGIC... USE IT!
REAL MAGIC?
THIS IS WHAT I'VE BEEN LEARNING IT ALL FOR?
FOR HIM?
FOR HER?
REAL MAGIC.
...DEAD CTHLULHU WAITS DREAMING...
...YET HE SHALL RISE...
I GUESS IT'S MY DESTINY TO SAVE YOU.

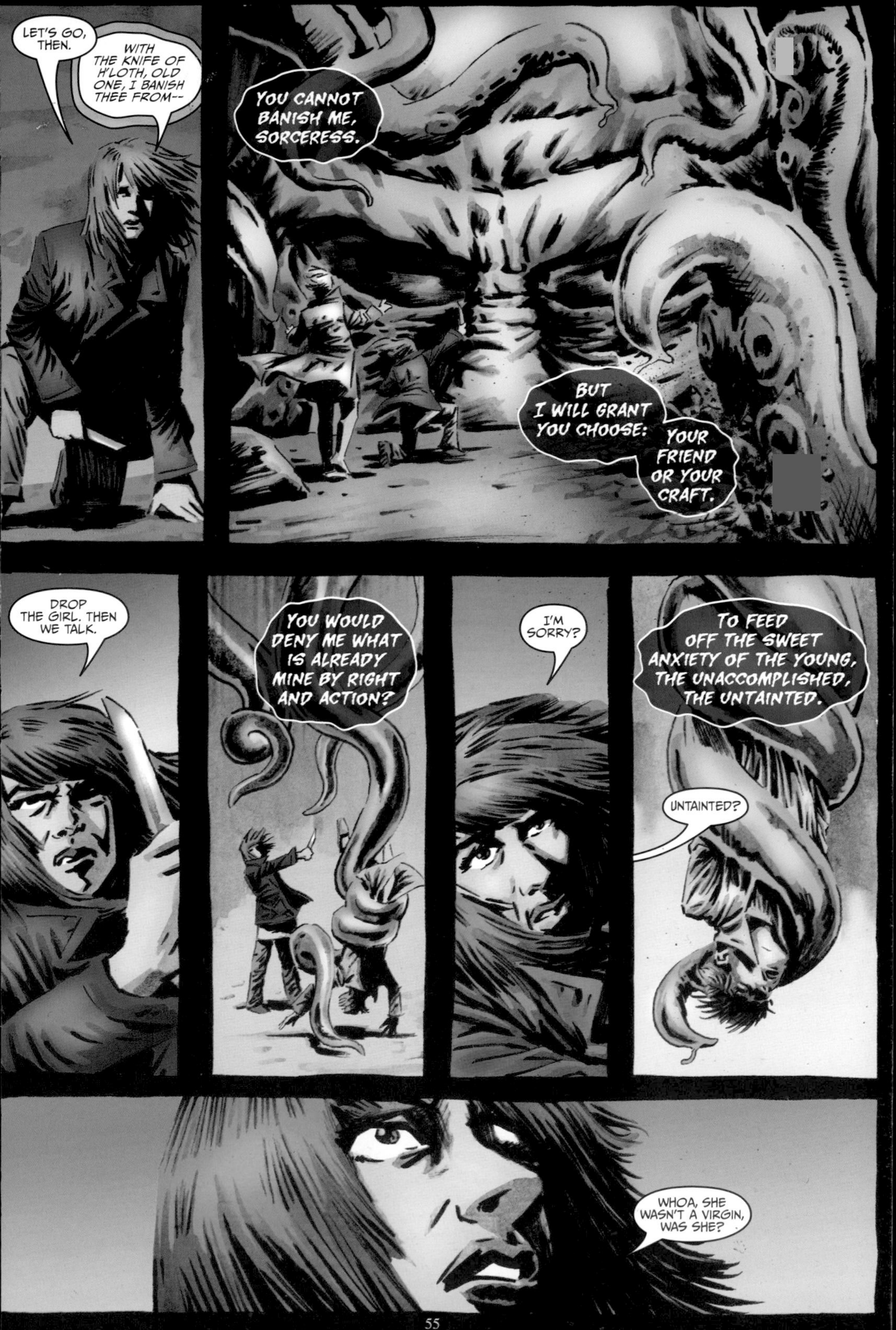
LET'S GO, THEN.
WITH THE KNIFE OF H'LOTH, OLD ONE, I BANISH THEE FROM--
YOU CANNOT BANISH ME, SORCERESS.
BUT I WILL GRANT YOU CHOOSE:
YOUR FRIEND OR YOUR CRAFT.
DROP THE GIRL. THEN WE TALK.
YOU WOULD DENY ME WHAT IS ALREADY MINE BY RIGHT AND ACTION?
I'M SORRY?
TO FEED OFF THE SWEET ANXIETY OF THE YOUNG, THE UNACCOMPLISHED, THE UNTAINTED.
UNTAINTED?
WHOA, SHE WASN'T A VIRGIN, WAS SHE?

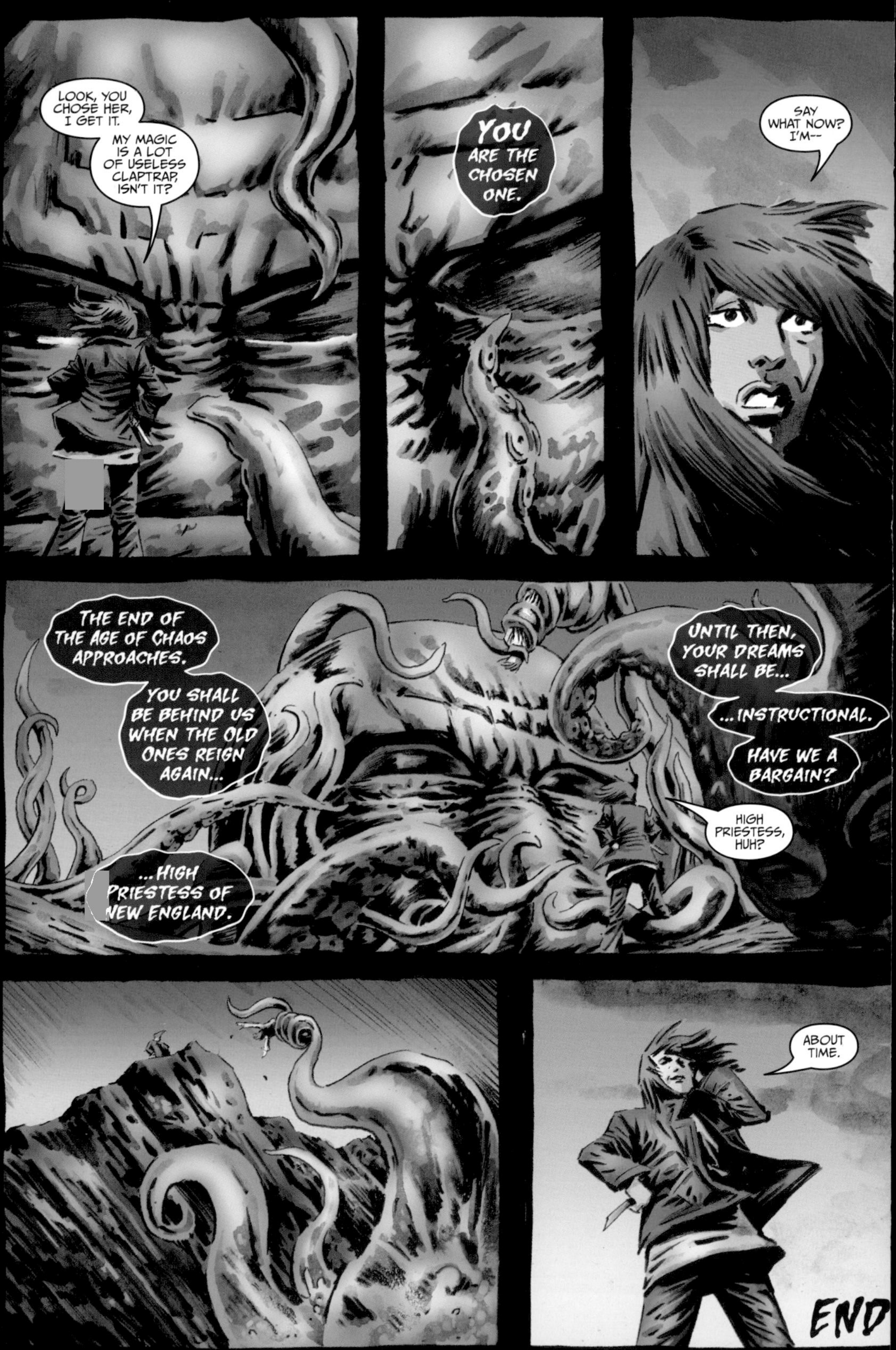
LOOK, YOU CHOSE HER, I GET IT.
MY MAGIC IS A LOT OF USELESS CLAPTRAP, ISN'T IT?
YOU ARE THE CHOSEN ONE.
SAY WHAT NOW? I'M--
THE END OF THE AGE OF CHAOS APPROACHES.
YOU SHALL BE BEHIND US WHEN THE OLD ONES REIGN AGAIN...
...HIGH PRIESTESS OF NEW ENGLAND.
UNTIL THEN, YOUR DREAMS SHALL BE...
...INSTRUCTIONAL.
HAVE WE A BARGAIN?
HIGH PRIESTESS, HUH?
ABOUT TIME.
END

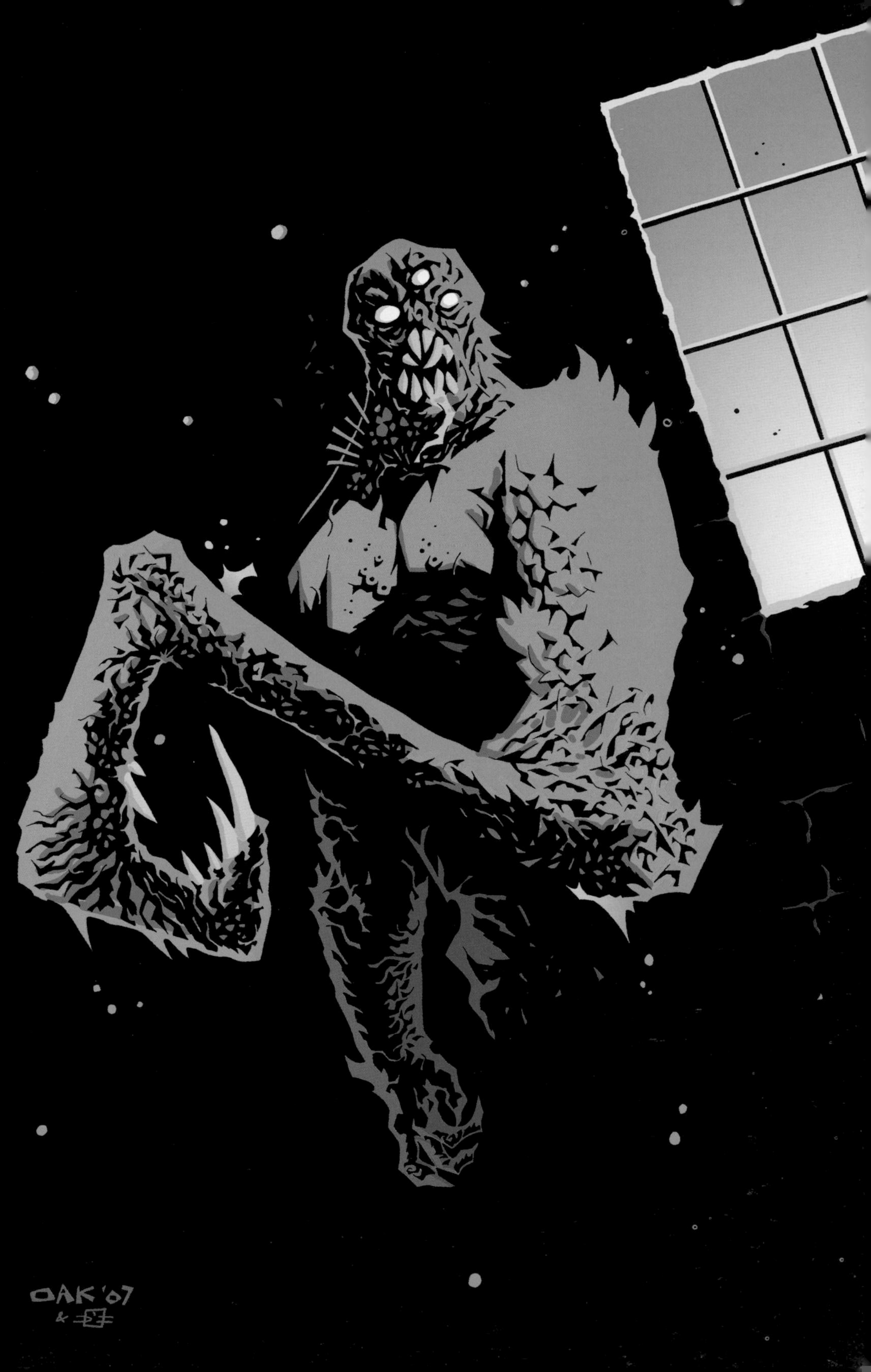
OAK '07

5

47°9'S 126°43'W

It burst from the water with such force, the ship threatened to capsize. I fought to control the ship, but the engine died. We stood on the forecastle and watched the creature lumbering through the depths. The wind was still and, but on the wake of the creature the seas dead calm. The figure of the thing pulled at the sanity of my crew.

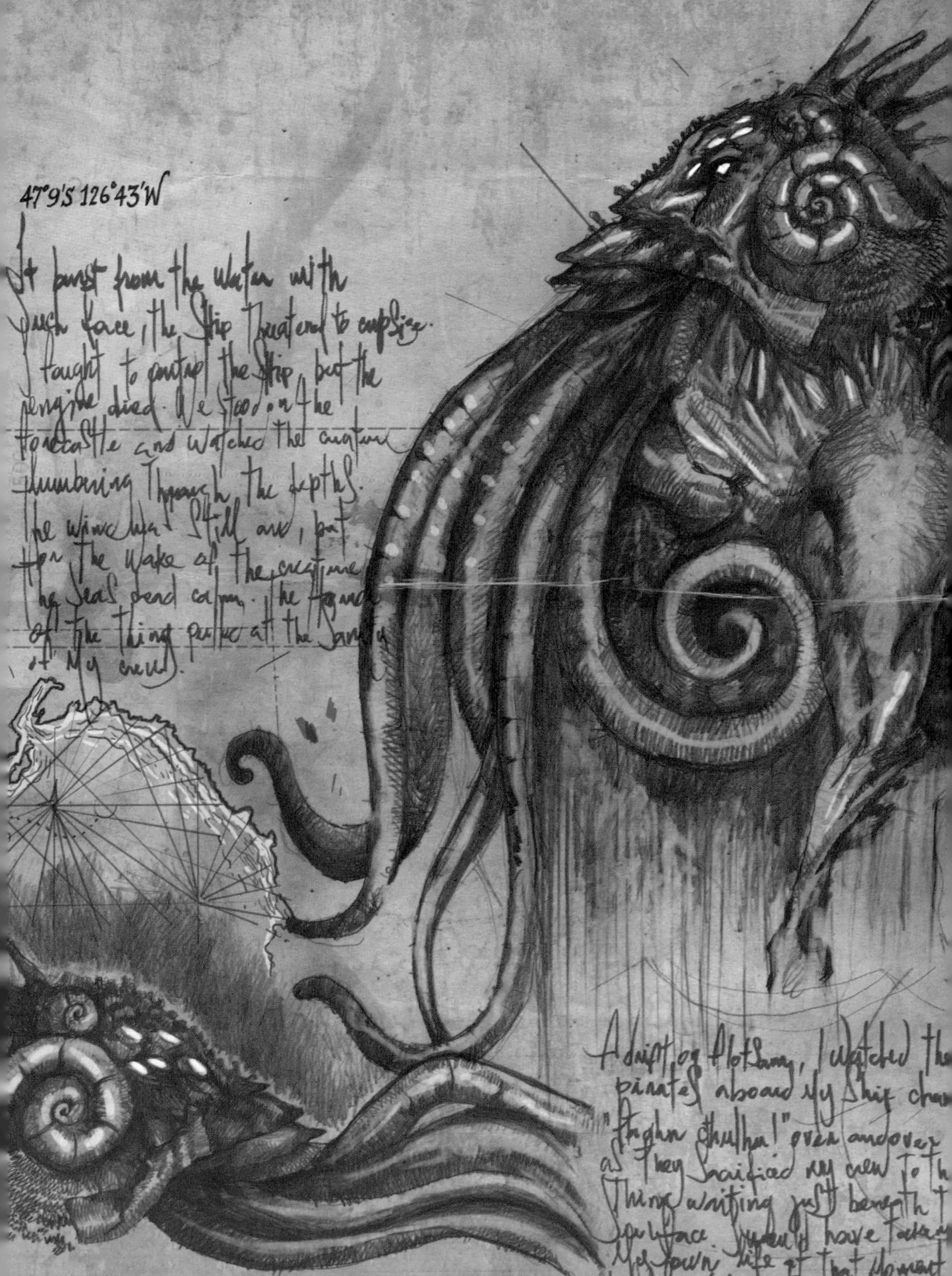

Adrift on flotsam, I watched the pirates aboard my ship chant "Fhtagn Cthulhu!" over and over as they sacrificed my crew to the Thing waiting just beneath the surface. I would have taken my own life at that moment had I not been too terrified to move

ALIMENTARY,
MY DEAR CTHULHU
STORY WILLIAM MESSNER-LOEBS
ART ANDREW RITCHIE

ON THE WAGON
STORY MICHAEL ALAN NELSON
ART EDUARDO FERIGATO

THE CRUISE OF CTHULHU
STORY TODD LEPRE
ART CHEE

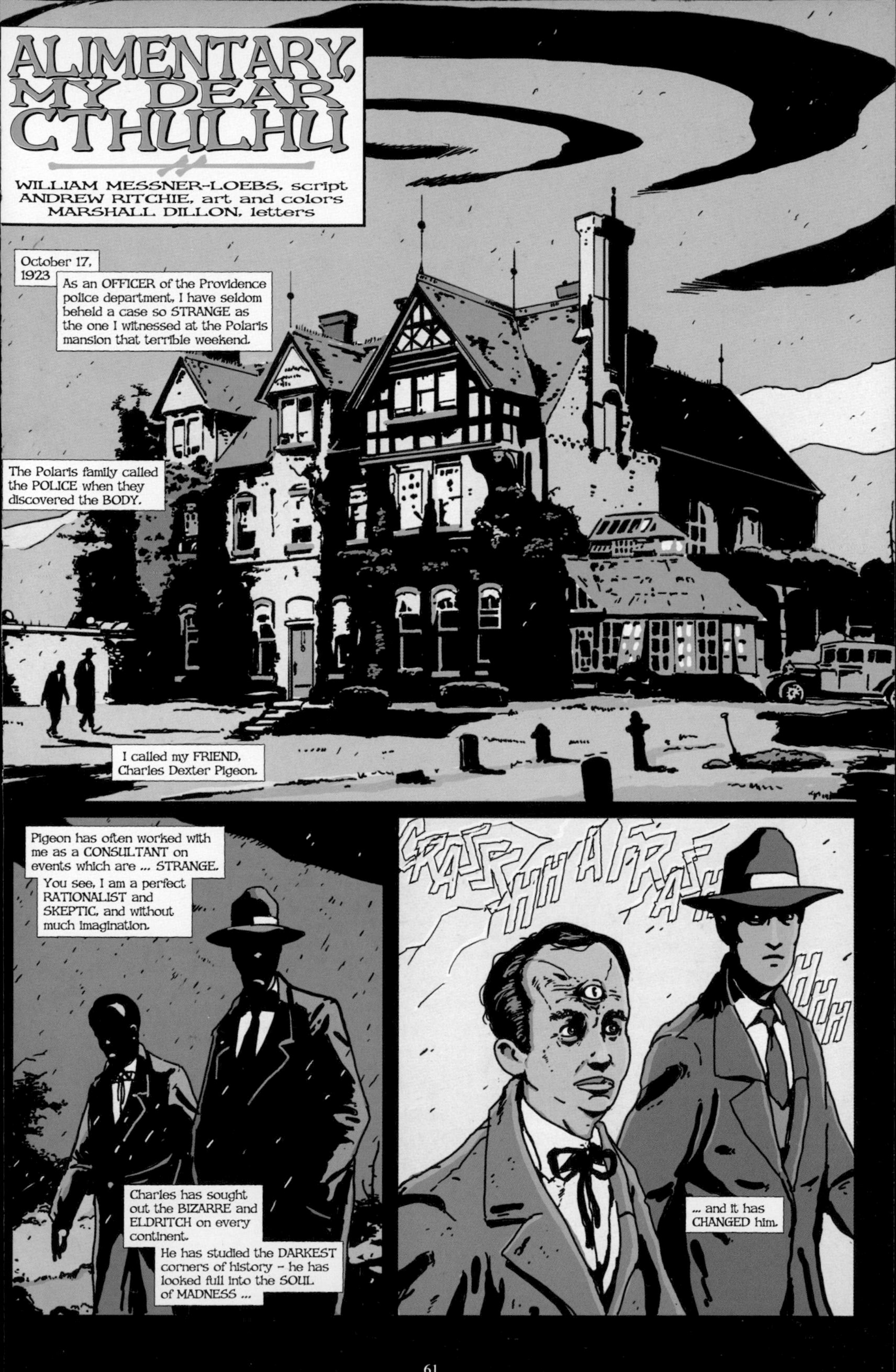
ALIMENTARY, MY DEAR CTHULHU
WILLIAM MESSNER-LOEBS, script
ANDREW RITCHIE, art and colors
MARSHALL DILLON, letters
October 17, 1923
As an OFFICER of the Providence police department, I have seldom beheld a case so STRANGE as the one I witnessed at the Polaris mansion that terrible weekend.
The Polaris family called the POLICE when they discovered the BODY.
I called my FRIEND, Charles Dexter Pigeon.
Pigeon has often worked with me as a CONSULTANT on events which are ... STRANGE.
You see, I am a perfect RATIONALIST and SKEPTIC, and without much imagination.
Charles has sought out the BIZARRE and ELDRITCH on every continent.
He has studied the DARKEST corners of history - he has looked full into the SOUL of MADNESS ...
... and it has CHANGED him.

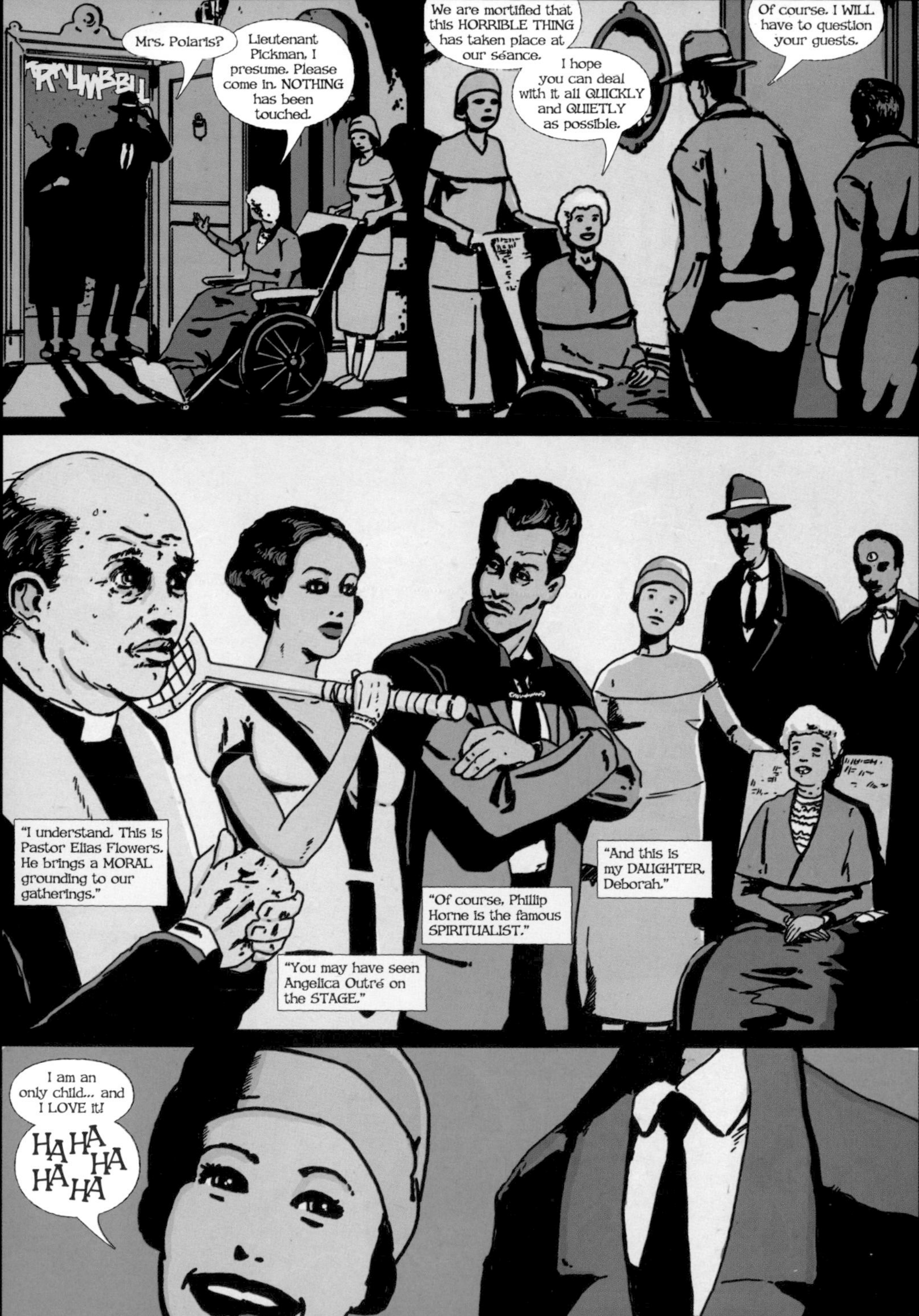
TRRUMBBLL
Mrs. Polaris?
Lieutenant Pickman, I presume. Please come in. NOTHING has been touched.
We are mortified that this HORRIBLE THING has taken place at our séance.
I hope you can deal with it all QUICKLY and QUIETLY as possible.
Of course. I WILL have to question your guests.
"I understand. This is Pastor Elias Flowers. He brings a MORAL grounding to our gatherings."
"You may have seen Angelica Outré on the STAGE."
"Of course, Phillip Horne is the famous SPIRITUALIST."
"And this is my DAUGHTER, Deborah."
I am an only child... and I LOVE it!
HA HA HA HA HA

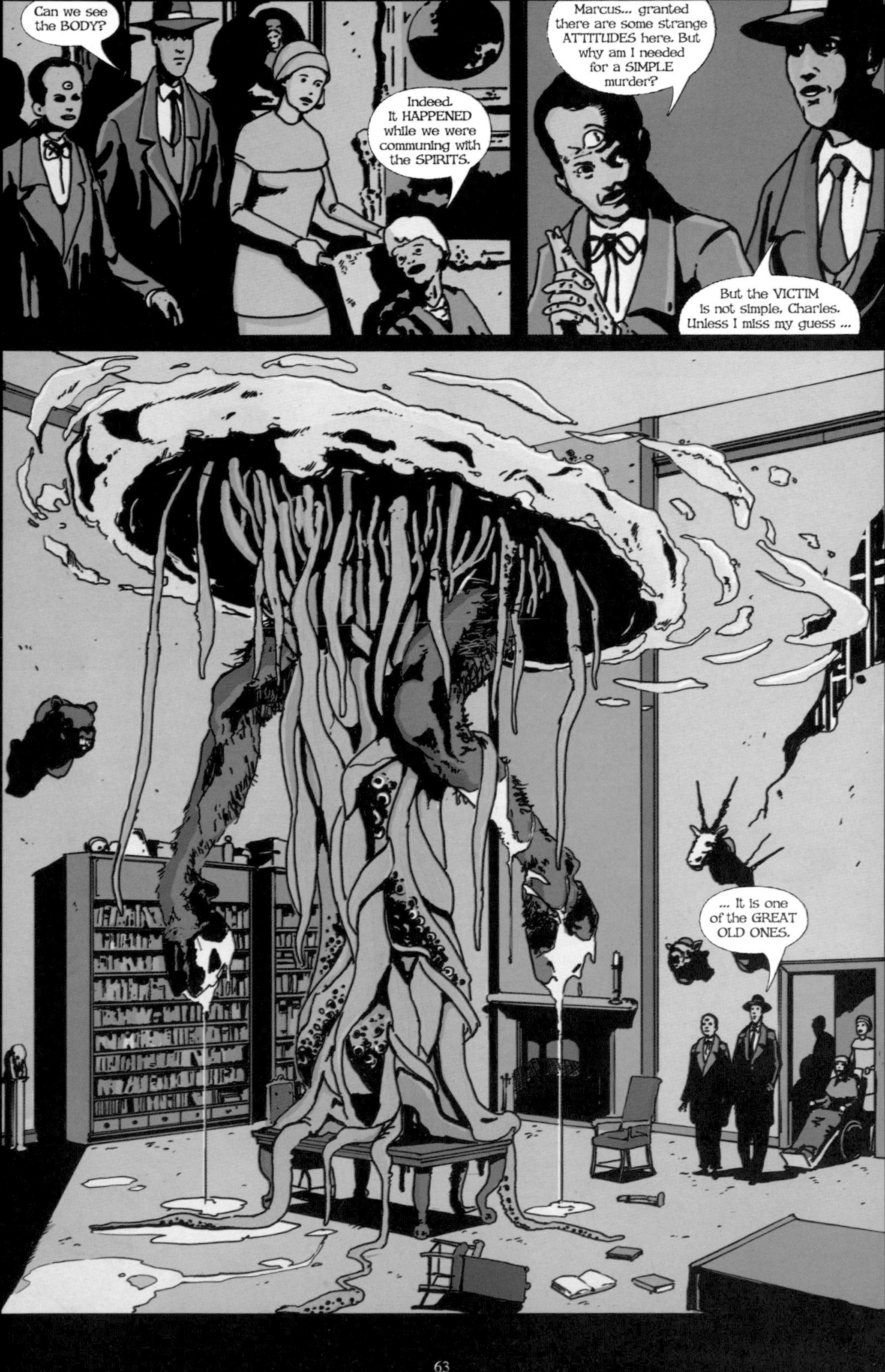
Can we see the BODY?
Indeed. It HAPPENED while we were communing with the SPIRITS.
Marcus... granted there are some strange ATTITUDES here. But why am I needed for a SIMPLE murder?
But the VICTIM is not simple, Charles. Unless I miss my guess ...
... It is one of the GREAT OLD ONES.

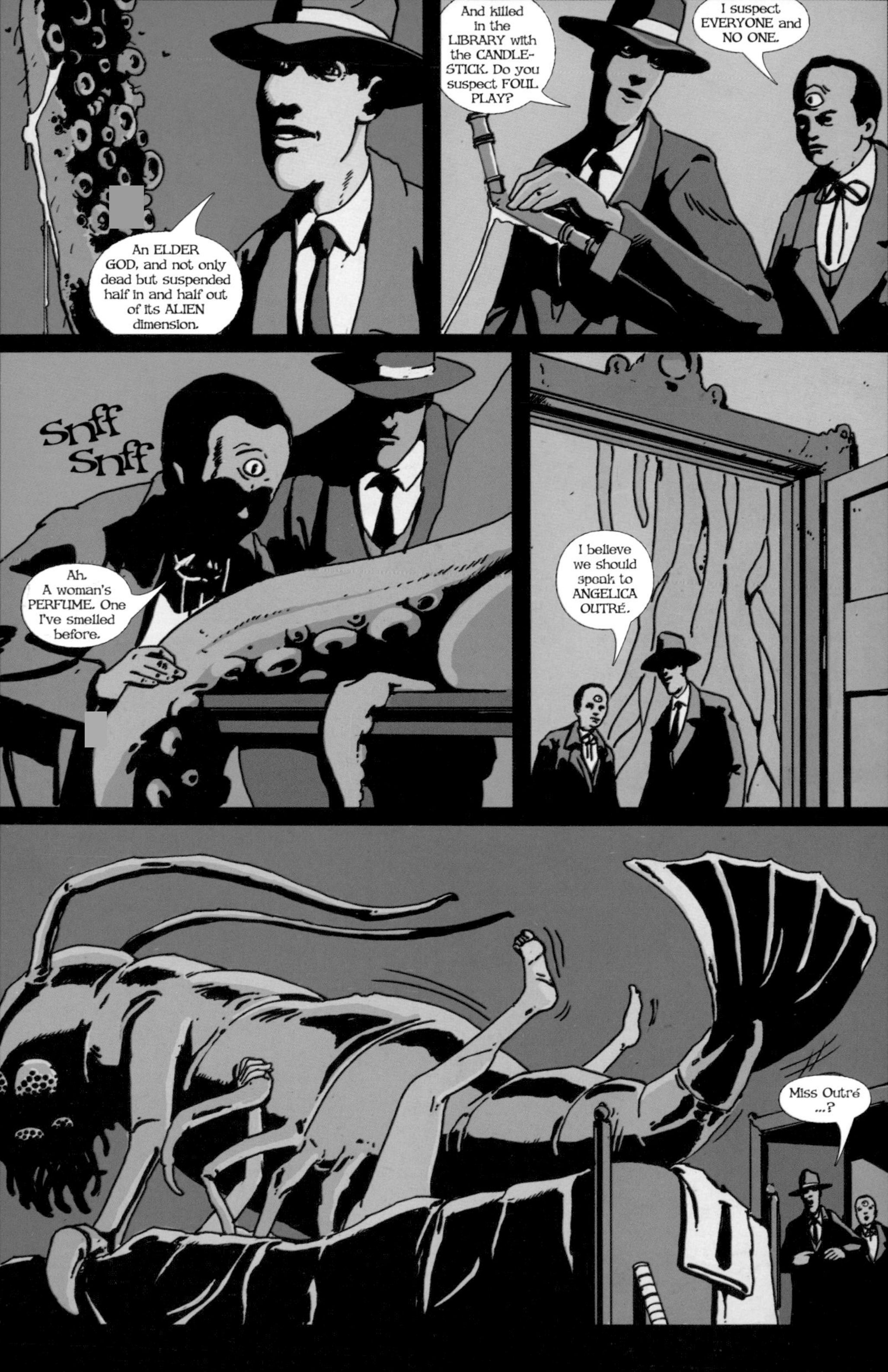
An ELDER GOD, and not only dead but suspended half in and half out of its ALIEN dimension.
And killed in the LIBRARY with the CANDLE-STICK. Do you suspect FOUL PLAY?
I suspect EVERYONE and NO ONE.
Snff Snff
Ah. A woman's PERFUME. One I've smelled before.
I believe we should speak to ANGELICA OUTRÉ.
Miss Outré ...?

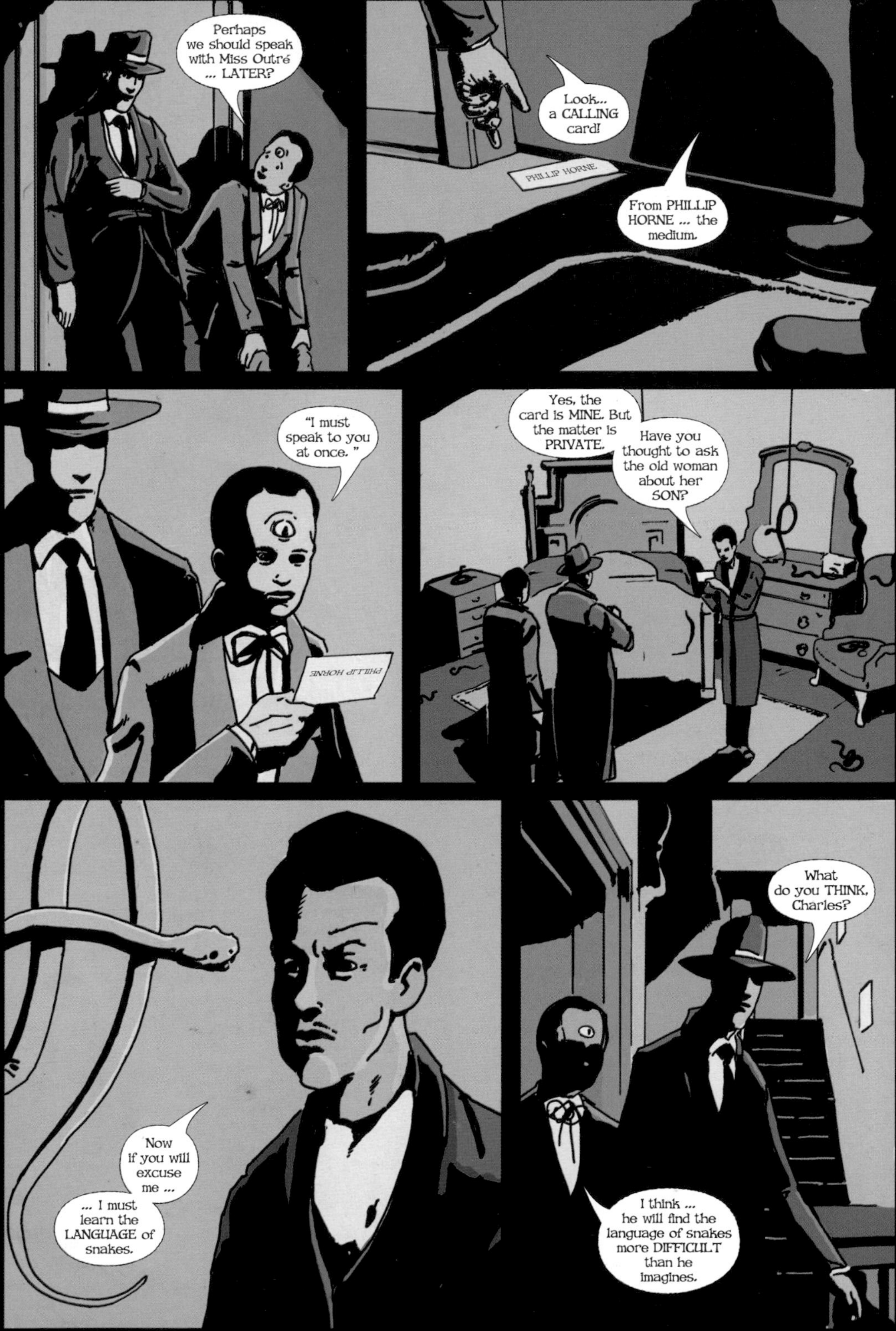
Perhaps we should speak with Miss Outré ... LATER?
Look... a CALLING card!
PHILLIP HORNE
From PHILLIP HORNE ... the medium.
"I must speak to you at once."
PHILLIP HORNE
Yes, the card is MINE. But the matter is PRIVATE.
Have you thought to ask the old woman about her SON?
Now if you will excuse me ...
... I must learn the LANGUAGE of snakes.
What do you THINK, Charles?
I think ... he will find the language of snakes more DIFFICULT than he imagines.

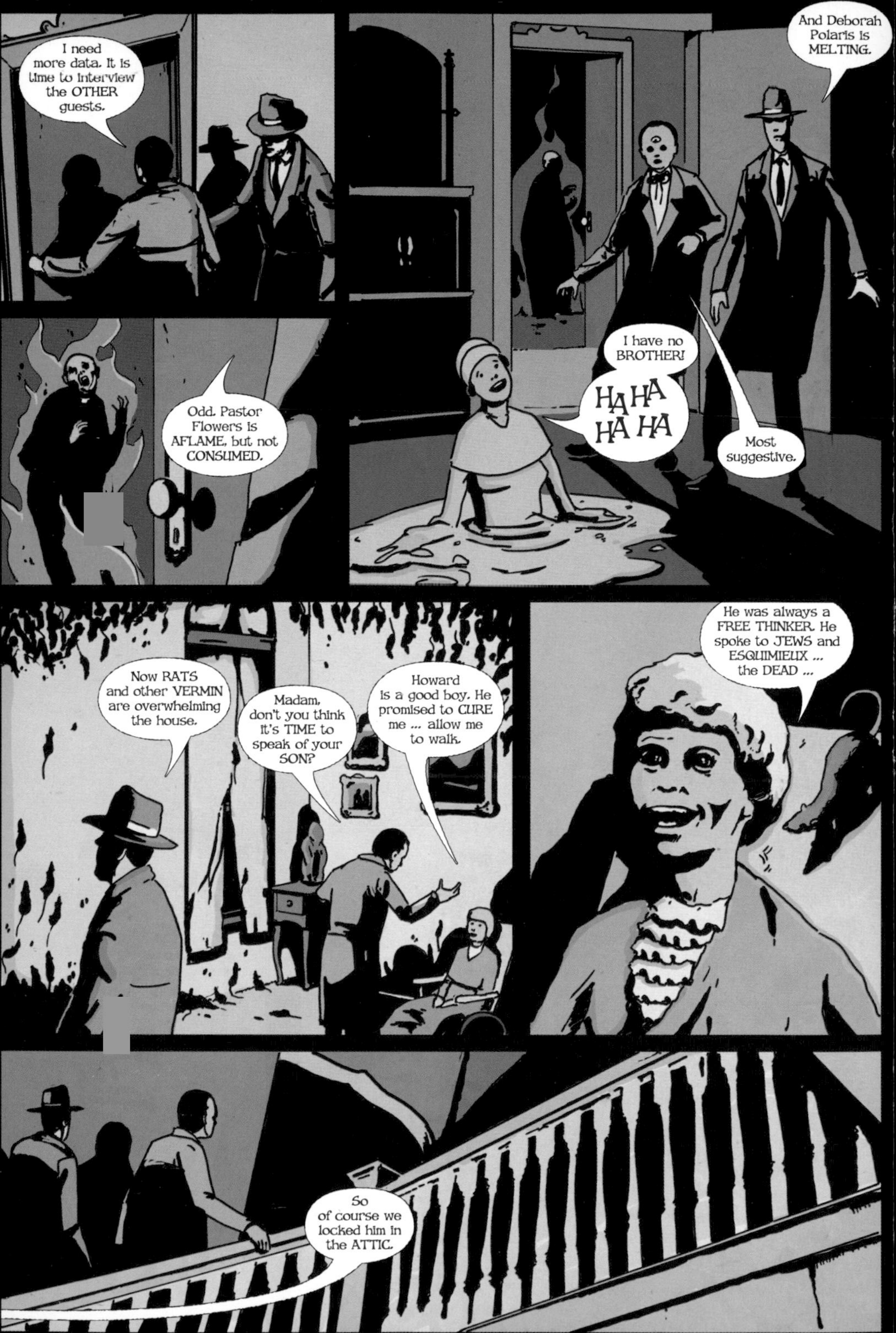
I need more data. It is time to interview the OTHER guests.
And Deborah Polaris is MELTING.
Odd. Pastor Flowers is AFLAME, but not CONSUMED.
I have no BROTHER!
HA HA HA HA
Most suggestive.
Now RATS and other VERMIN are overwhelming the house.
Madam, don't you think it's TIME to speak of your SON?
Howard is a good boy. He promised to CURE me ... allow me to walk.
He was always a FREE THINKER. He spoke to JEWS and ESQUIMIEUX ... the DEAD ...
So of course we locked him in the ATTIC.

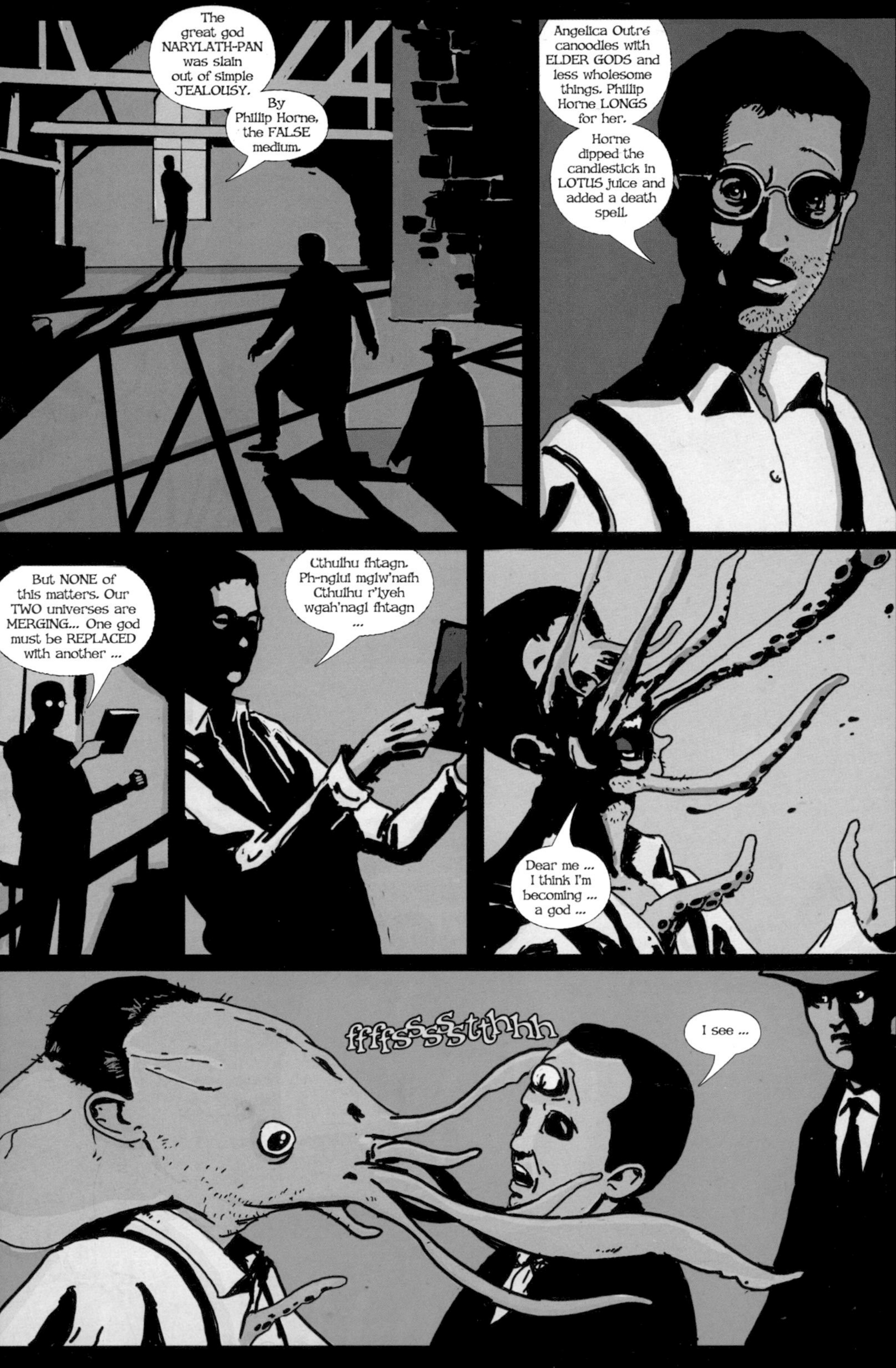
The great god NARYLATH-PAN was slain out of simple JEALOUSY.
By Phillip Horne, the FALSE medium.
Angelica Outré canoodles with ELDER GODS and less wholesome things. Phillip Horne LONGS for her.
Horne dipped the candlestick in LOTUS juice and added a death spell.
But NONE of this matters. Our TWO universes are MERGING... One god must be REPLACED with another ...
Cthulhu fhtagn. Ph-nglui mglw'nafh Cthulhu r'lyeh wgah'nagl fhtagn ...
Dear me ... I think I'm becoming ... a god ...
ffffsSSStthhh
I see ...

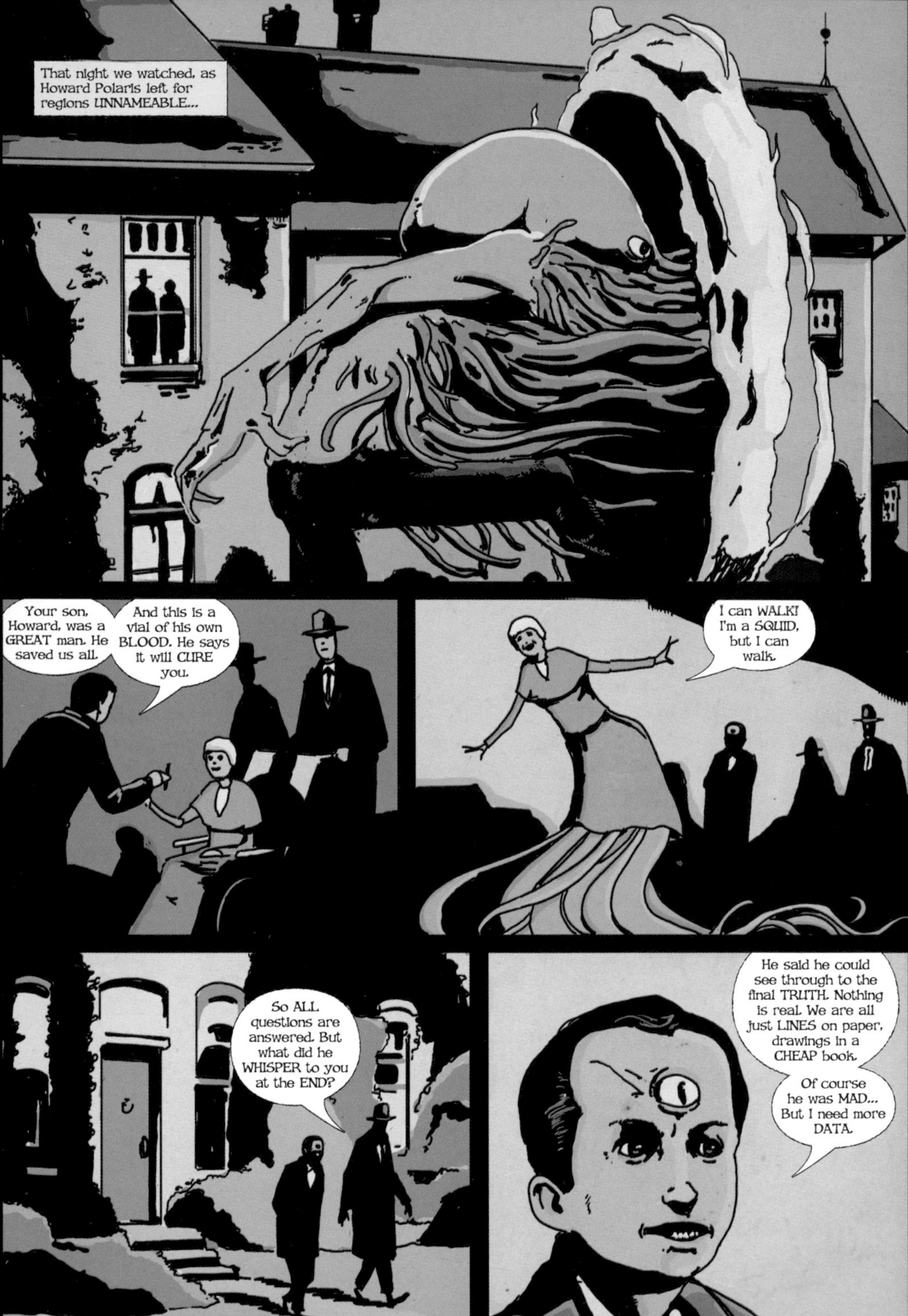
That night we watched, as Howard Polaris left for regions UNNAMEABLE...
Your son, Howard, was a GREAT man. He saved us all.
And this is a vial of his own BLOOD. He says it will CURE you.
I can WALK! I'm a SQUID, but I can walk.
So ALL questions are answered. But what did he WHISPER to you at the END?
He said he could see through to the final TRUTH. Nothing is real. We are all just LINES on paper, drawings in a CHEAP book.
Of course he was MAD... But I need more DATA.
END

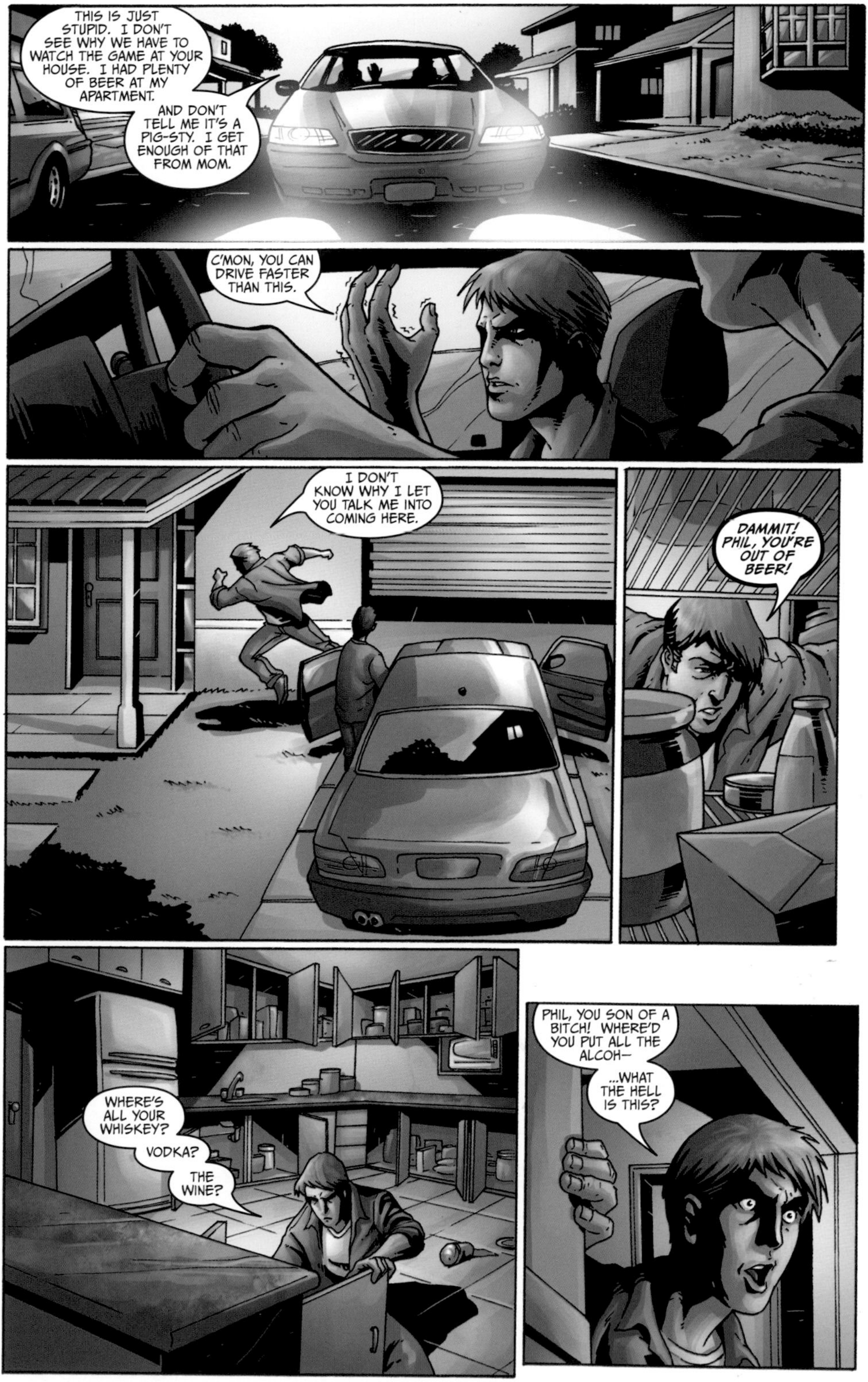
THIS IS JUST STUPID. I DON'T SEE WHY WE HAVE TO WATCH THE GAME AT YOUR HOUSE. I HAD PLENTY OF BEER AT MY APARTMENT.
AND DON'T TELL ME IT'S A PIG-STY. I GET ENOUGH OF THAT FROM MOM.
C'MON, YOU CAN DRIVE FASTER THAN THIS.
I DON'T KNOW WHY I LET YOU TALK ME INTO COMING HERE.
DAMMIT! PHIL, YOU'RE OUT OF BEER!
WHERE'S ALL YOUR WHISKEY?
VODKA?
THE WINE?
PHIL, YOU SON OF A BITCH! WHERE'D YOU PUT ALL THE ALCOH—
...WHAT THE HELL IS THIS?

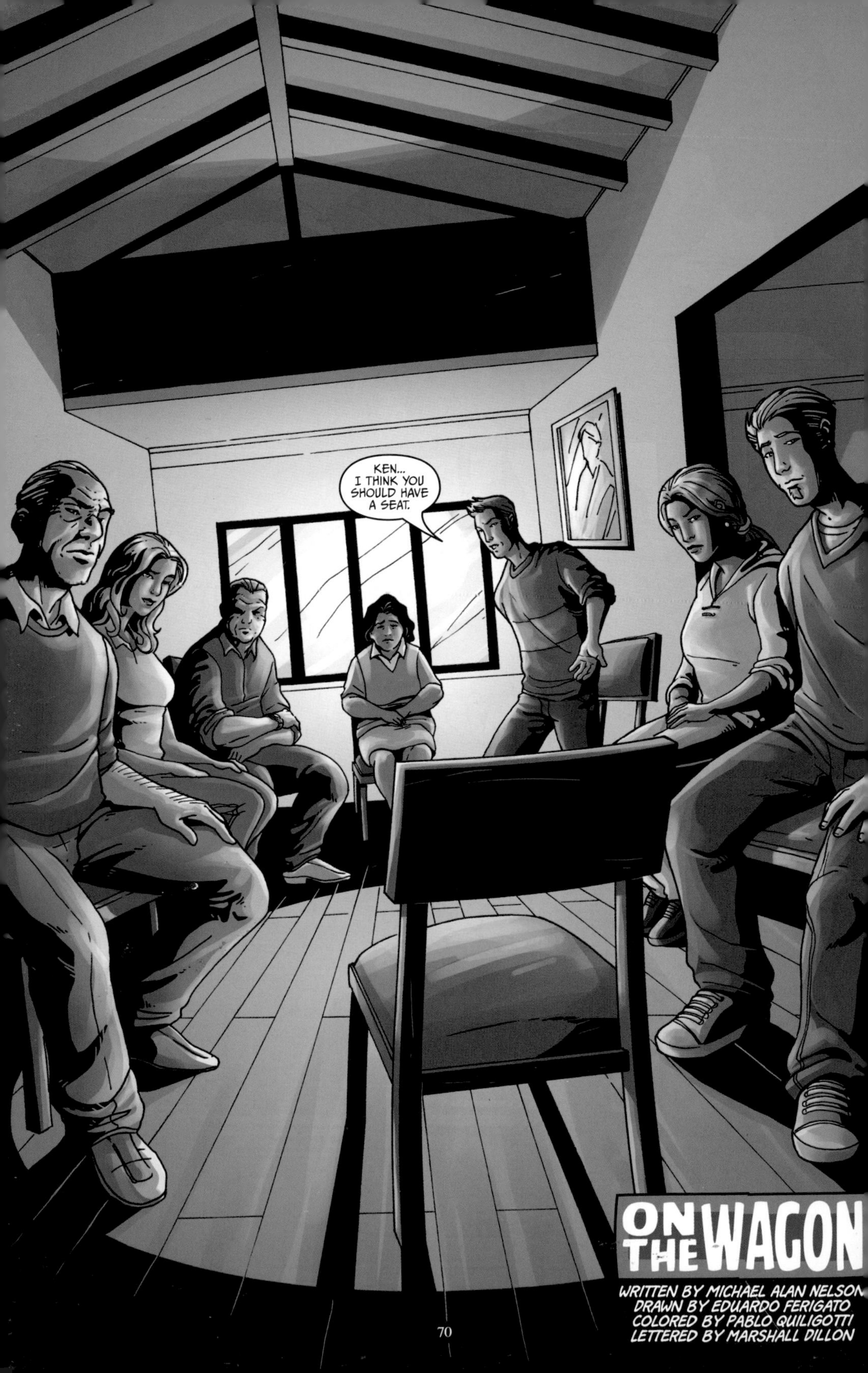
KEN... I THINK YOU SHOULD HAVE A SEAT.
ON THE WAGON
WRITTEN BY MICHAEL ALAN NELSON
DRAWN BY EDUARDO FERIGATO
COLORED BY PABLO QUILIGOTTI
LETTERED BY MARSHALL DILLON

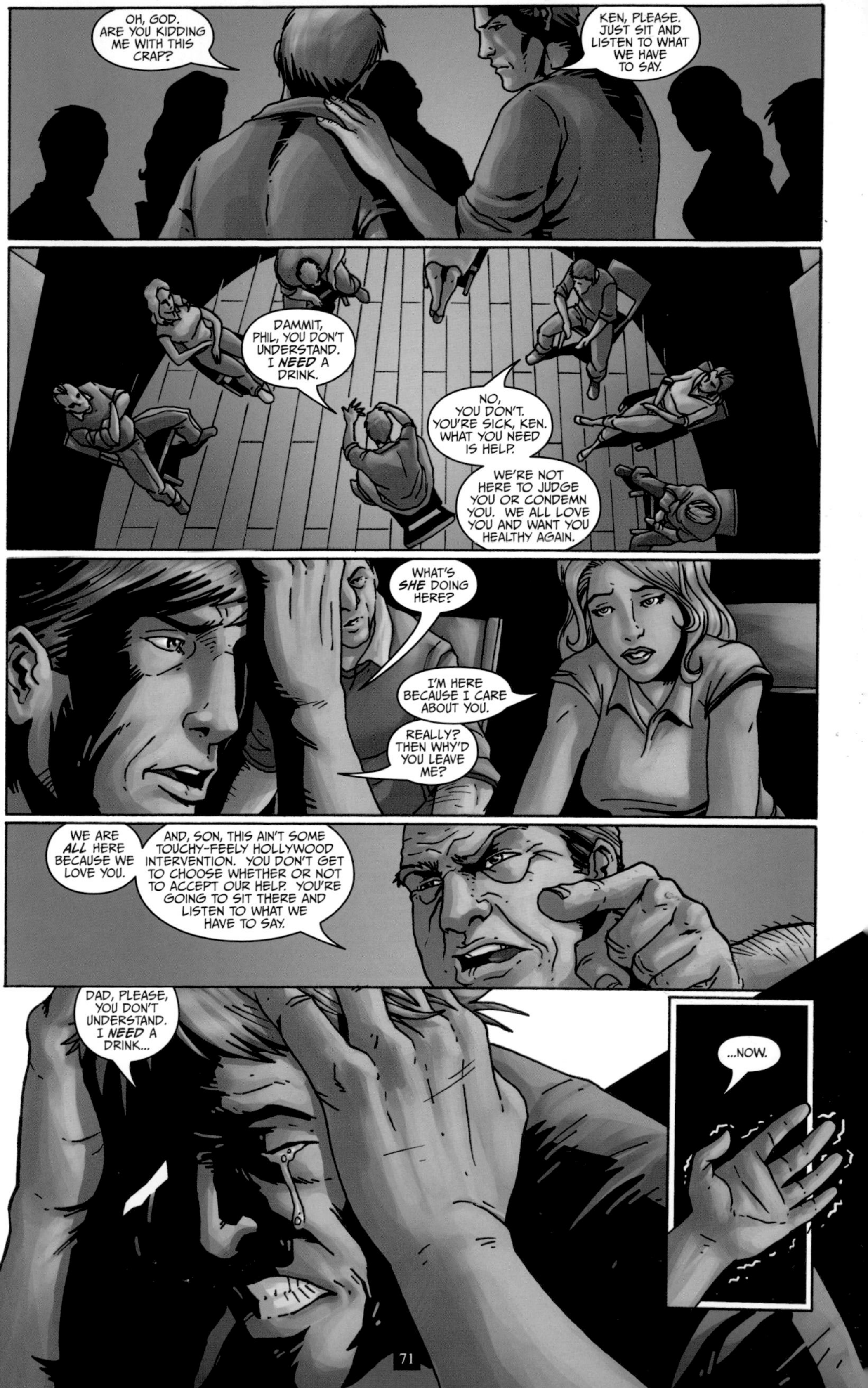
OH, GOD. ARE YOU KIDDING ME WITH THIS CRAP?
KEN, PLEASE. JUST SIT AND LISTEN TO WHAT WE HAVE TO SAY.
DAMMIT, PHIL, YOU DON'T UNDERSTAND. I *NEED* A DRINK.
NO, YOU DON'T. YOU'RE SICK, KEN. WHAT YOU NEED IS HELP.
WE'RE NOT HERE TO JUDGE YOU OR CONDEMN YOU. WE ALL LOVE YOU AND WANT YOU HEALTHY AGAIN.
WHAT'S *SHE* DOING HERE?
I'M HERE BECAUSE I CARE ABOUT YOU.
REALLY? THEN WHY'D YOU LEAVE ME?
WE ARE *ALL* HERE BECAUSE WE LOVE YOU.
AND, SON, THIS AIN'T SOME TOUCHY-FEELY HOLLYWOOD INTERVENTION. YOU DON'T GET TO CHOOSE WHETHER OR NOT TO ACCEPT OUR HELP. YOU'RE GOING TO SIT THERE AND LISTEN TO WHAT WE HAVE TO SAY.
DAD, PLEASE, YOU DON'T UNDERSTAND. I *NEED* A DRINK...
...NOW.

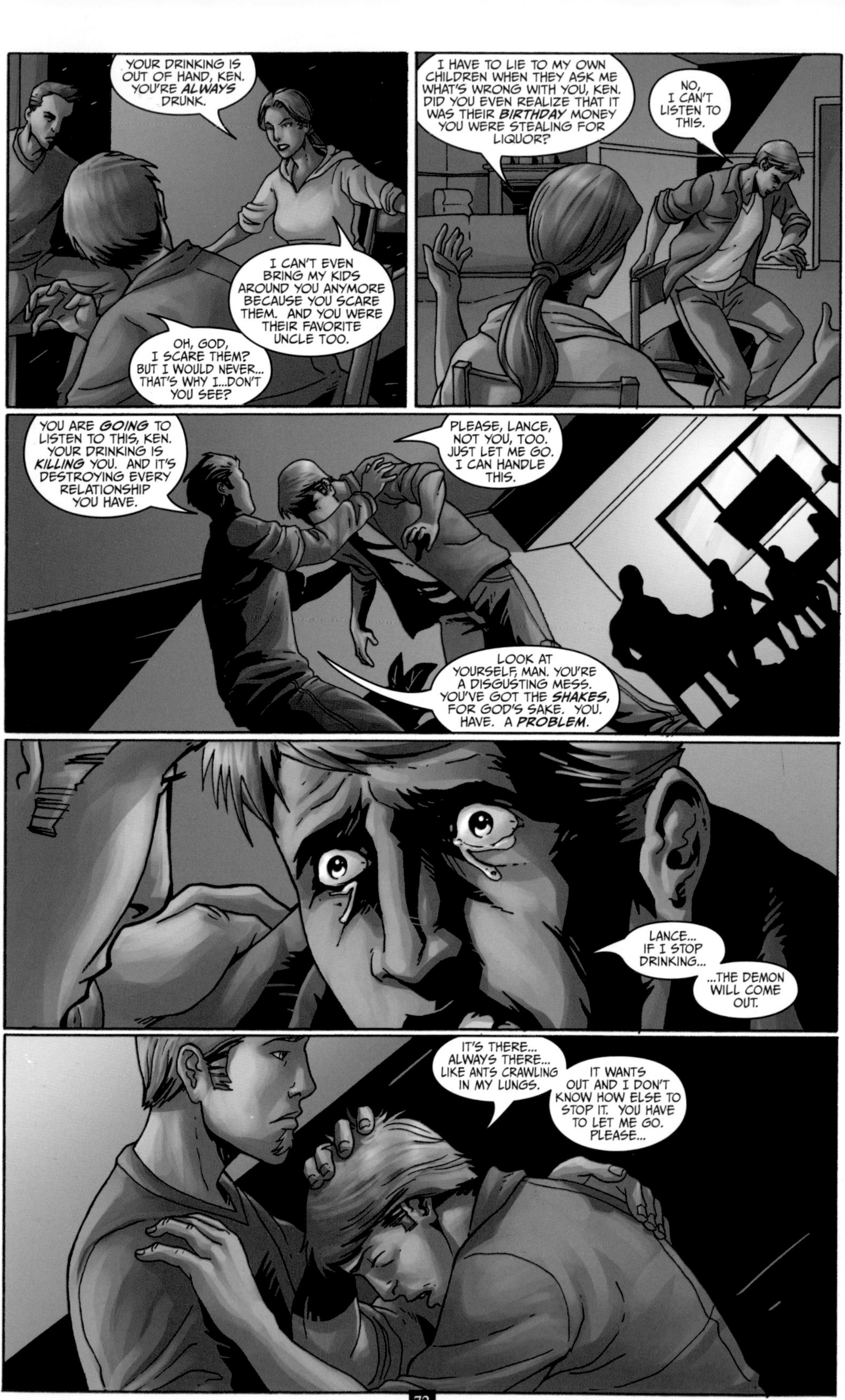
YOUR DRINKING IS OUT OF HAND, KEN. YOU'RE ALWAYS DRUNK.
I CAN'T EVEN BRING MY KIDS AROUND YOU ANYMORE BECAUSE YOU SCARE THEM. AND YOU WERE THEIR FAVORITE UNCLE TOO.
OH, GOD, I SCARE THEM? BUT I WOULD NEVER... THAT'S WHY I...DON'T YOU SEE?
I HAVE TO LIE TO MY OWN CHILDREN WHEN THEY ASK ME WHAT'S WRONG WITH YOU, KEN. DID YOU EVEN REALIZE THAT IT WAS THEIR BIRTHDAY MONEY YOU WERE STEALING FOR LIQUOR?
NO, I CAN'T LISTEN TO THIS.
YOU ARE GOING TO LISTEN TO THIS, KEN. YOUR DRINKING IS KILLING YOU. AND IT'S DESTROYING EVERY RELATIONSHIP YOU HAVE.
PLEASE, LANCE, NOT YOU, TOO. JUST LET ME GO. I CAN HANDLE THIS.
LOOK AT YOURSELF, MAN. YOU'RE A DISGUSTING MESS. YOU'VE GOT THE SHAKES, FOR GOD'S SAKE. YOU. HAVE. A PROBLEM.
LANCE... IF I STOP DRINKING...
...THE DEMON WILL COME OUT.
IT'S THERE... ALWAYS THERE... LIKE ANTS CRAWLING IN MY LUNGS.
IT WANTS OUT AND I DON'T KNOW HOW ELSE TO STOP IT. YOU HAVE TO LET ME GO. PLEASE...

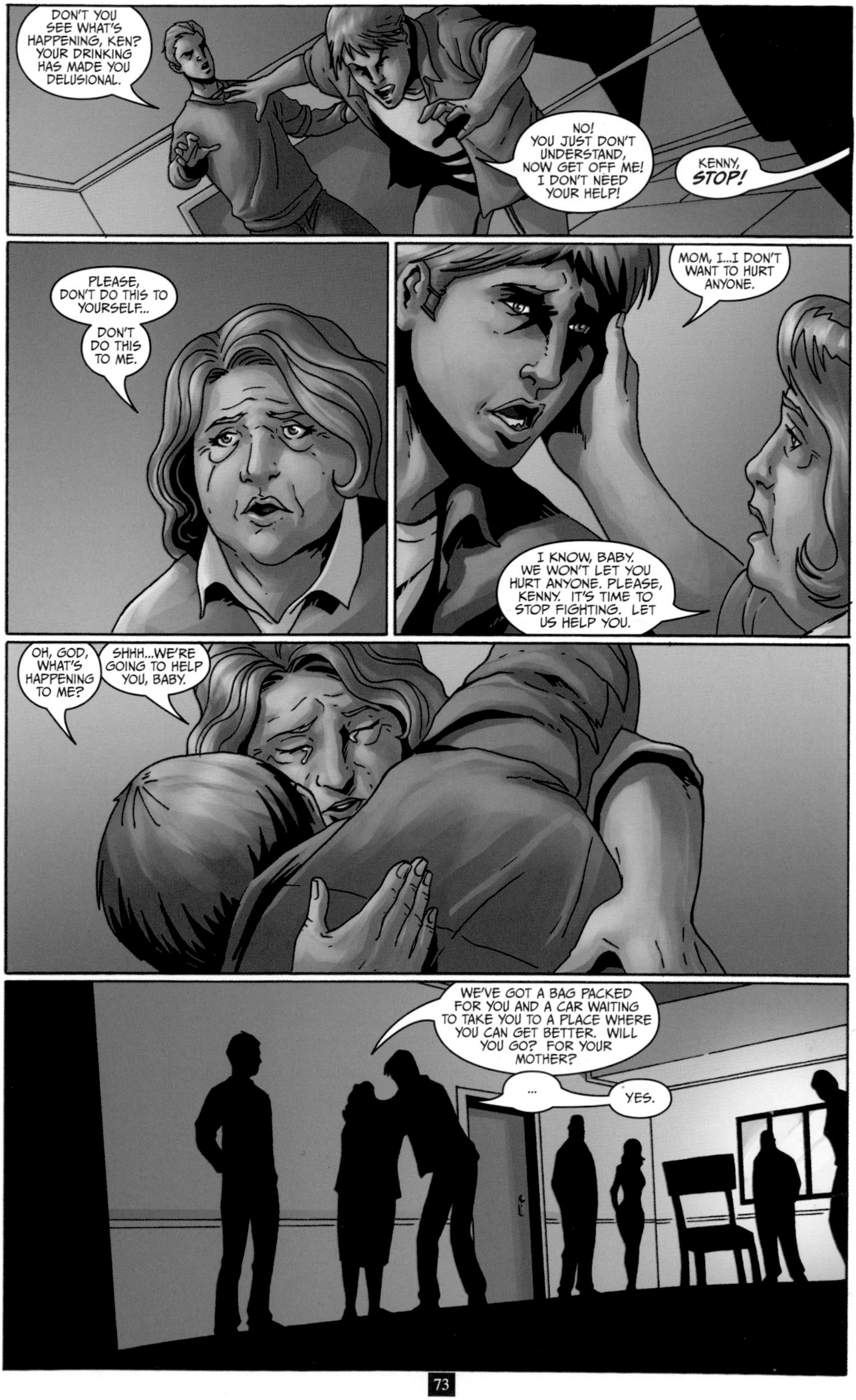
DON'T YOU SEE WHAT'S HAPPENING, KEN? YOUR DRINKING HAS MADE YOU DELUSIONAL.
NO! YOU JUST DON'T UNDERSTAND, NOW GET OFF ME! I DON'T NEED YOUR HELP!
KENNY, STOP!
PLEASE, DON'T DO THIS TO YOURSELF...
DON'T DO THIS TO ME.
MOM, I...I DON'T WANT TO HURT ANYONE.
I KNOW, BABY. WE WON'T LET YOU HURT ANYONE. PLEASE, KENNY. IT'S TIME TO STOP FIGHTING. LET US HELP YOU.
OH, GOD, WHAT'S HAPPENING TO ME?
SHHH...WE'RE GOING TO HELP YOU, BABY.
WE'VE GOT A BAG PACKED FOR YOU AND A CAR WAITING TO TAKE YOU TO A PLACE WHERE YOU CAN GET BETTER. WILL YOU GO? FOR YOUR MOTHER?
...
YES.

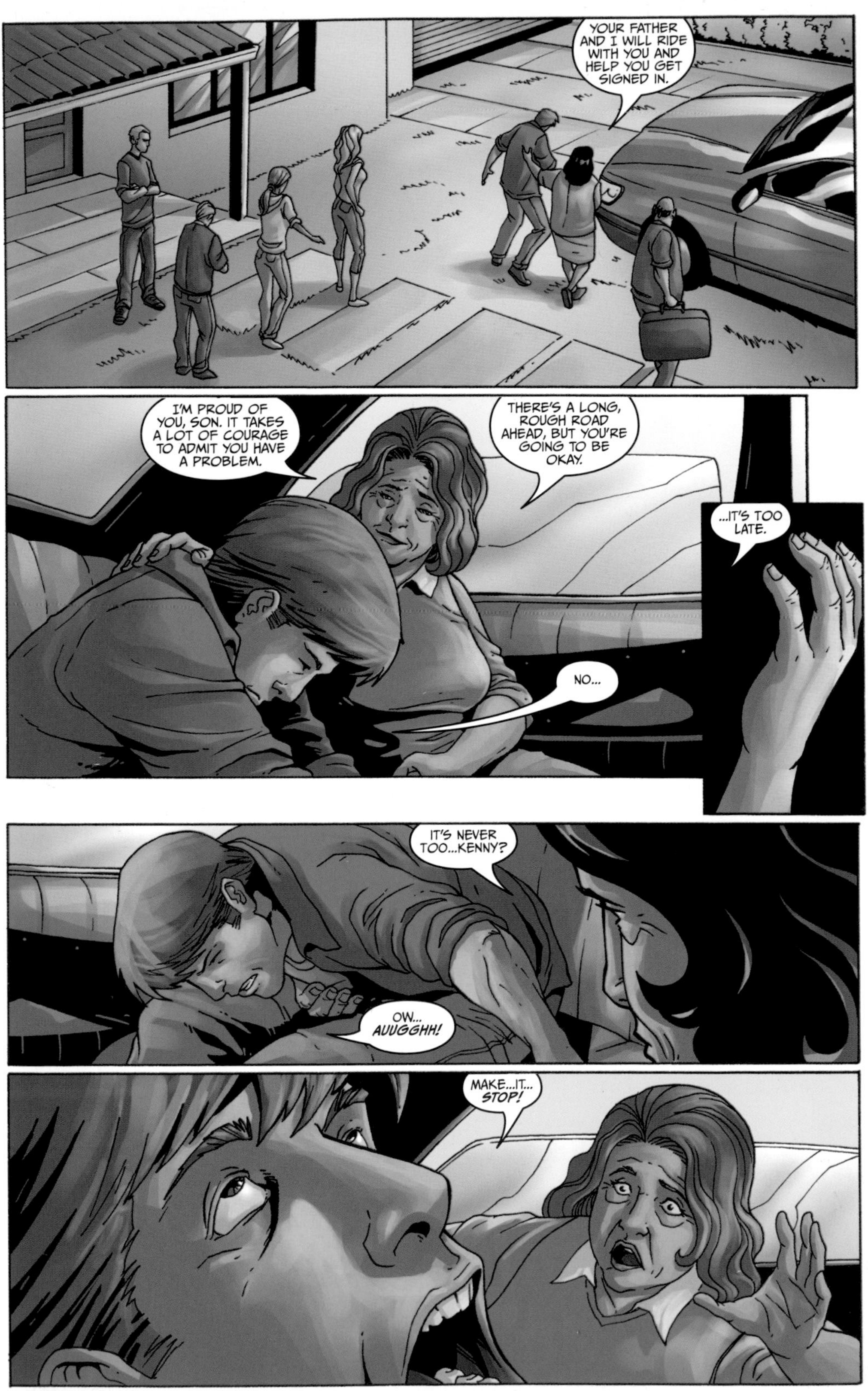
YOUR FATHER AND I WILL RIDE WITH YOU AND HELP YOU GET SIGNED IN.
I'M PROUD OF YOU, SON. IT TAKES A LOT OF COURAGE TO ADMIT YOU HAVE A PROBLEM.
THERE'S A LONG, ROUGH ROAD AHEAD, BUT YOU'RE GOING TO BE OKAY.
NO...
...IT'S TOO LATE.
IT'S NEVER TOO...KENNY?
OW... AUUGGHH!
MAKE...IT... STOP!

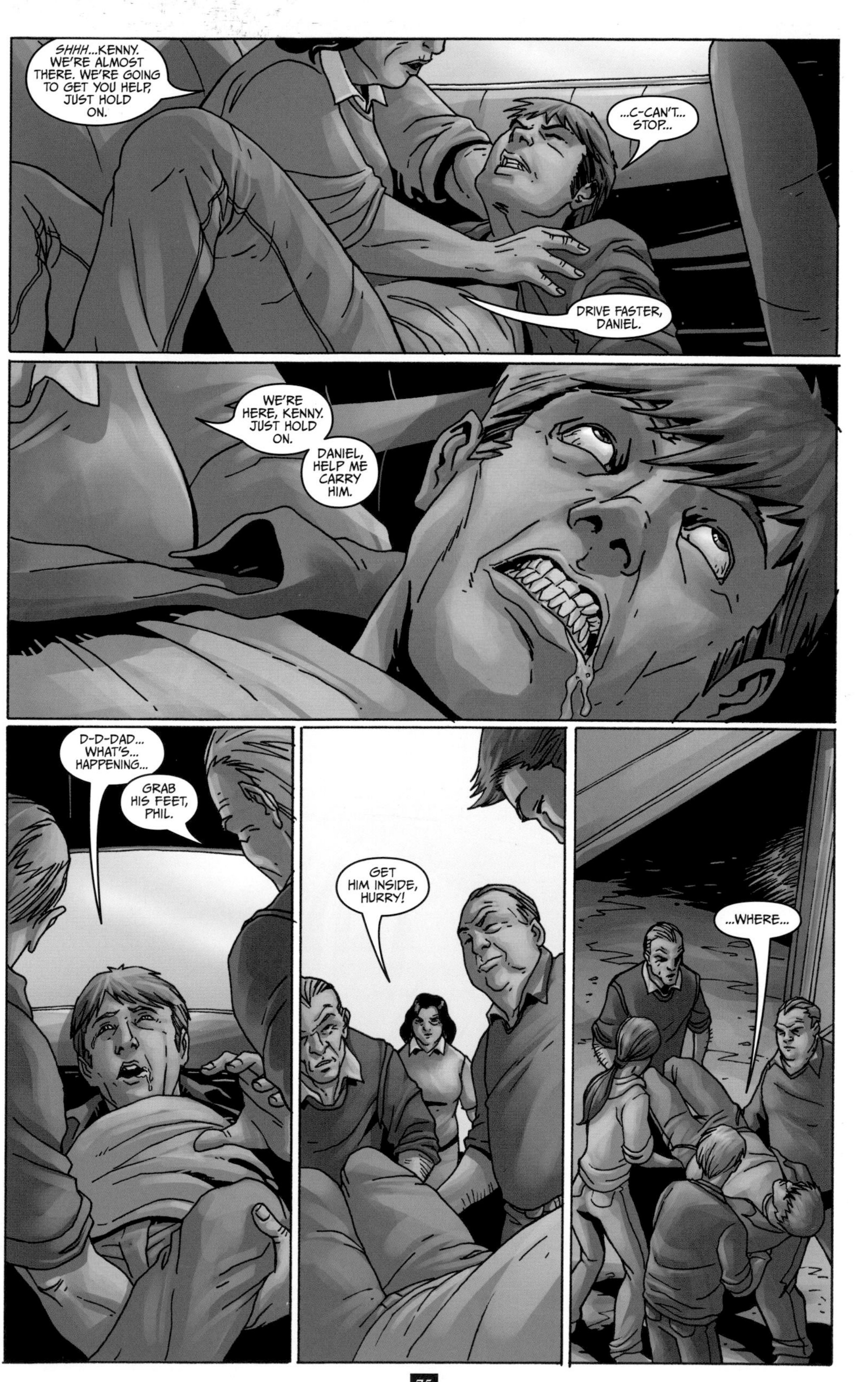
SHHH...KENNY. WE'RE ALMOST THERE. WE'RE GOING TO GET YOU HELP, JUST HOLD ON.
...C-CAN'T... STOP...
DRIVE FASTER, DANIEL.
WE'RE HERE, KENNY. JUST HOLD ON.
DANIEL, HELP ME CARRY HIM.
D-D-DAD... WHAT'S... HAPPENING...
GRAB HIS FEET, PHIL.
GET HIM INSIDE, HURRY!
...WHERE...

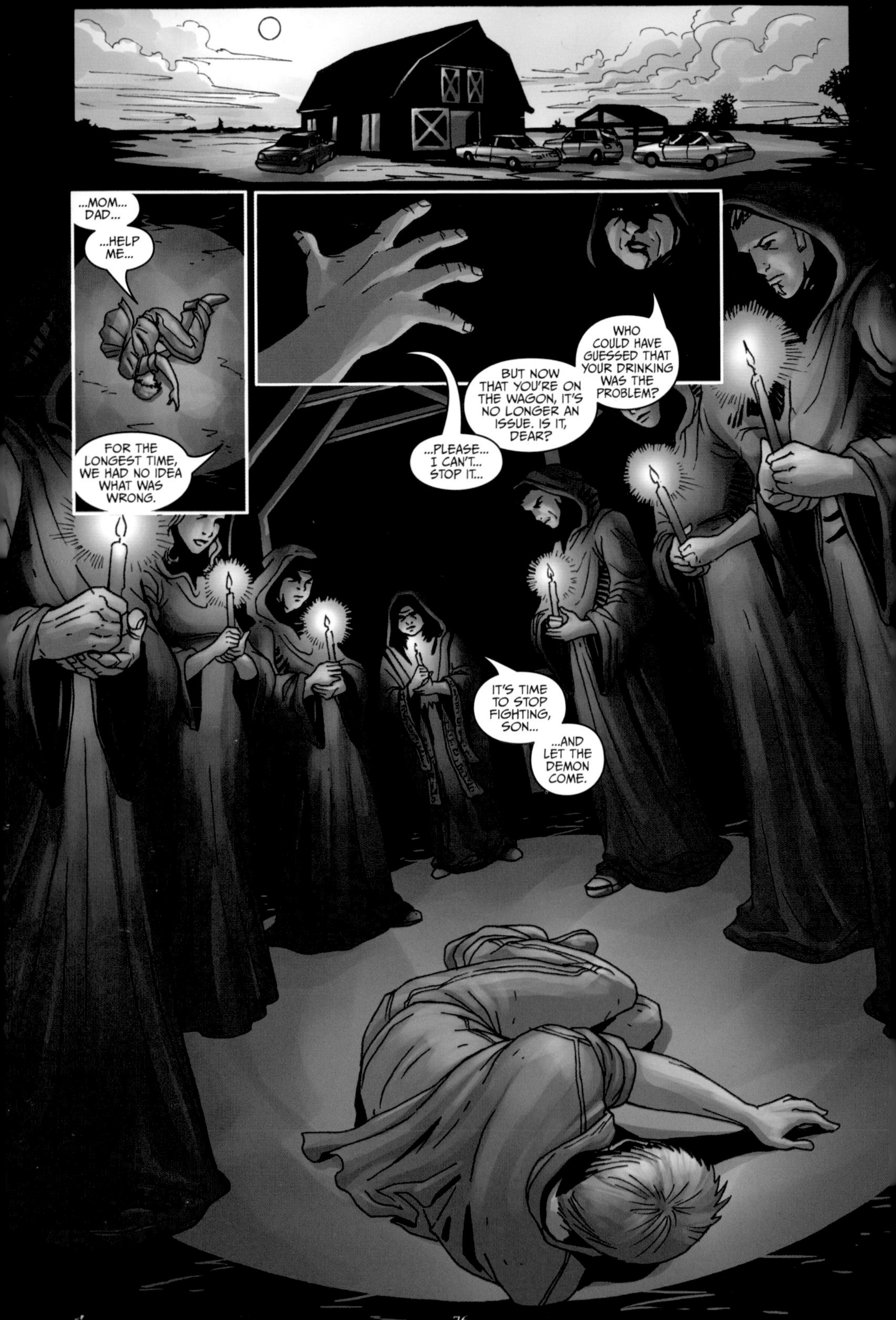
...MOM... DAD...
...HELP ME...
FOR THE LONGEST TIME, WE HAD NO IDEA WHAT WAS WRONG.
WHO COULD HAVE GUESSED THAT YOUR DRINKING WAS THE PROBLEM?
BUT NOW THAT YOU'RE ON THE WAGON, IT'S NO LONGER AN ISSUE. IS IT, DEAR?
...PLEASE... I CAN'T... STOP IT...
IT'S TIME TO STOP FIGHTING, SON...
...AND LET THE DEMON COME.

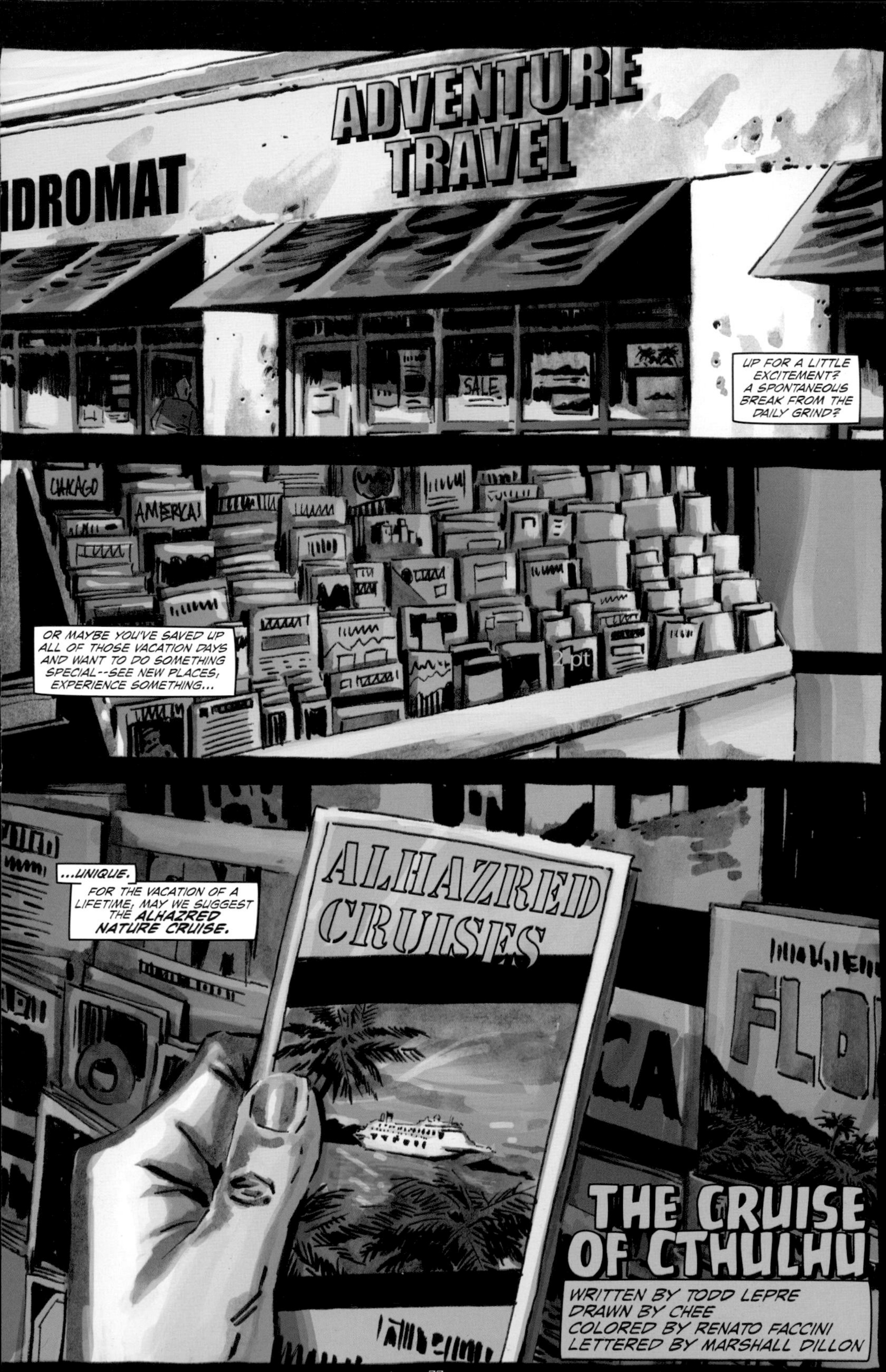
ADVENTURE TRAVEL
DROMAT
SALE
UP FOR A LITTLE EXCITEMENT? A SPONTANEOUS BREAK FROM THE DAILY GRIND?
CHICAGO
AMERICA!
OR MAYBE YOU'VE SAVED UP ALL OF THOSE VACATION DAYS AND WANT TO DO SOMETHING SPECIAL--SEE NEW PLACES, EXPERIENCE SOMETHING...
...UNIQUE.
FOR THE VACATION OF A LIFETIME, MAY WE SUGGEST THE ALHAZRED NATURE CRUISE.
ALHAZRED CRUISES
FLO
THE CRUISE OF CTHULHU
WRITTEN BY TODD LEPRE
DRAWN BY CHEE
COLORED BY RENATO FACCINI
LETTERED BY MARSHALL DILLON

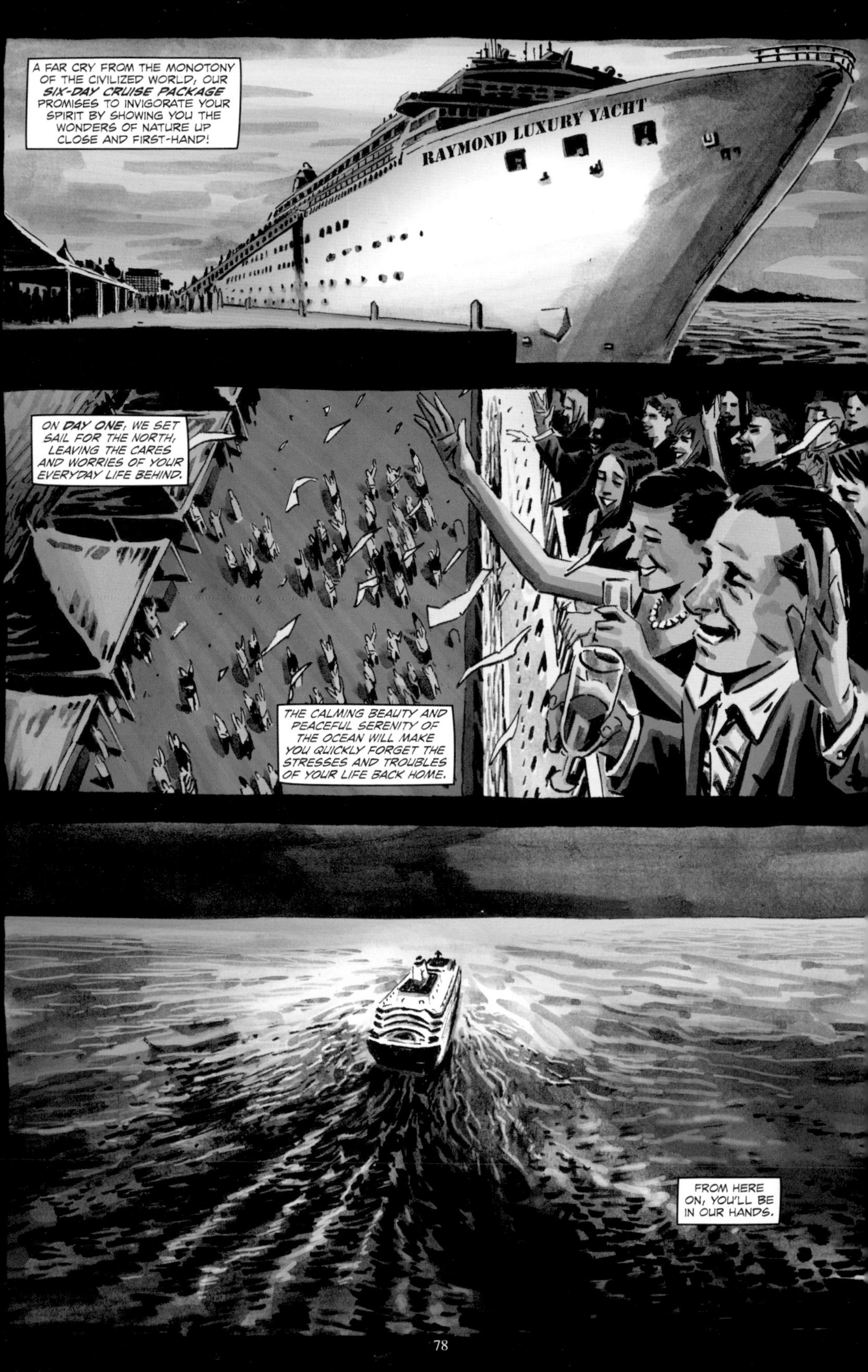
A FAR CRY FROM THE MONOTONY OF THE CIVILIZED WORLD, OUR *SIX-DAY CRUISE PACKAGE* PROMISES TO INVIGORATE YOUR SPIRIT BY SHOWING YOU THE WONDERS OF NATURE UP CLOSE AND FIRST-HAND!
RAYMOND LUXURY YACHT
ON *DAY ONE*, WE SET SAIL FOR THE NORTH, LEAVING THE CARES AND WORRIES OF YOUR EVERYDAY LIFE BEHIND.
THE CALMING BEAUTY AND PEACEFUL SERENITY OF THE OCEAN WILL MAKE YOU QUICKLY FORGET THE STRESSES AND TROUBLES OF YOUR LIFE BACK HOME.
FROM HERE ON, YOU'LL BE IN OUR HANDS.

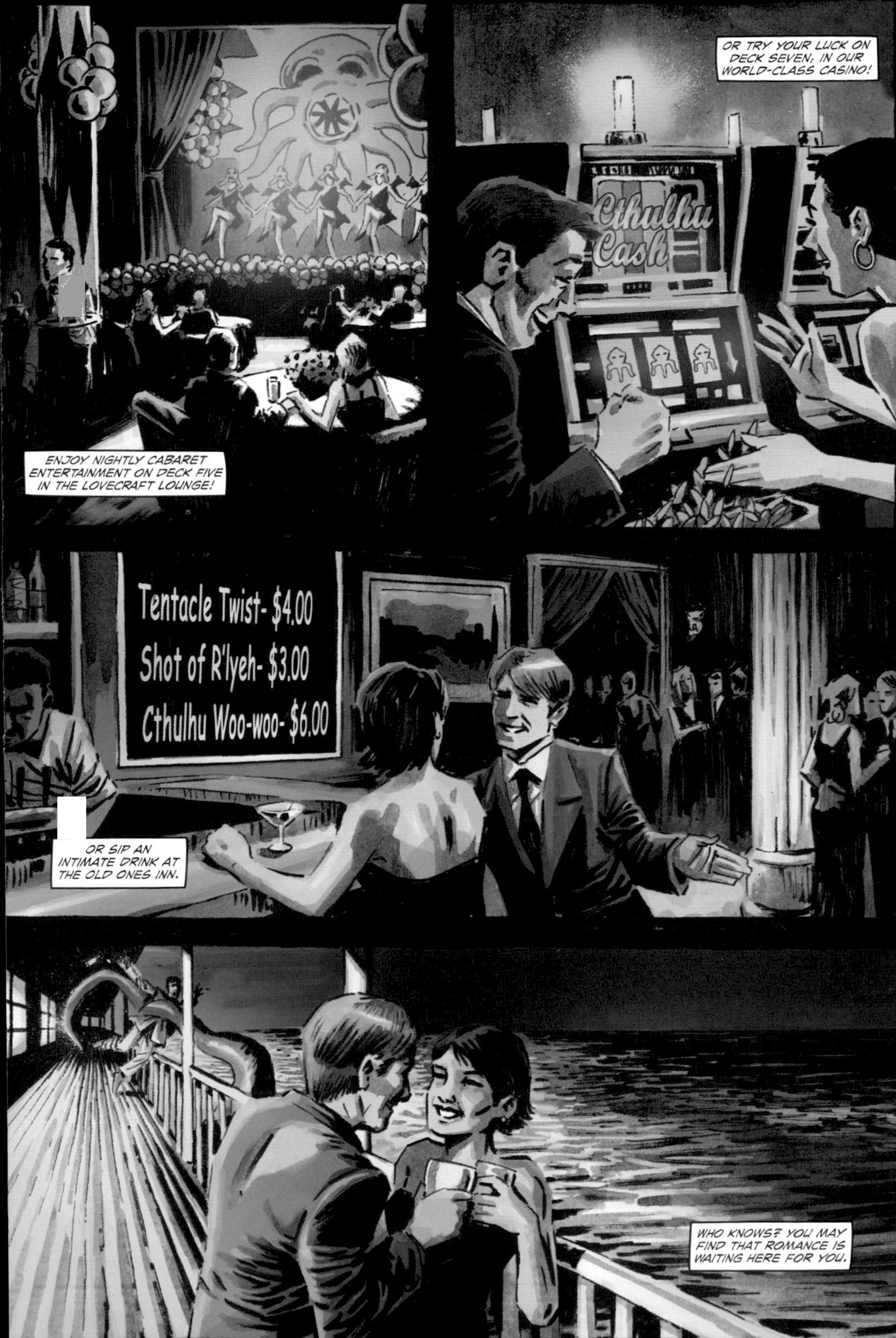
ENJOY NIGHTLY CABARET ENTERTAINMENT ON DECK FIVE IN THE LOVECRAFT LOUNGE!
OR TRY YOUR LUCK ON DECK SEVEN, IN OUR WORLD-CLASS CASINO!
Cthulhu Cash
Tentacle Twist- $4.00
Shot of R'lyeh- $3.00
Cthulhu Woo-woo- $6.00
OR SIP AN INTIMATE DRINK AT THE OLD ONES INN.
WHO KNOWS? YOU MAY FIND THAT ROMANCE IS WAITING HERE FOR YOU.

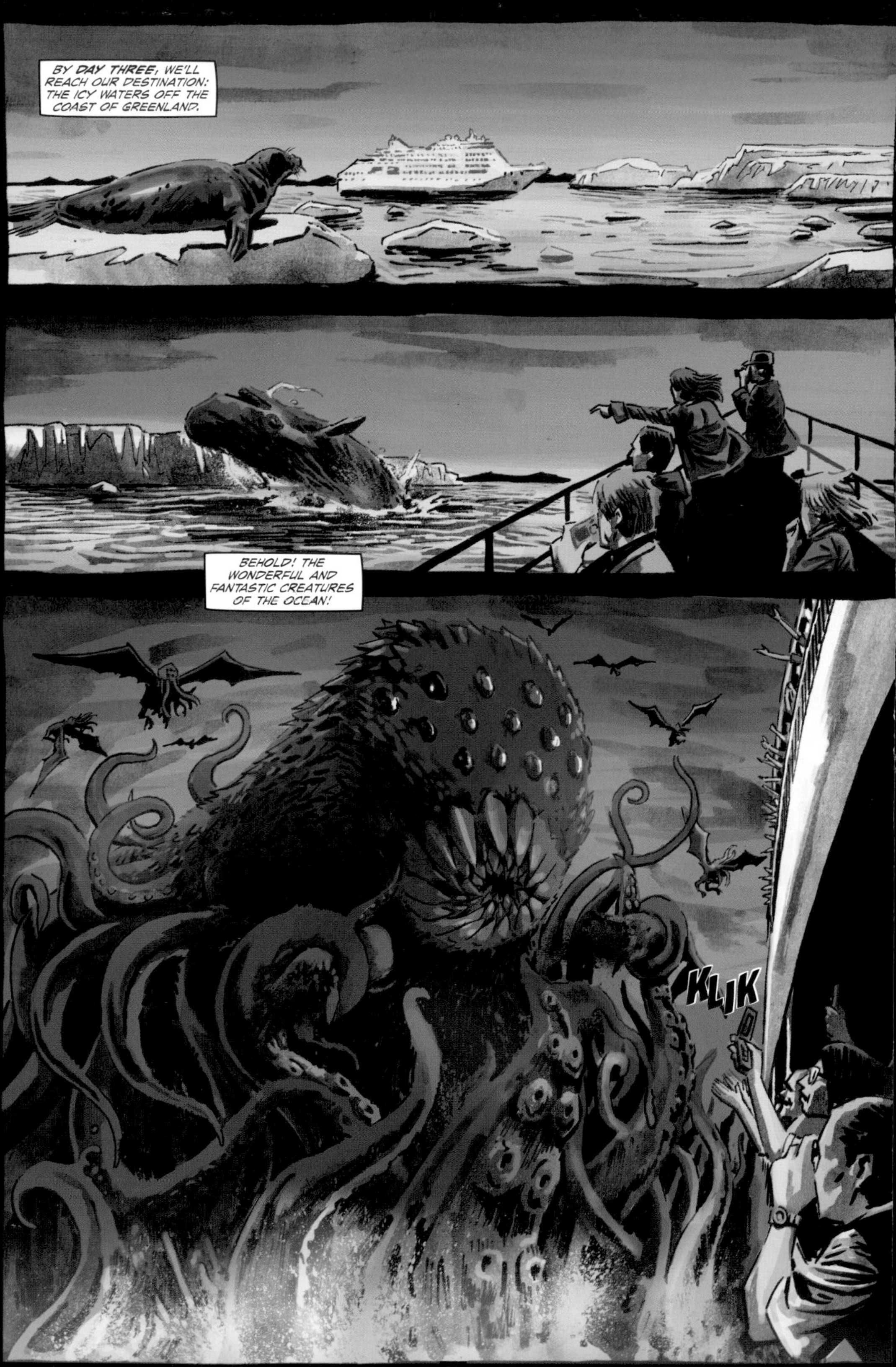
BY DAY THREE, WE'LL REACH OUR DESTINATION: THE ICY WATERS OFF THE COAST OF GREENLAND.
BEHOLD! THE WONDERFUL AND FANTASTIC CREATURES OF THE OCEAN!
KLIK

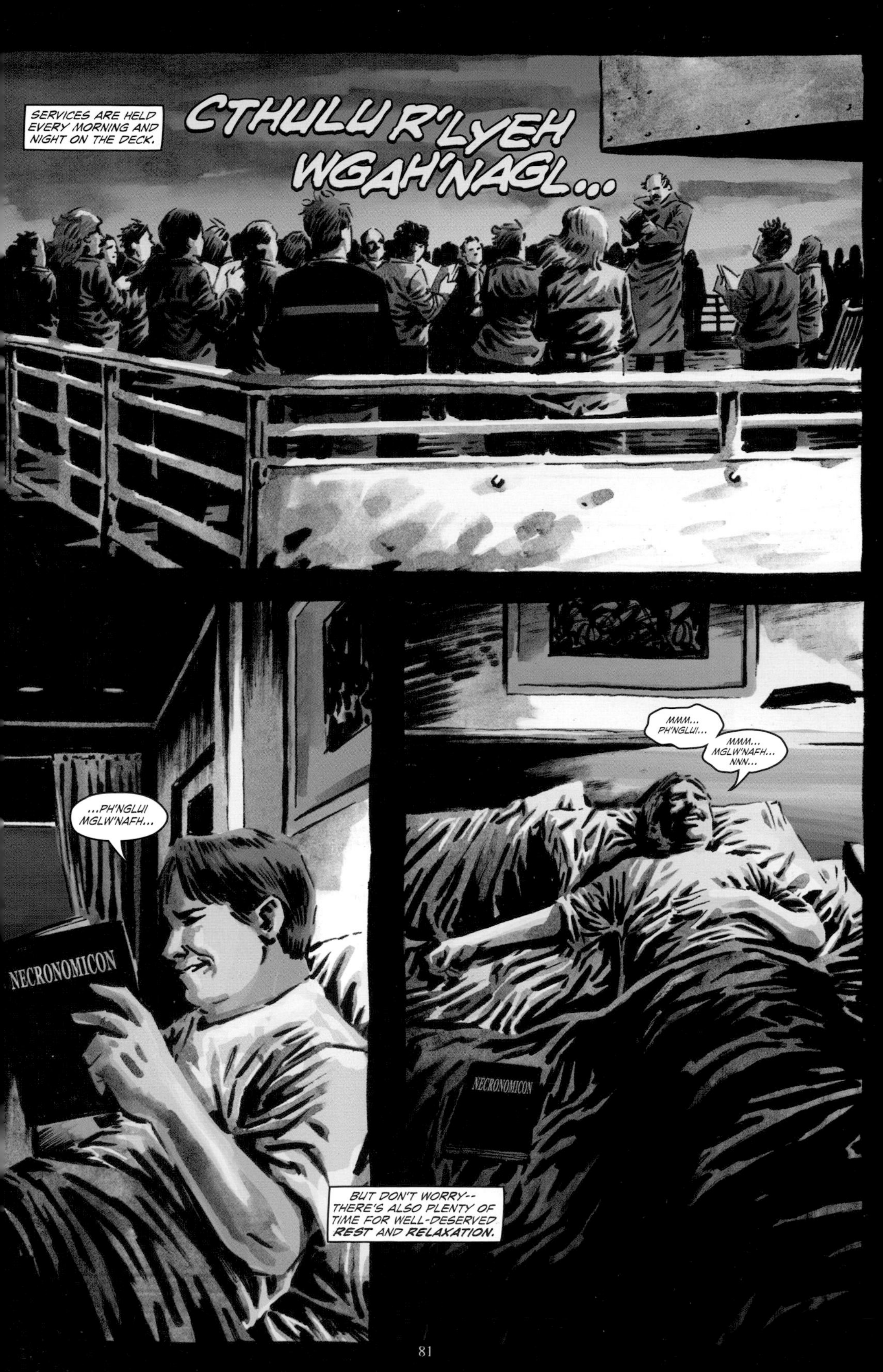
SERVICES ARE HELD EVERY MORNING AND NIGHT ON THE DECK.
CTHULU R'LYEH WGAH'NAGL...
...PH'NGLUI MGLW'NAFH...
NECRONOMICON
BUT DON'T WORRY-- THERE'S ALSO PLENTY OF TIME FOR WELL-DESERVED REST AND RELAXATION.
MMM... PH'NGLUI...
MMM... MGLW'NAFH... NNN...
NECRONOMICON

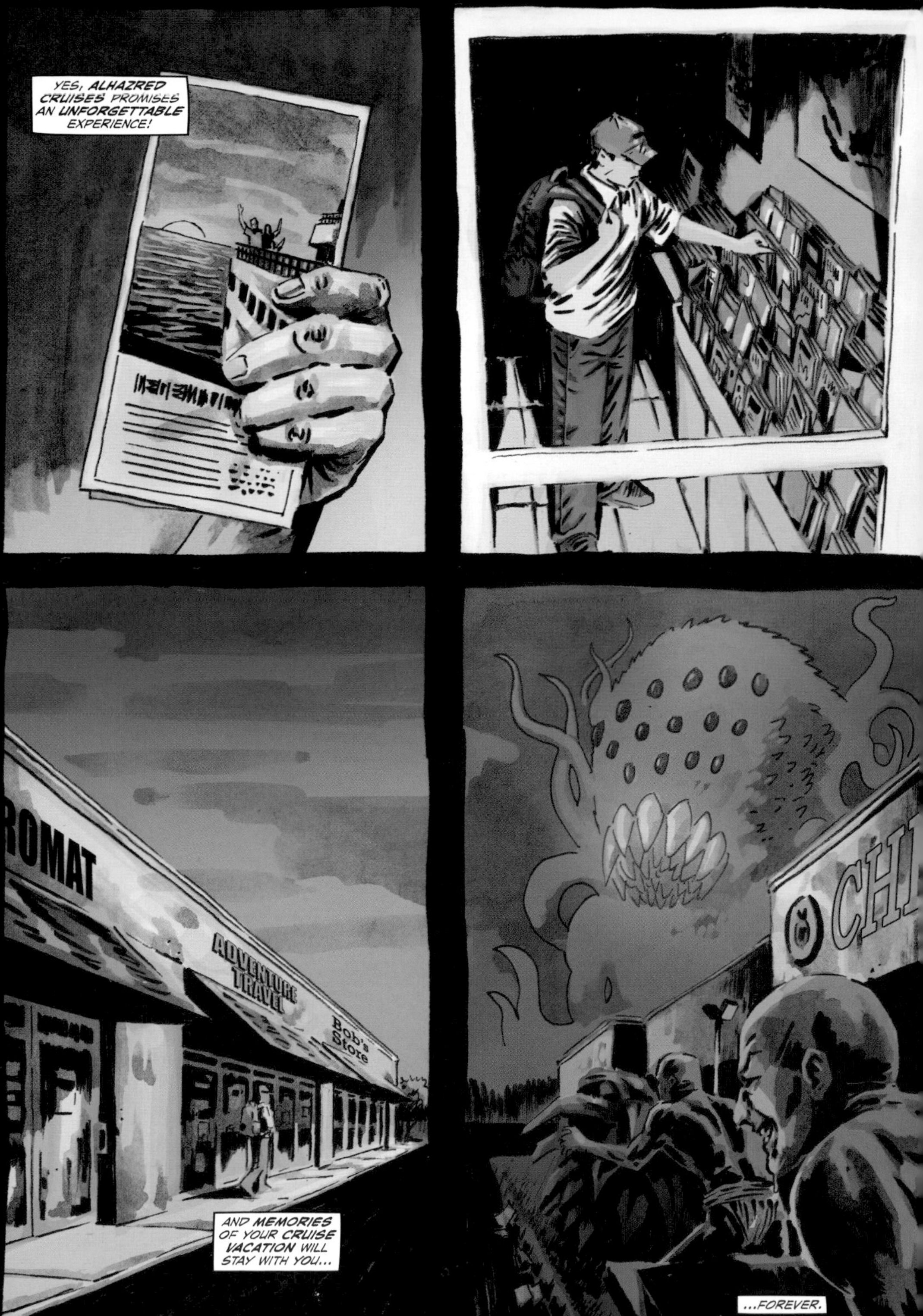
YES, ALHAZRED CRUISES PROMISES AN UNFORGETTABLE EXPERIENCE!
ROMAT
ADVENTURE TRAVEL
Bob's Store
AND MEMORIES OF YOUR CRUISE VACATION WILL STAY WITH YOU...
...FOREVER.

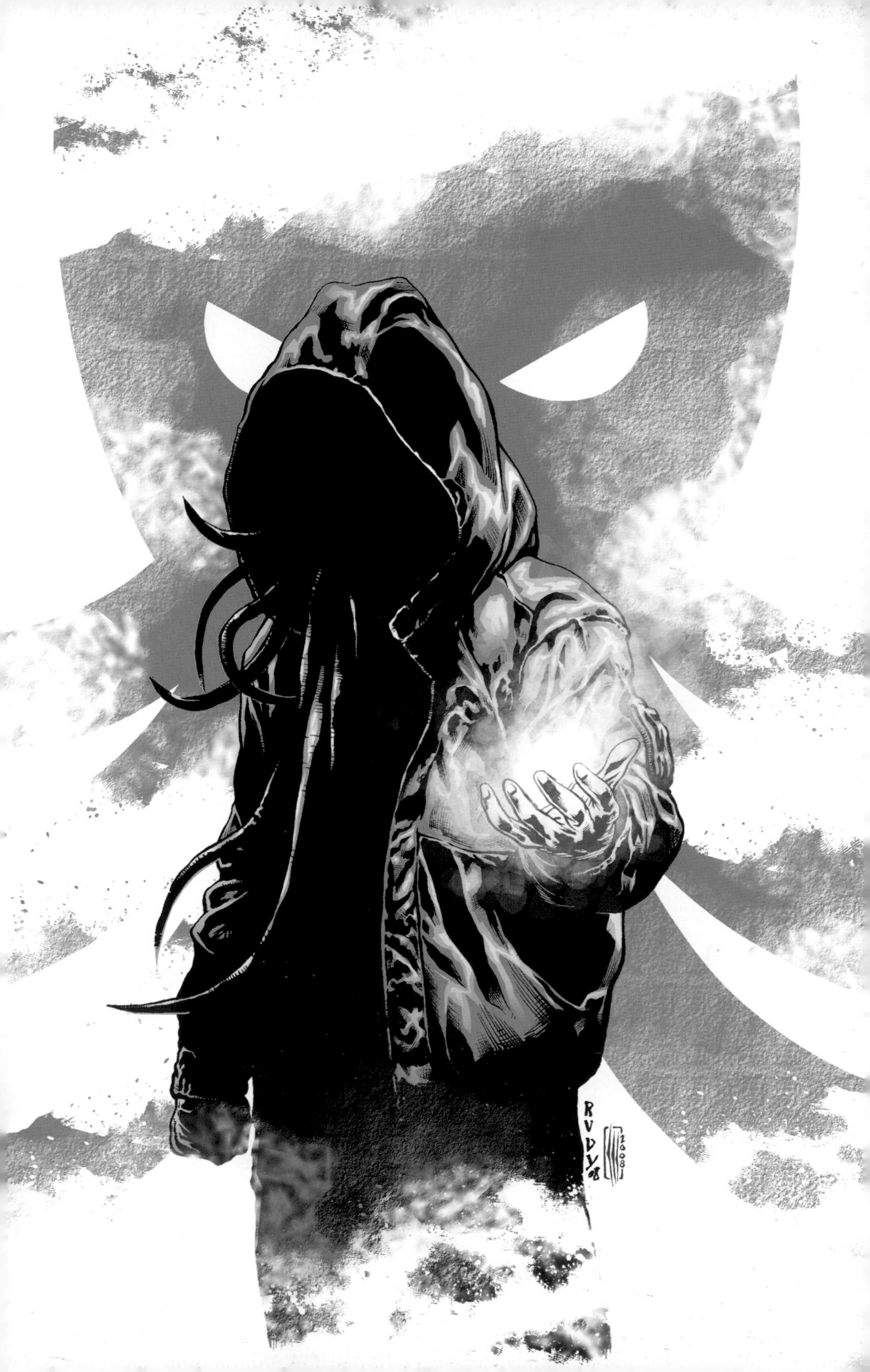

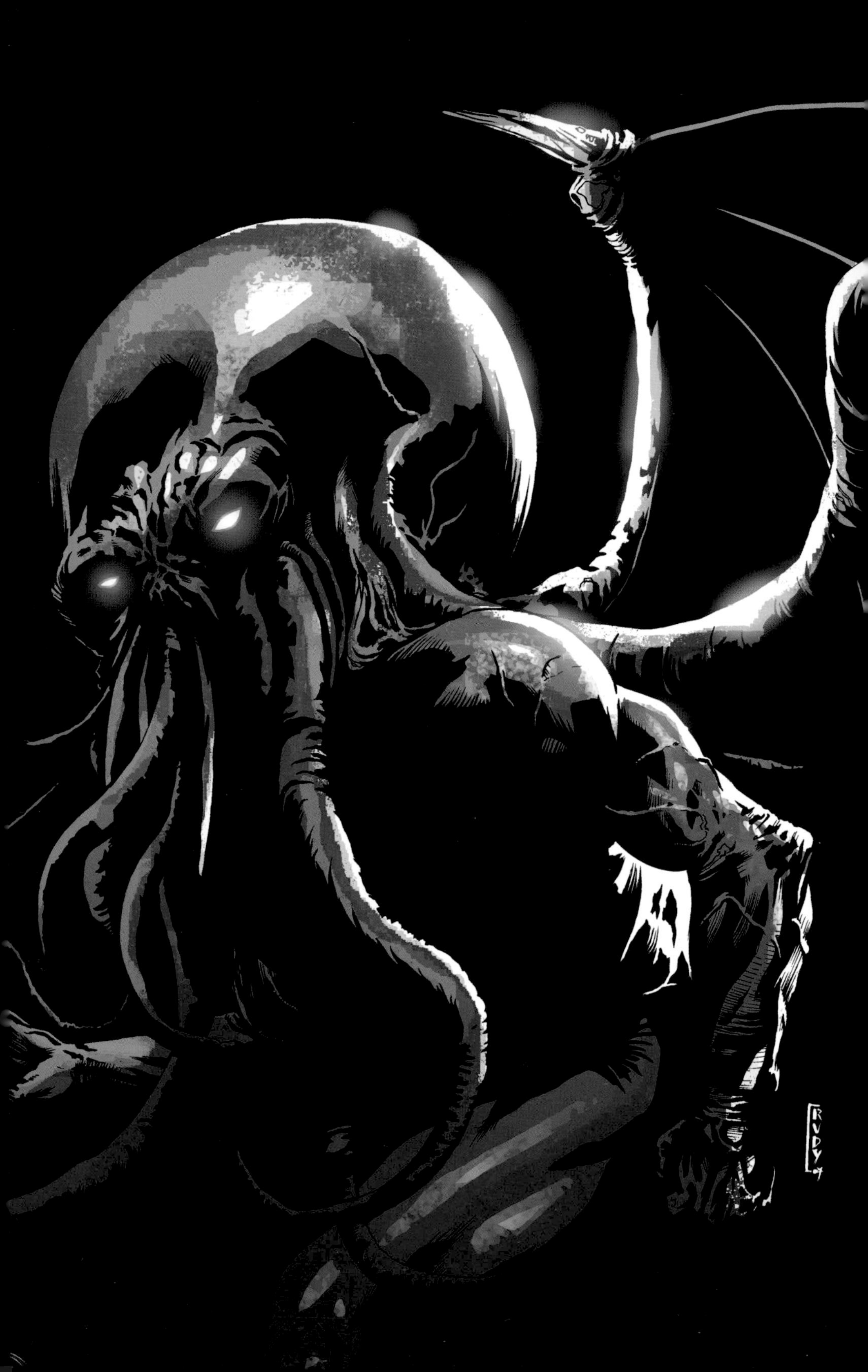
RUDY

IN THE π OF THE BEHOLDER

STORY **MARK WAID**

ART **CHEE**

THERE WILL BE BLOOD

STORY **MARK SABLE**

ART **SERGIO CARRERA**

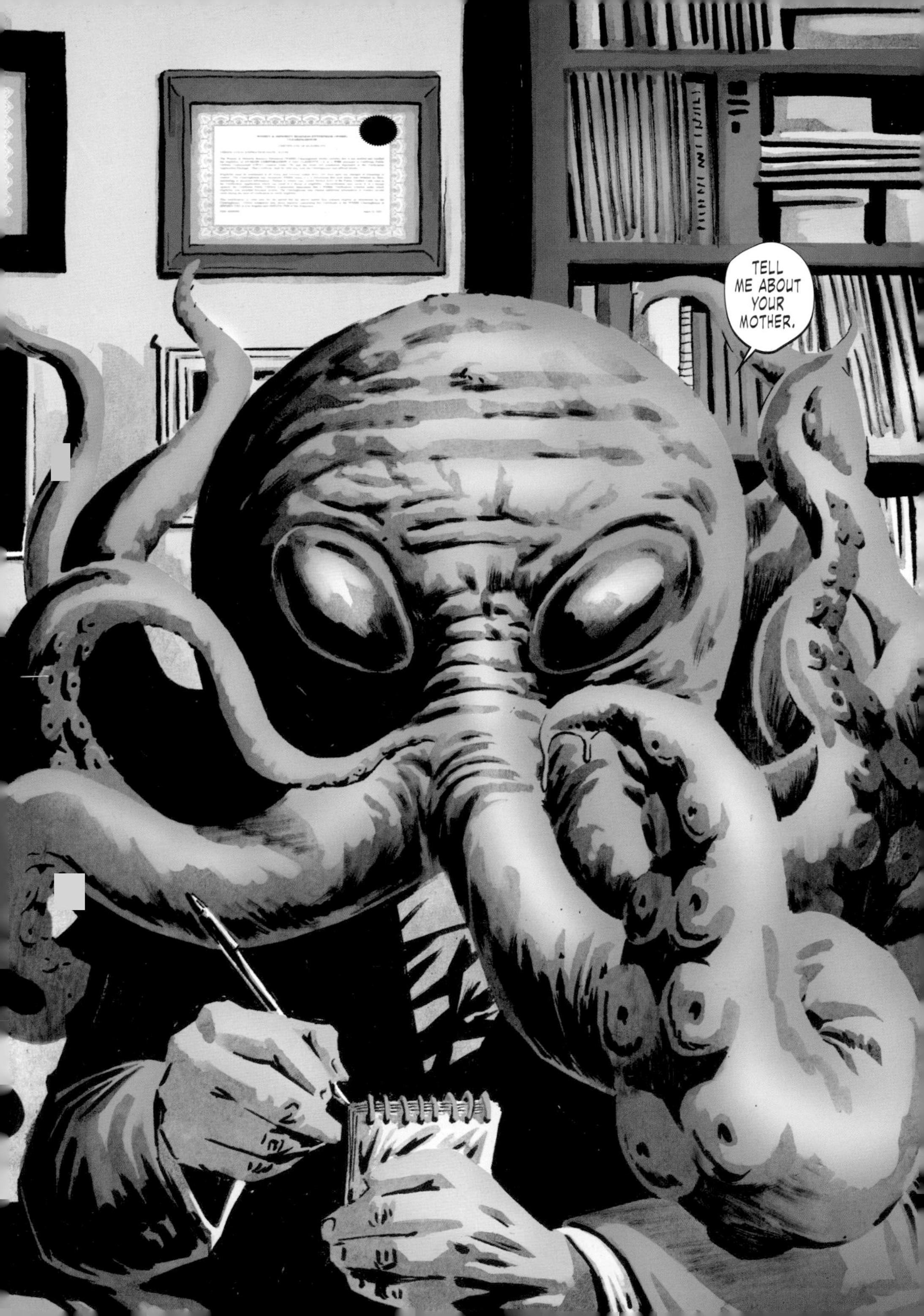
TELL ME ABOUT YOUR MOTHER.

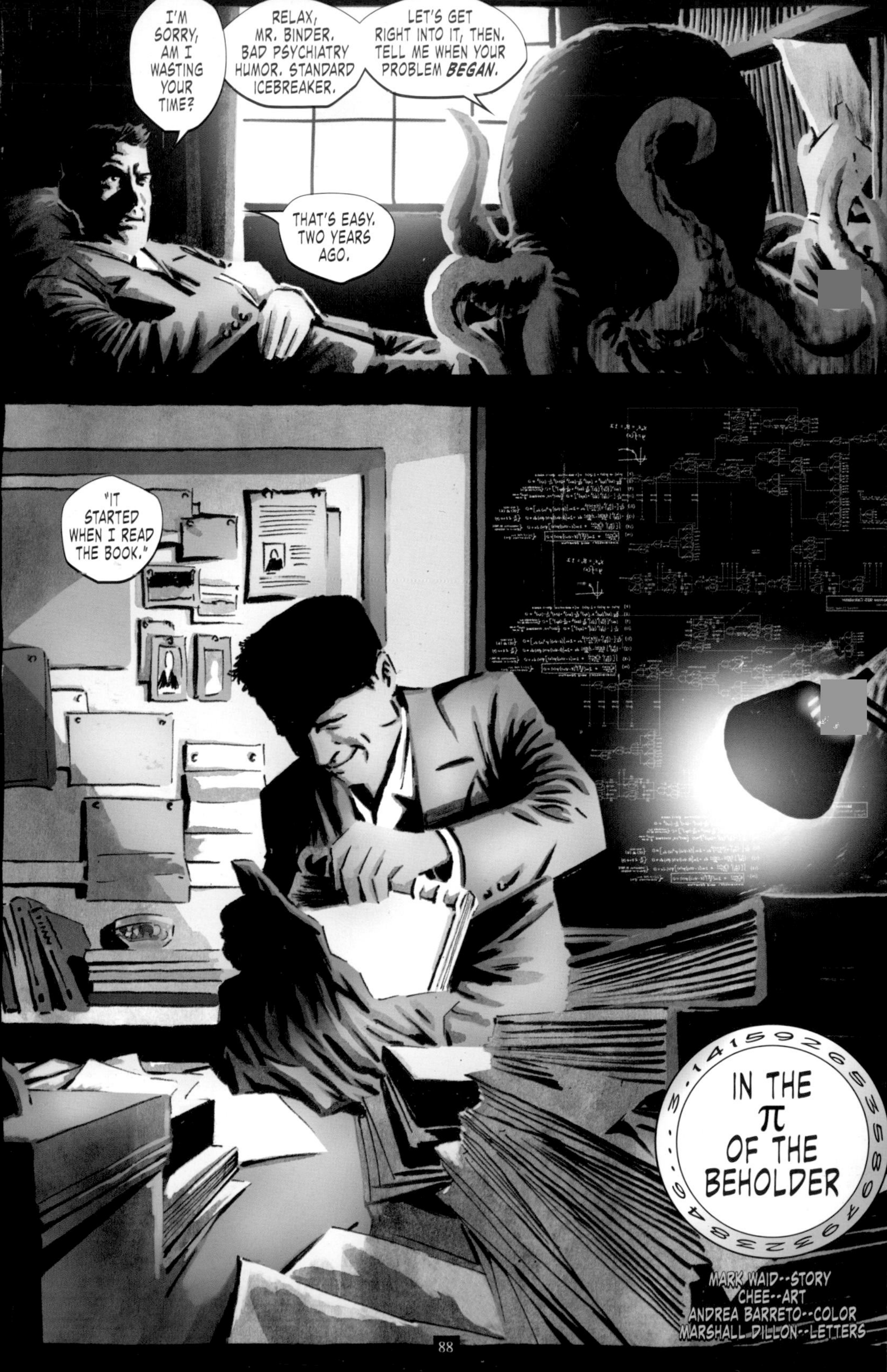
I'M SORRY, AM I WASTING YOUR TIME?
RELAX, MR. BINDER. BAD PSYCHIATRY HUMOR. STANDARD ICEBREAKER.
LET'S GET RIGHT INTO IT, THEN. TELL ME WHEN YOUR PROBLEM *BEGAN.*
THAT'S EASY. TWO YEARS AGO.
"IT STARTED WHEN I READ THE BOOK."
3.14159265358979323846...
IN THE π OF THE BEHOLDER
MARK WAID--STORY
CHEE--ART
ANDREA BARRETO--COLOR
MARSHALL DILLON--LETTERS

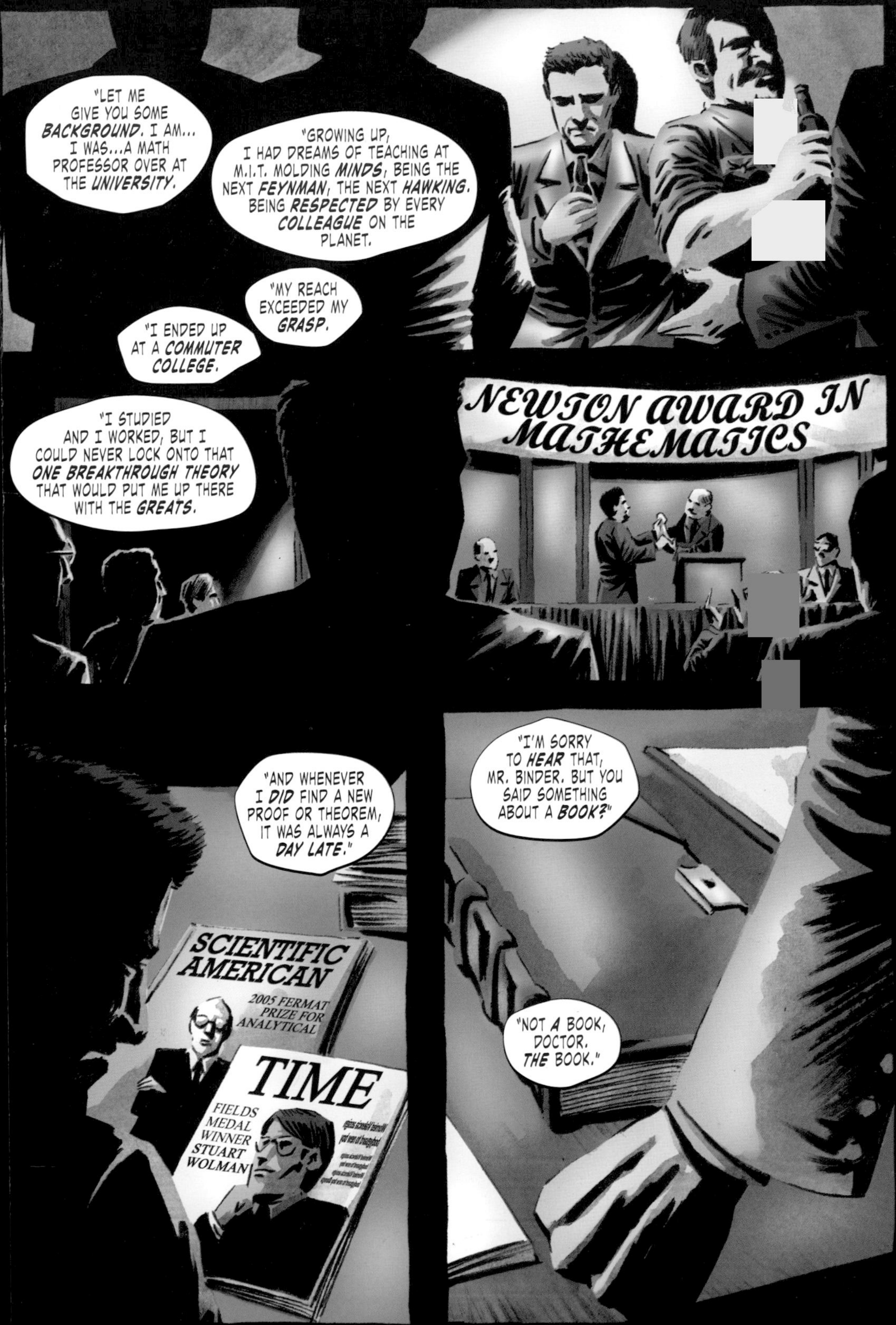
"LET ME GIVE YOU SOME BACKGROUND. I AM... I WAS...A MATH PROFESSOR OVER AT THE UNIVERSITY.
"GROWING UP, I HAD DREAMS OF TEACHING AT M.I.T. MOLDING MINDS, BEING THE NEXT FEYNMAN, THE NEXT HAWKING. BEING RESPECTED BY EVERY COLLEAGUE ON THE PLANET.
"MY REACH EXCEEDED MY GRASP.
"I ENDED UP AT A COMMUTER COLLEGE.
"I STUDIED AND I WORKED, BUT I COULD NEVER LOCK ONTO THAT ONE BREAKTHROUGH THEORY THAT WOULD PUT ME UP THERE WITH THE GREATS.
NEWTON AWARD IN MATHEMATICS
"AND WHENEVER I DID FIND A NEW PROOF OR THEOREM, IT WAS ALWAYS A DAY LATE."
SCIENTIFIC AMERICAN
2005 FERMAT PRIZE FOR ANALYTICAL
TIME
FIELDS MEDAL WINNER STUART WOLMAN
"I'M SORRY TO HEAR THAT, MR. BINDER. BUT YOU SAID SOMETHING ABOUT A BOOK?"
"NOT A BOOK, DOCTOR. THE BOOK."

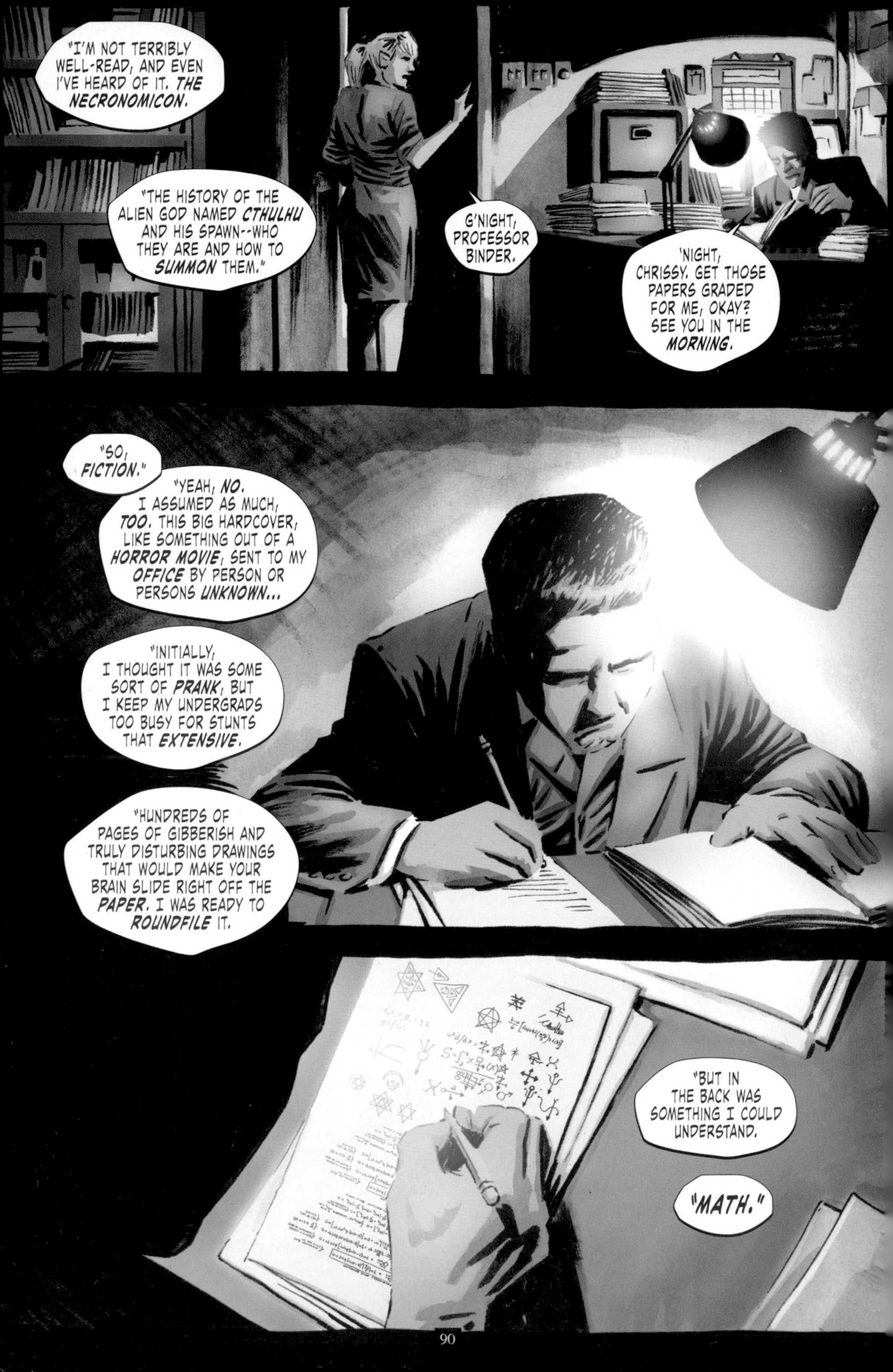
"I'M NOT TERRIBLY WELL-READ, AND EVEN I'VE HEARD OF IT. THE NECRONOMICON.
"THE HISTORY OF THE ALIEN GOD NAMED CTHULHU AND HIS SPAWN--WHO THEY ARE AND HOW TO SUMMON THEM."
G'NIGHT, PROFESSOR BINDER.
'NIGHT, CHRISSY. GET THOSE PAPERS GRADED FOR ME, OKAY? SEE YOU IN THE MORNING.
"SO, FICTION."
"YEAH, NO. I ASSUMED AS MUCH, TOO. THIS BIG HARDCOVER, LIKE SOMETHING OUT OF A HORROR MOVIE, SENT TO MY OFFICE BY PERSON OR PERSONS UNKNOWN...
"INITIALLY, I THOUGHT IT WAS SOME SORT OF PRANK, BUT I KEEP MY UNDERGRADS TOO BUSY FOR STUNTS THAT EXTENSIVE.
"HUNDREDS OF PAGES OF GIBBERISH AND TRULY DISTURBING DRAWINGS THAT WOULD MAKE YOUR BRAIN SLIDE RIGHT OFF THE PAPER. I WAS READY TO ROUNDFILE IT.
"BUT IN THE BACK WAS SOMETHING I COULD UNDERSTAND.
"MATH."

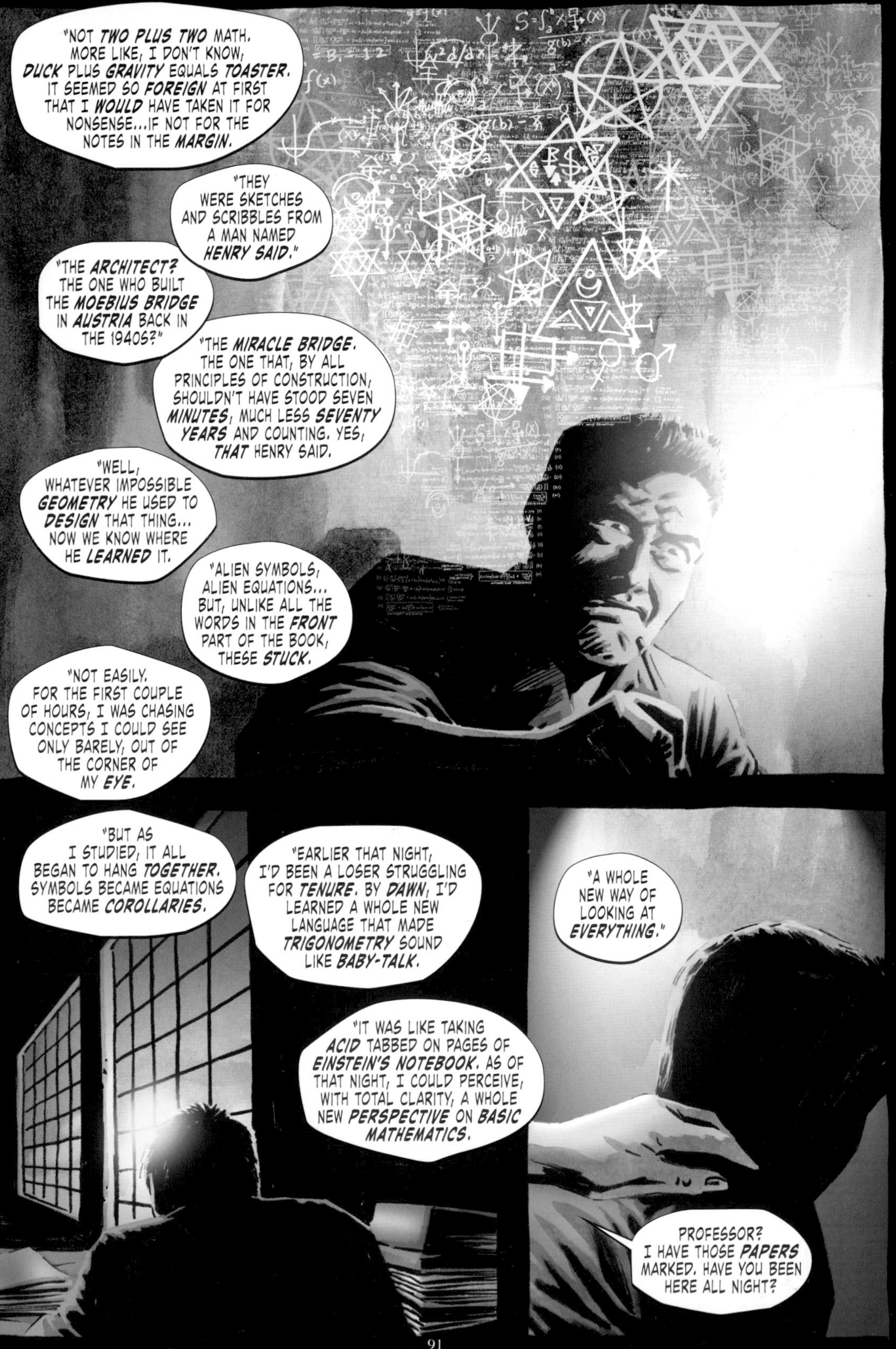
"NOT TWO PLUS TWO MATH. MORE LIKE, I DON'T KNOW, DUCK PLUS GRAVITY EQUALS TOASTER. IT SEEMED SO FOREIGN AT FIRST THAT I WOULD HAVE TAKEN IT FOR NONSENSE...IF NOT FOR THE NOTES IN THE MARGIN.
"THEY WERE SKETCHES AND SCRIBBLES FROM A MAN NAMED HENRY SAID."
"THE ARCHITECT? THE ONE WHO BUILT THE MOEBIUS BRIDGE IN AUSTRIA BACK IN THE 1940S?"
"THE MIRACLE BRIDGE. THE ONE THAT, BY ALL PRINCIPLES OF CONSTRUCTION, SHOULDN'T HAVE STOOD SEVEN MINUTES, MUCH LESS SEVENTY YEARS AND COUNTING. YES, THAT HENRY SAID.
"WELL, WHATEVER IMPOSSIBLE GEOMETRY HE USED TO DESIGN THAT THING... NOW WE KNOW WHERE HE LEARNED IT.
"ALIEN SYMBOLS, ALIEN EQUATIONS... BUT, UNLIKE ALL THE WORDS IN THE FRONT PART OF THE BOOK, THESE STUCK.
"NOT EASILY. FOR THE FIRST COUPLE OF HOURS, I WAS CHASING CONCEPTS I COULD SEE ONLY BARELY, OUT OF THE CORNER OF MY EYE.
"BUT AS I STUDIED, IT ALL BEGAN TO HANG TOGETHER. SYMBOLS BECAME EQUATIONS BECAME COROLLARIES.
"EARLIER THAT NIGHT, I'D BEEN A LOSER STRUGGLING FOR TENURE. BY DAWN, I'D LEARNED A WHOLE NEW LANGUAGE THAT MADE TRIGONOMETRY SOUND LIKE BABY-TALK.
"IT WAS LIKE TAKING ACID TABBED ON PAGES OF EINSTEIN'S NOTEBOOK. AS OF THAT NIGHT, I COULD PERCEIVE, WITH TOTAL CLARITY, A WHOLE NEW PERSPECTIVE ON BASIC MATHEMATICS.
"A WHOLE NEW WAY OF LOOKING AT EVERYTHING."
PROFESSOR? I HAVE THOSE PAPERS MARKED. HAVE YOU BEEN HERE ALL NIGHT?

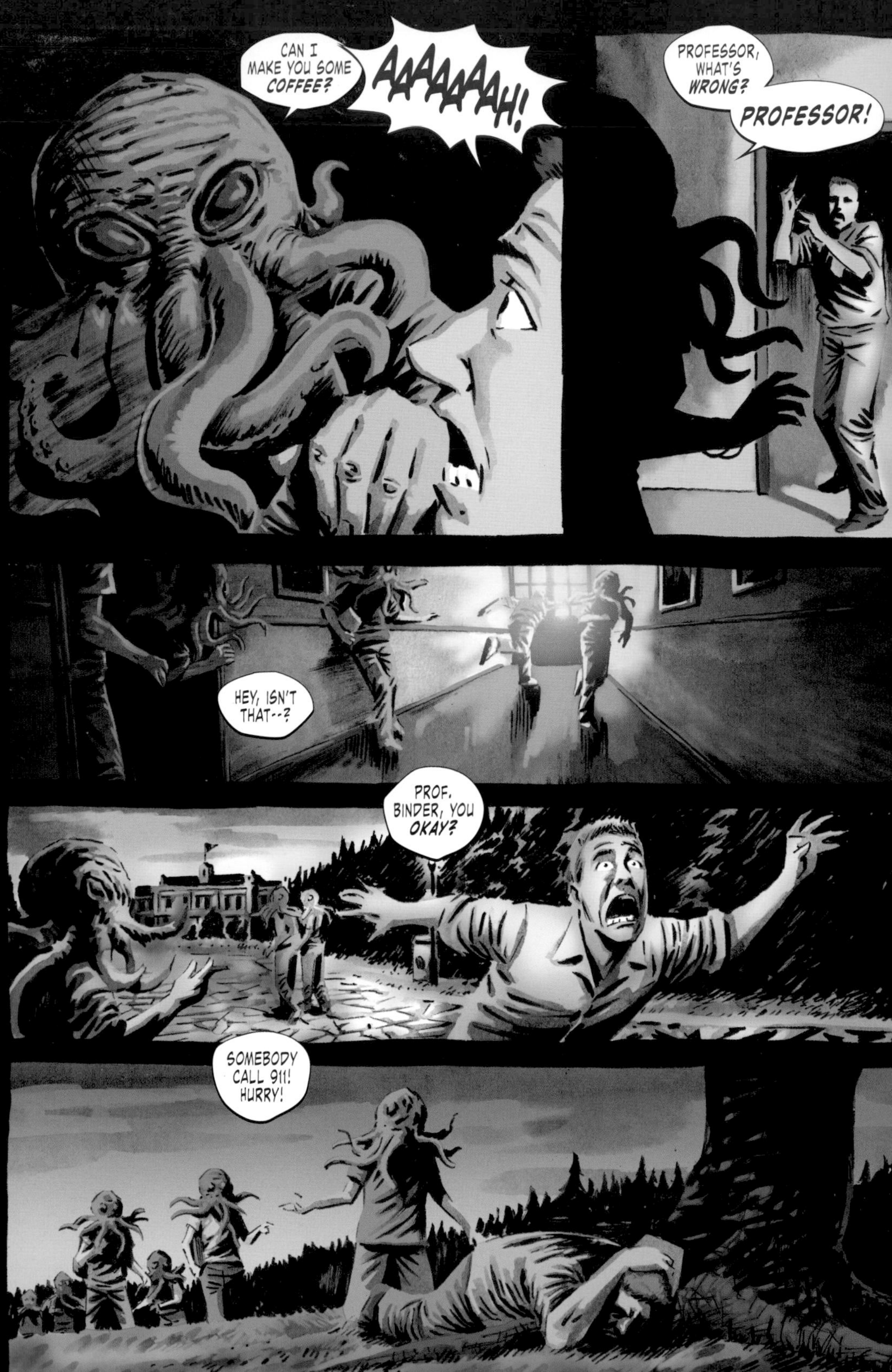
CAN I MAKE YOU SOME COFFEE?
AAAAAAAH!
PROFESSOR, WHAT'S WRONG?
PROFESSOR!
HEY, ISN'T THAT--?
PROF. BINDER, YOU OKAY?
SOMEBODY CALL 911! HURRY!

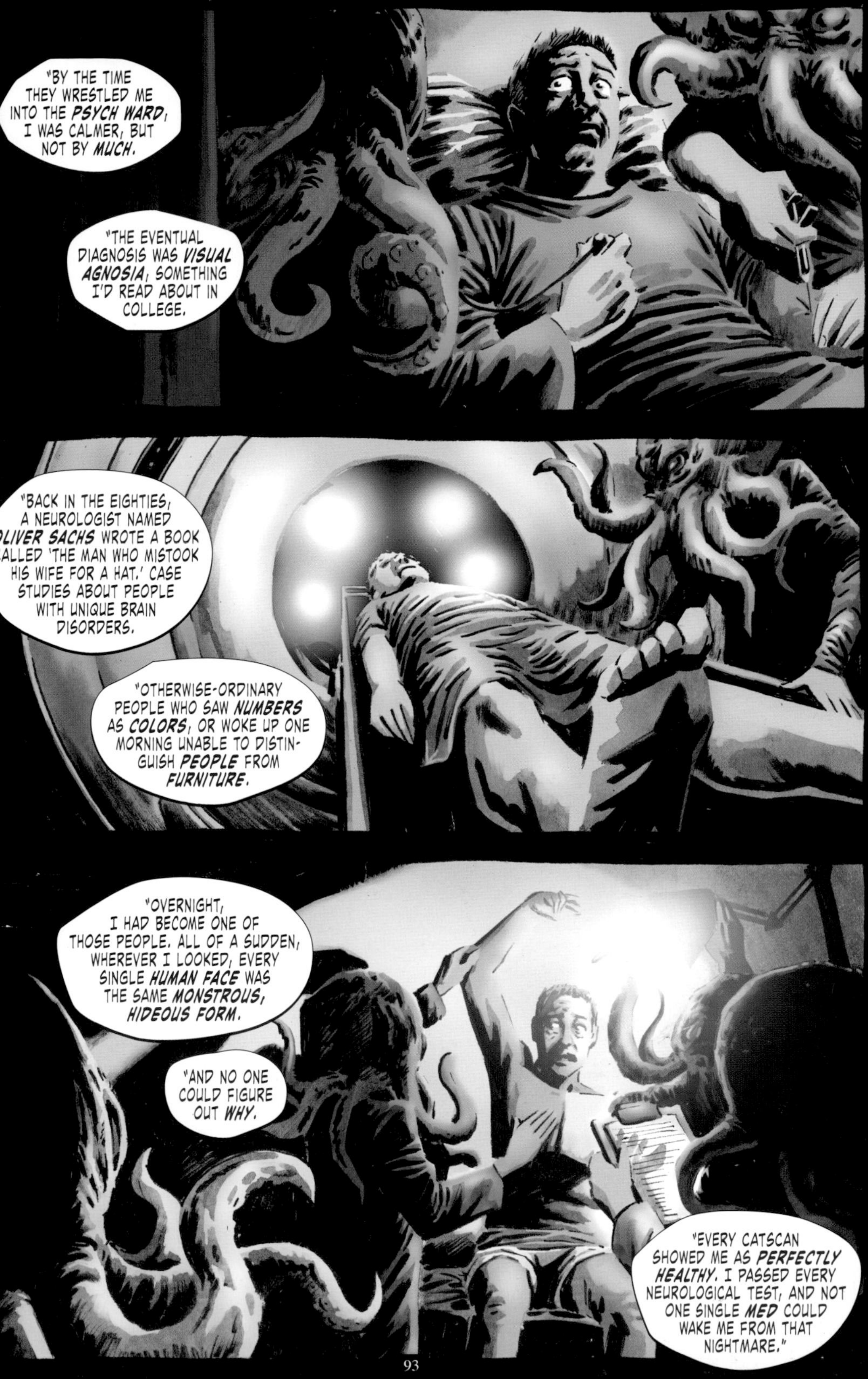
"BY THE TIME THEY WRESTLED ME INTO THE PSYCH WARD, I WAS CALMER, BUT NOT BY MUCH.
"THE EVENTUAL DIAGNOSIS WAS VISUAL AGNOSIA, SOMETHING I'D READ ABOUT IN COLLEGE.
"BACK IN THE EIGHTIES, A NEUROLOGIST NAMED OLIVER SACHS WROTE A BOOK CALLED 'THE MAN WHO MISTOOK HIS WIFE FOR A HAT.' CASE STUDIES ABOUT PEOPLE WITH UNIQUE BRAIN DISORDERS.
"OTHERWISE-ORDINARY PEOPLE WHO SAW NUMBERS AS COLORS, OR WOKE UP ONE MORNING UNABLE TO DISTIN-GUISH PEOPLE FROM FURNITURE.
"OVERNIGHT, I HAD BECOME ONE OF THOSE PEOPLE. ALL OF A SUDDEN, WHEREVER I LOOKED, EVERY SINGLE HUMAN FACE WAS THE SAME MONSTROUS, HIDEOUS FORM.
"AND NO ONE COULD FIGURE OUT WHY.
"EVERY CATSCAN SHOWED ME AS PERFECTLY HEALTHY. I PASSED EVERY NEUROLOGICAL TEST, AND NOT ONE SINGLE MED COULD WAKE ME FROM THAT NIGHTMARE."

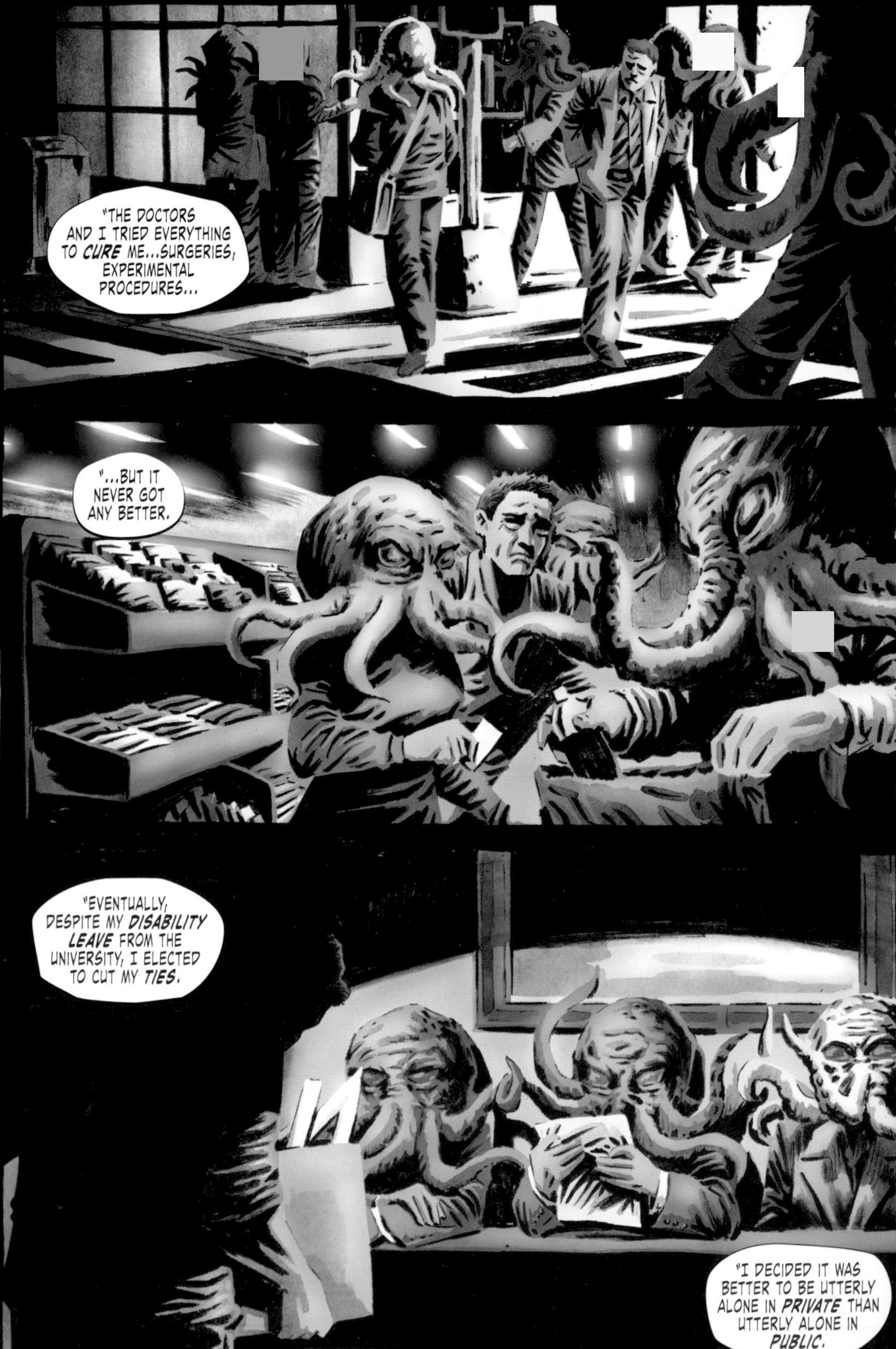
"THE DOCTORS AND I TRIED EVERYTHING TO CURE ME...SURGERIES, EXPERIMENTAL PROCEDURES...
"...BUT IT NEVER GOT ANY BETTER.
"EVENTUALLY, DESPITE MY DISABILITY LEAVE FROM THE UNIVERSITY, I ELECTED TO CUT MY TIES.
"I DECIDED IT WAS BETTER TO BE UTTERLY ALONE IN PRIVATE THAN UTTERLY ALONE IN PUBLIC.

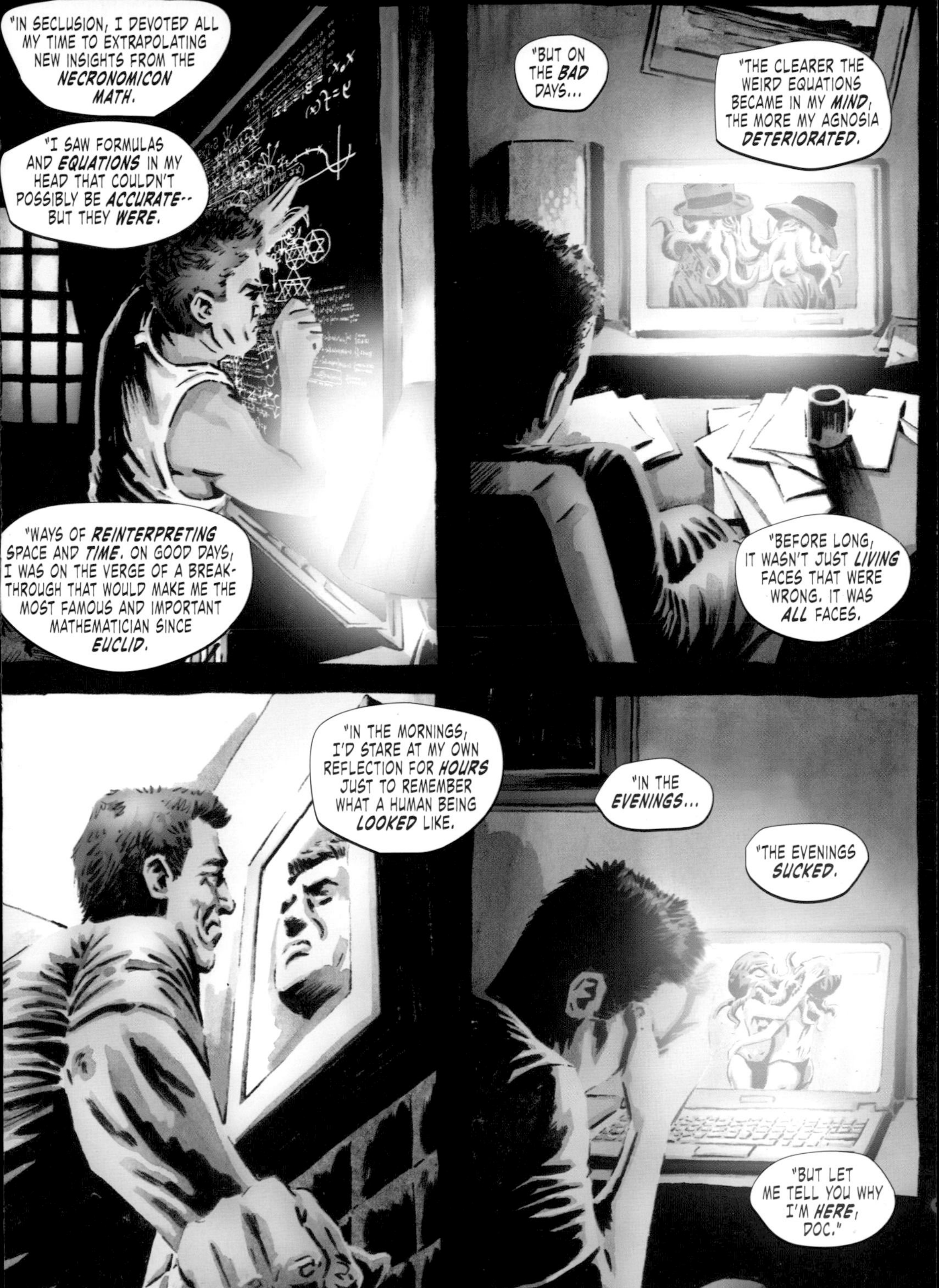
"IN SECLUSION, I DEVOTED ALL MY TIME TO EXTRAPOLATING NEW INSIGHTS FROM THE NECRONOMICON MATH.
"I SAW FORMULAS AND EQUATIONS IN MY HEAD THAT COULDN'T POSSIBLY BE ACCURATE-- BUT THEY WERE.
"WAYS OF REINTERPRETING SPACE AND TIME. ON GOOD DAYS, I WAS ON THE VERGE OF A BREAK-THROUGH THAT WOULD MAKE ME THE MOST FAMOUS AND IMPORTANT MATHEMATICIAN SINCE EUCLID.
"BUT ON THE BAD DAYS...
"THE CLEARER THE WEIRD EQUATIONS BECAME IN MY MIND, THE MORE MY AGNOSIA DETERIORATED.
"BEFORE LONG, IT WASN'T JUST LIVING FACES THAT WERE WRONG. IT WAS ALL FACES.
"IN THE MORNINGS, I'D STARE AT MY OWN REFLECTION FOR HOURS JUST TO REMEMBER WHAT A HUMAN BEING LOOKED LIKE.
"IN THE EVENINGS...
"THE EVENINGS SUCKED.
"BUT LET ME TELL YOU WHY I'M HERE, DOC."

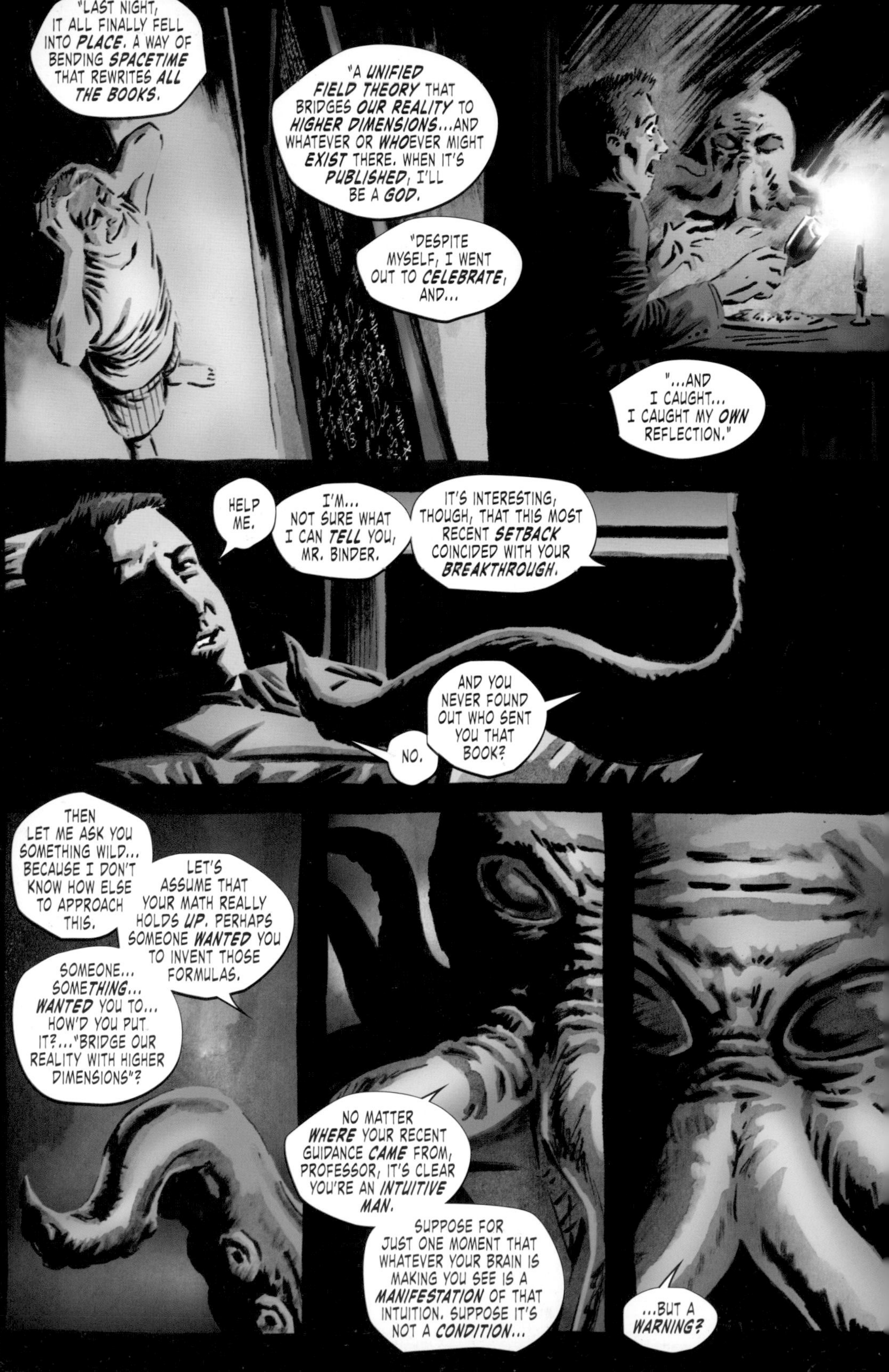
"LAST NIGHT, IT ALL FINALLY FELL INTO PLACE. A WAY OF BENDING SPACETIME THAT REWRITES ALL THE BOOKS.
"A UNIFIED FIELD THEORY THAT BRIDGES OUR REALITY TO HIGHER DIMENSIONS...AND WHATEVER OR WHOEVER MIGHT EXIST THERE. WHEN IT'S PUBLISHED, I'LL BE A GOD.
"DESPITE MYSELF, I WENT OUT TO CELEBRATE, AND...
"...AND I CAUGHT... I CAUGHT MY OWN REFLECTION."
HELP ME.
I'M... NOT SURE WHAT I CAN TELL YOU, MR. BINDER.
IT'S INTERESTING, THOUGH, THAT THIS MOST RECENT SETBACK COINCIDED WITH YOUR BREAKTHROUGH.
AND YOU NEVER FOUND OUT WHO SENT YOU THAT BOOK?
NO.
THEN LET ME ASK YOU SOMETHING WILD... BECAUSE I DON'T KNOW HOW ELSE TO APPROACH THIS.
LET'S ASSUME THAT YOUR MATH REALLY HOLDS UP. PERHAPS SOMEONE WANTED YOU TO INVENT THOSE FORMULAS.
SOMEONE... SOMETHING... WANTED YOU TO... HOW'D YOU PUT IT?..."BRIDGE OUR REALITY WITH HIGHER DIMENSIONS"?
NO MATTER WHERE YOUR RECENT GUIDANCE CAME FROM, PROFESSOR, IT'S CLEAR YOU'RE AN INTUITIVE MAN.
SUPPOSE FOR JUST ONE MOMENT THAT WHATEVER YOUR BRAIN IS MAKING YOU SEE IS A MANIFESTATION OF THAT INTUITION. SUPPOSE IT'S NOT A CONDITION...
...BUT A WARNING?

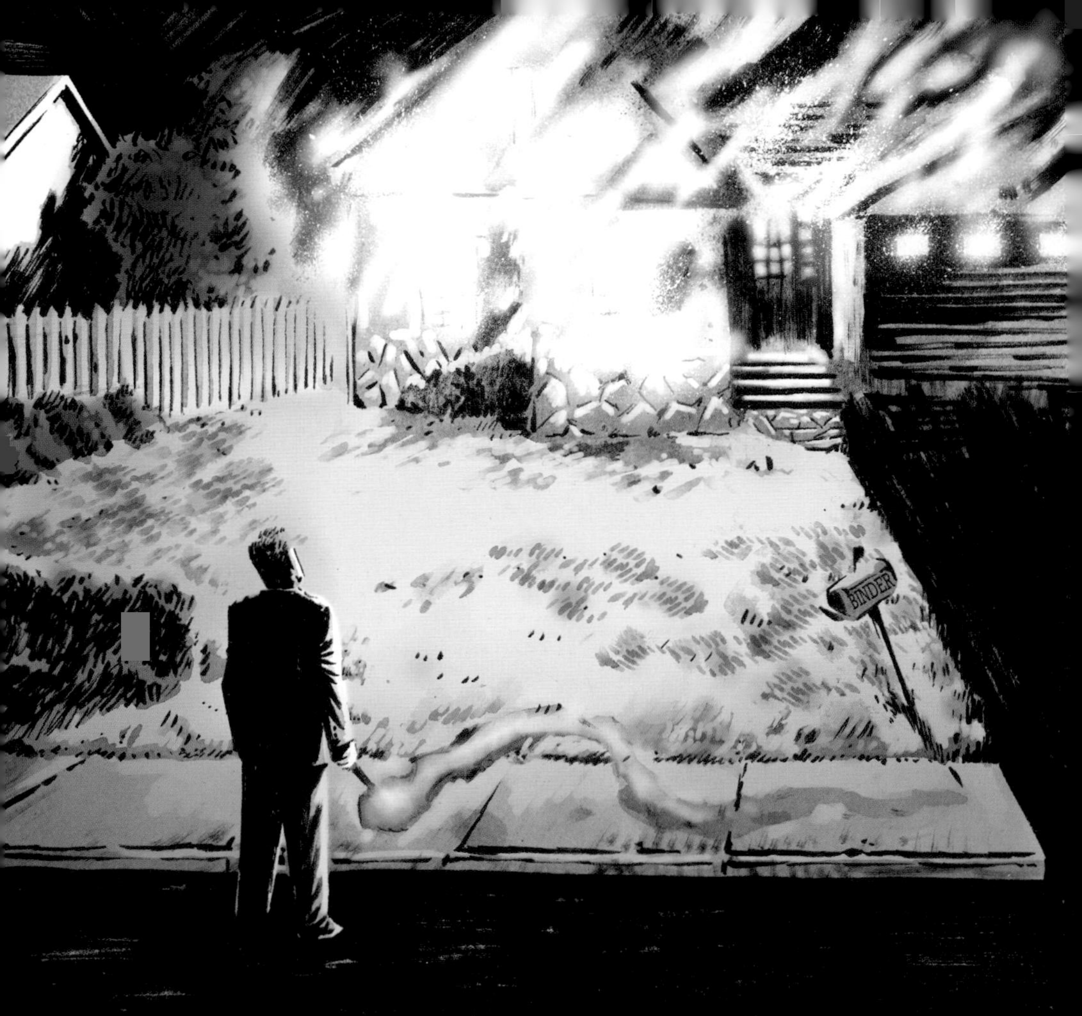
BINDER

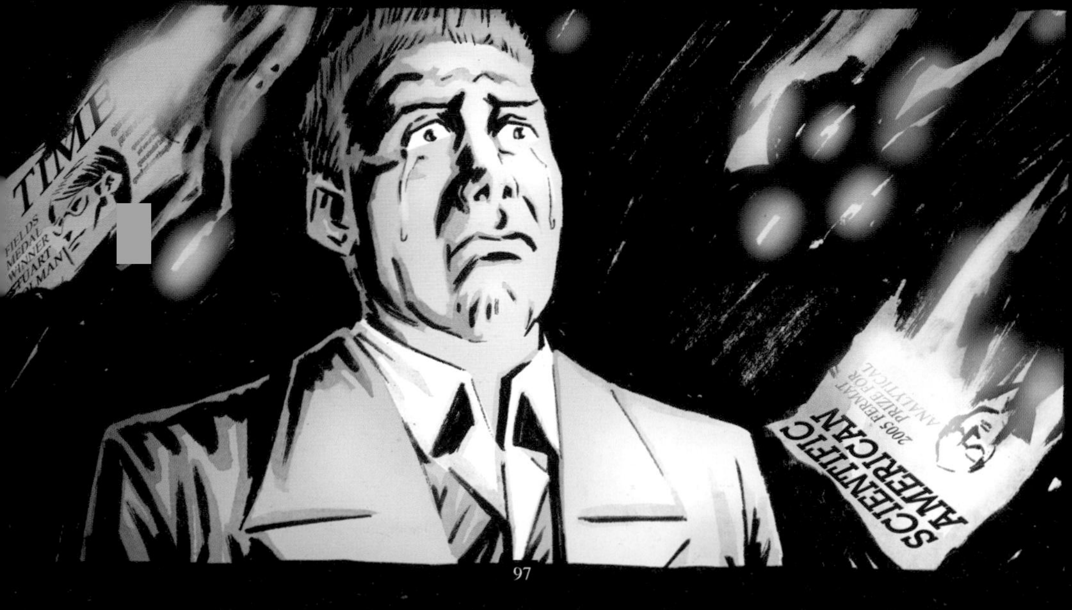
TIME
FIELDS
MEDAL
WINNER
SCIENTIFIC
AMERICAN
2005 FERMAT
PRIZE FOR
ANALYTICAL

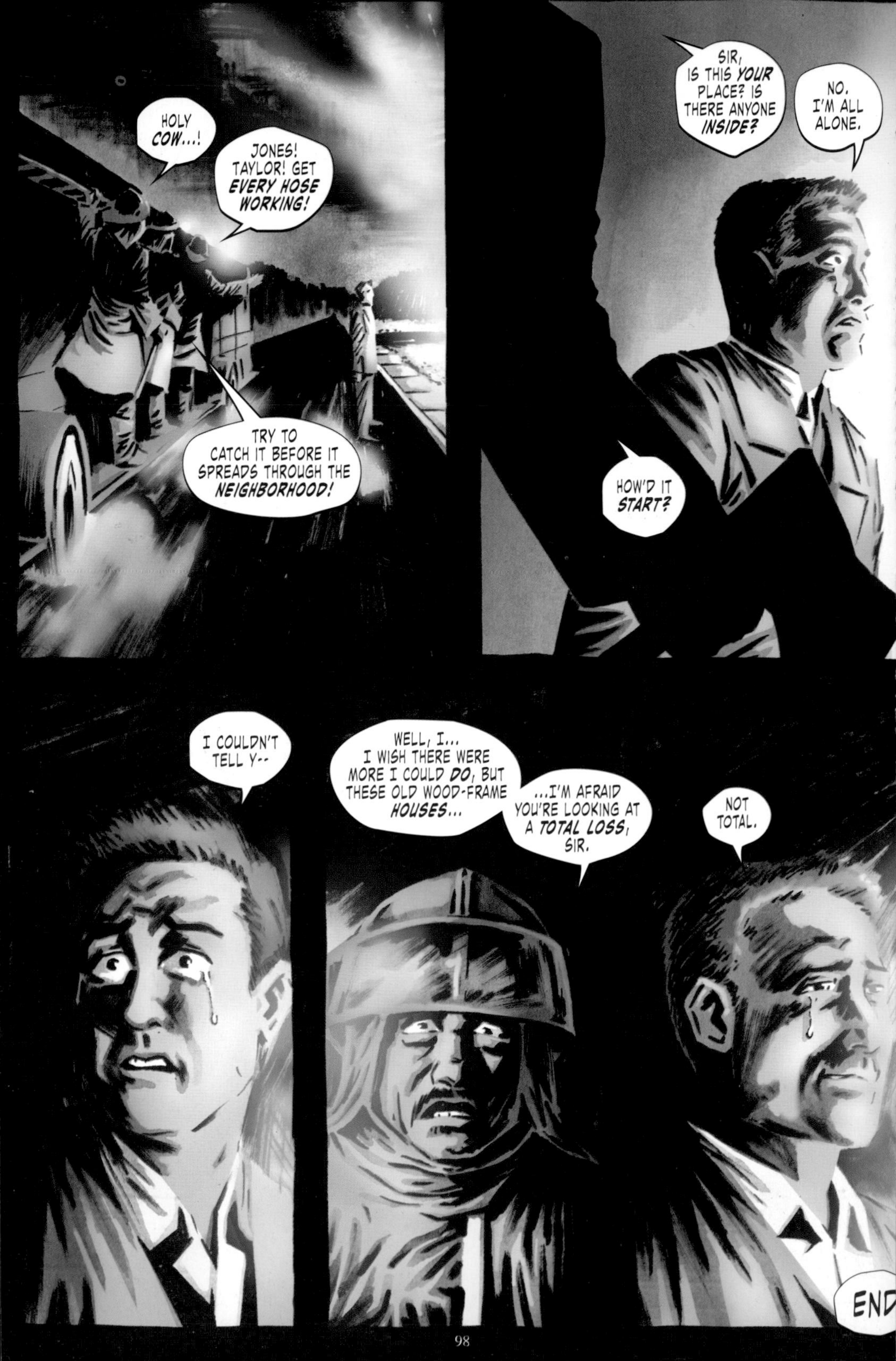
HOLY COW...!
JONES! TAYLOR! GET EVERY HOSE WORKING!
TRY TO CATCH IT BEFORE IT SPREADS THROUGH THE NEIGHBORHOOD!
SIR, IS THIS YOUR PLACE? IS THERE ANYONE INSIDE?
NO. I'M ALL ALONE.
HOW'D IT START?
I COULDN'T TELL Y--
WELL, I... I WISH THERE WERE MORE I COULD DO, BUT THESE OLD WOOD-FRAME HOUSES...
...I'M AFRAID YOU'RE LOOKING AT A TOTAL LOSS, SIR.
NOT TOTAL.
END

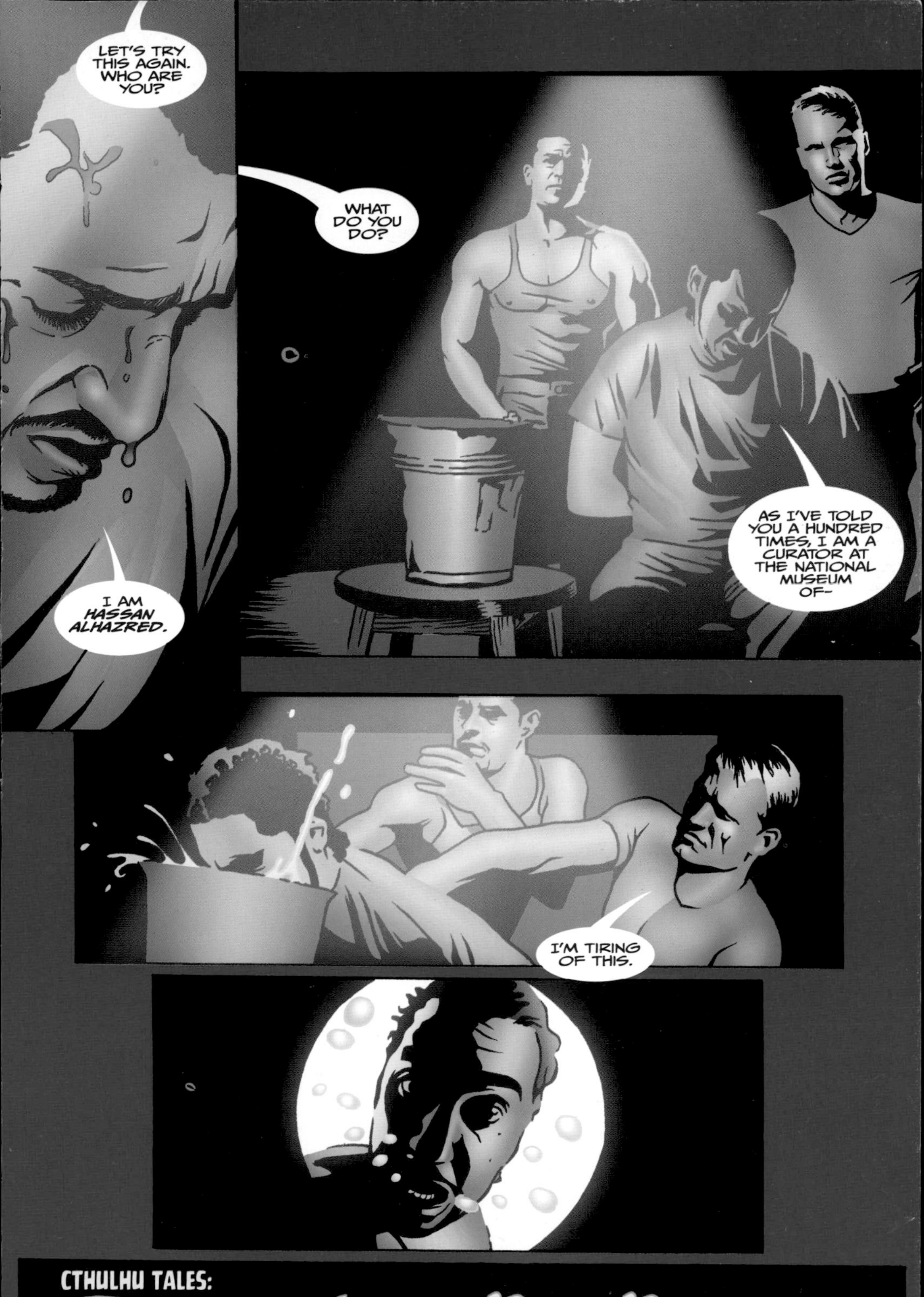
LET'S TRY THIS AGAIN. WHO ARE YOU?
I AM HASSAN ALHAZRED.
WHAT DO YOU DO?
AS I'VE TOLD YOU A HUNDRED TIMES, I AM A CURATOR AT THE NATIONAL MUSEUM OF-
I'M TIRING OF THIS.

CTHULHU TALES:

There Will Be Blood

WRITTEN BY MARK SABLE DRAWN BY SERGIO CARRERA COLORED BY ANDREW DALHOUSE LETTERED BY MARSHALL DILLON

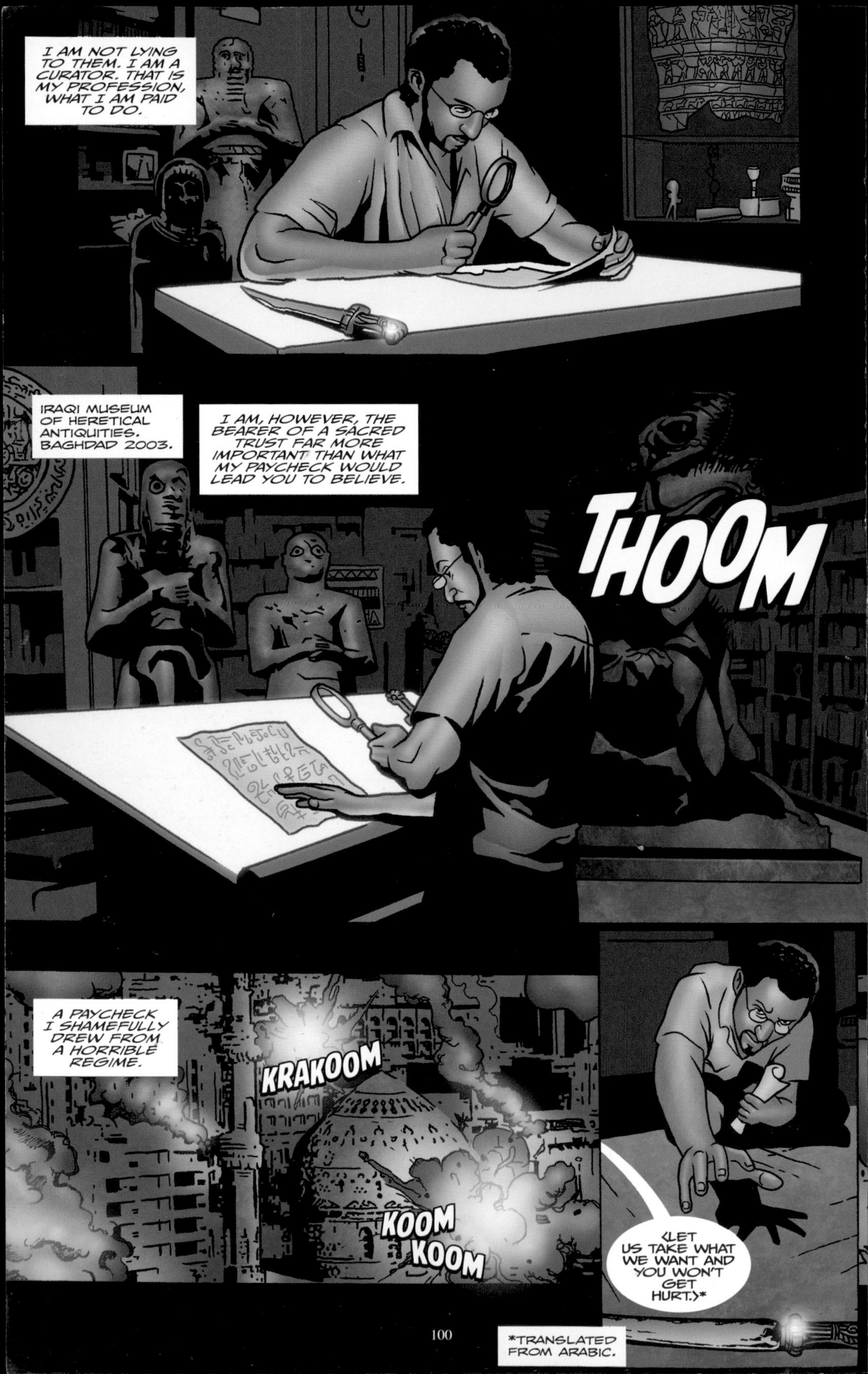
I AM NOT LYING TO THEM. I AM A CURATOR. THAT IS MY PROFESSION, WHAT I AM PAID TO DO.
IRAQI MUSEUM OF HERETICAL ANTIQUITIES. BAGHDAD 2003.
I AM, HOWEVER, THE BEARER OF A SACRED TRUST FAR MORE IMPORTANT THAN WHAT MY PAYCHECK WOULD LEAD YOU TO BELIEVE.
THOOM
A PAYCHECK I SHAMEFULLY DREW FROM A HORRIBLE REGIME.
KRAKOOM
KOOM KOOM
<LET US TAKE WHAT WE WANT AND YOU WON'T GET HURT.>*
*TRANSLATED FROM ARABIC.

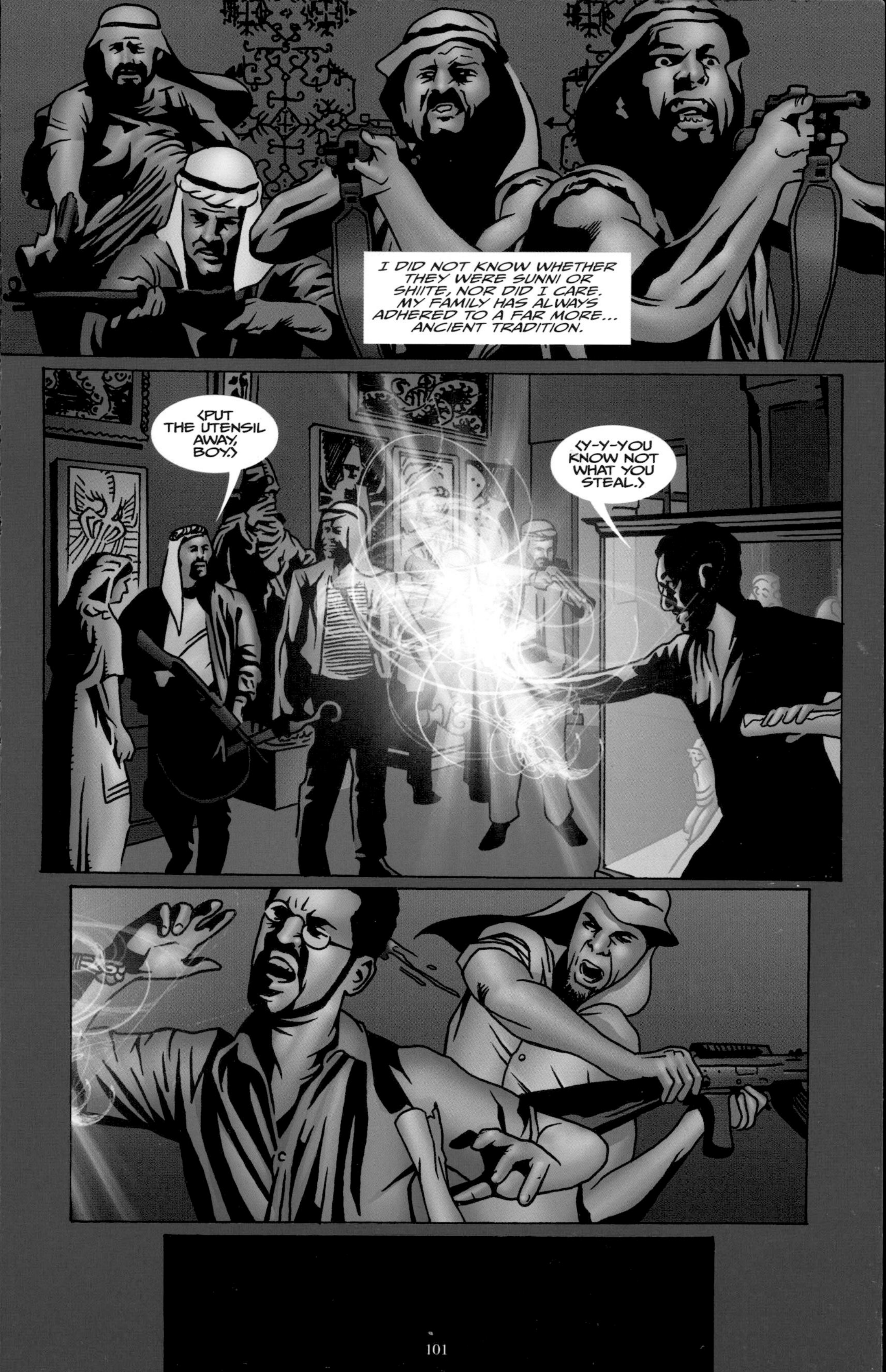
I DID NOT KNOW WHETHER THEY WERE SUNNI OR SHIITE, NOR DID I CARE. MY FAMILY HAS ALWAYS ADHERED TO A FAR MORE... ANCIENT TRADITION.
<PUT THE UTENSIL AWAY, BOY.>
<Y-Y-YOU KNOW NOT WHAT YOU STEAL.>

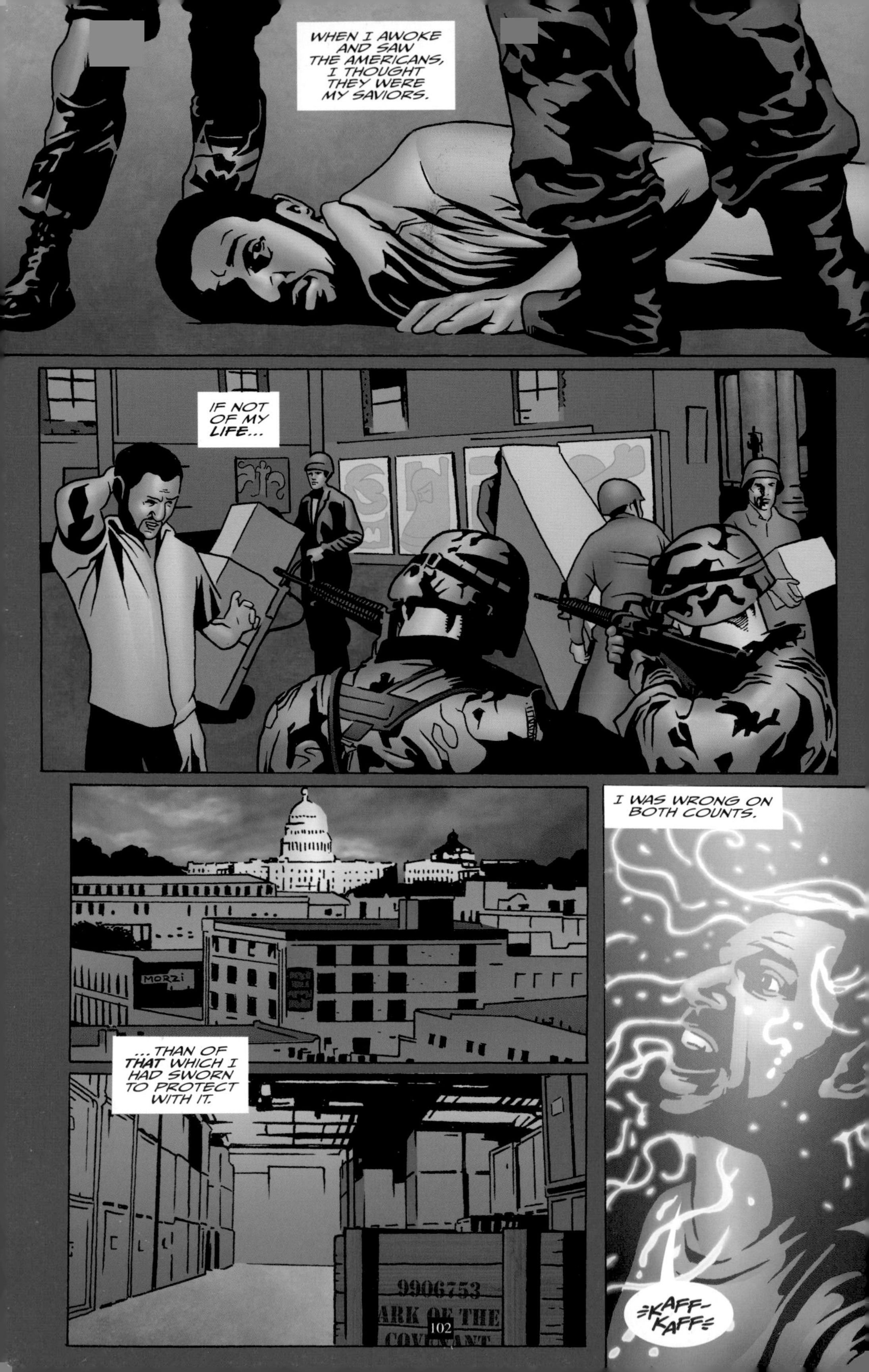
WHEN I AWOKE AND SAW THE AMERICANS, I THOUGHT THEY WERE MY SAVIORS.
IF NOT OF MY LIFE...
MORZI
...THAN OF THAT WHICH I HAD SWORN TO PROTECT WITH IT.
9906753
ARK OF THE
I WAS WRONG ON BOTH COUNTS.
KAFF- KAFF

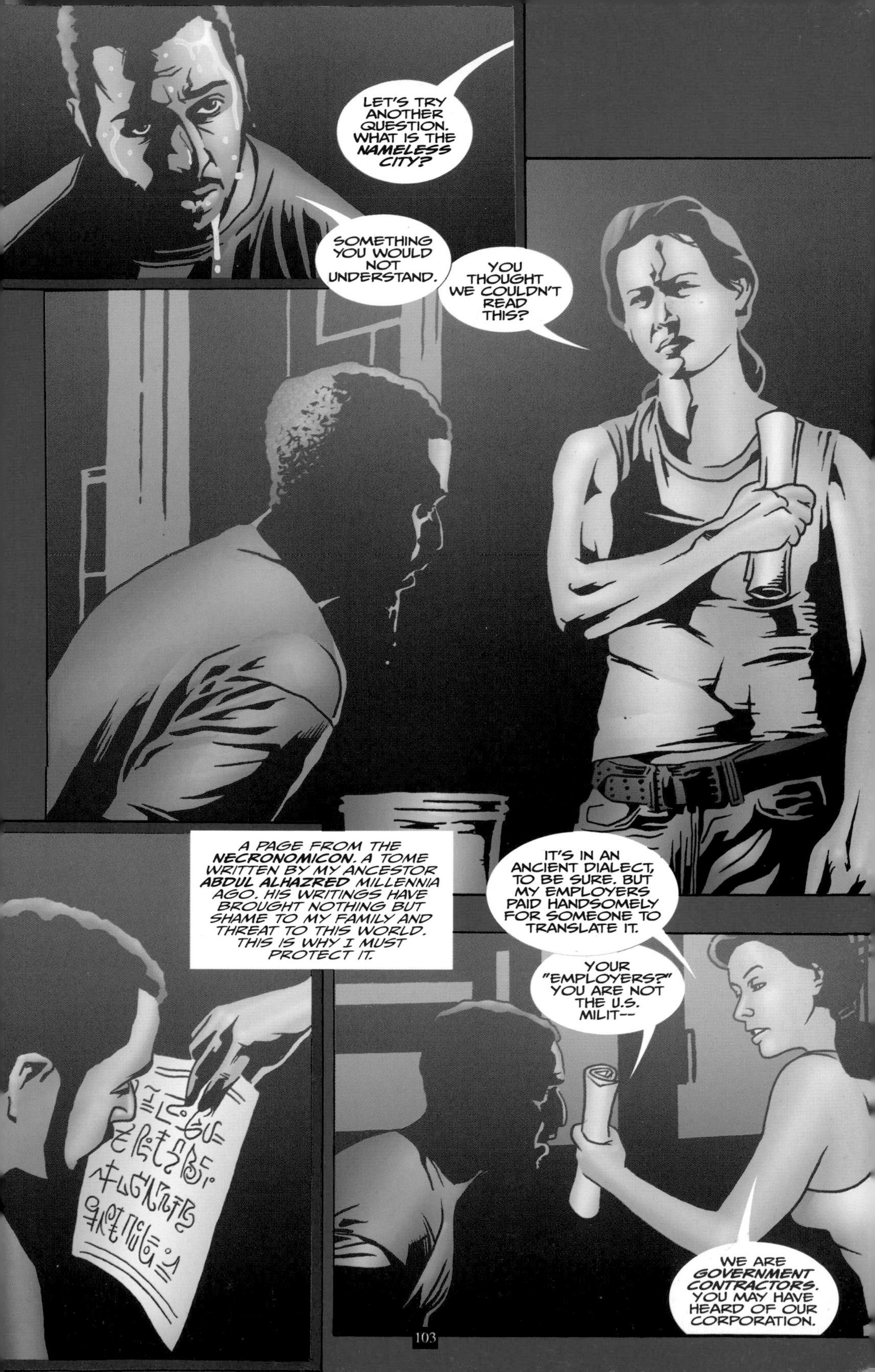
LET'S TRY ANOTHER QUESTION. WHAT IS THE NAMELESS CITY?
SOMETHING YOU WOULD NOT UNDERSTAND.
YOU THOUGHT WE COULDN'T READ THIS?
A PAGE FROM THE NECRONOMICON. A TOME WRITTEN BY MY ANCESTOR ABDUL ALHAZRED MILLENNIA AGO. HIS WRITINGS HAVE BROUGHT NOTHING BUT SHAME TO MY FAMILY AND THREAT TO THIS WORLD. THIS IS WHY I MUST PROTECT IT.
IT'S IN AN ANCIENT DIALECT, TO BE SURE. BUT MY EMPLOYERS PAID HANDSOMELY FOR SOMEONE TO TRANSLATE IT.
YOUR "EMPLOYERS?" YOU ARE NOT THE U.S. MILIT--
WE ARE GOVERNMENT CONTRACTORS. YOU MAY HAVE HEARD OF OUR CORPORATION.

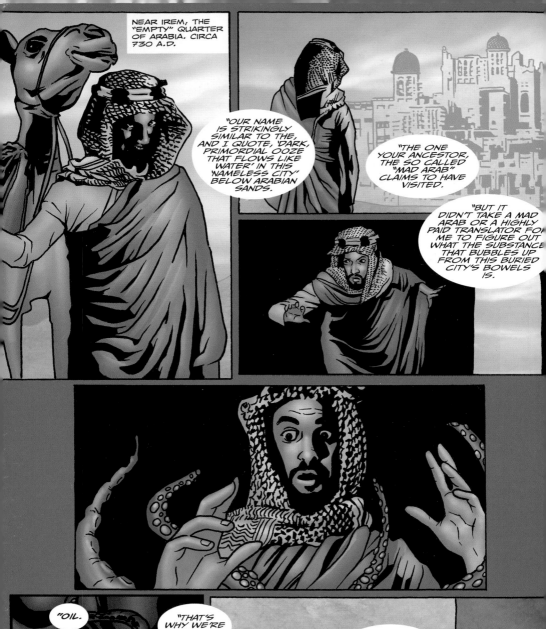

NEAR IREM, THE "EMPTY" QUARTER OF ARABIA. CIRCA 730 A.D.

"OUR NAME IS STRIKINGLY SIMILAR TO THE, AND I QUOTE, 'DARK, PRIMORDIAL OOZE THAT FLOWS LIKE WATER' IN THIS 'NAMELESS CITY' BELOW ARABIAN SANDS.

"THE ONE YOUR ANCESTOR, THE SO CALLED "MAD ARAB" CLAIMS TO HAVE VISITED.

"BUT IT DIDN'T TAKE A MAD ARAB OR A HIGHLY PAID TRANSLATOR FOR ME TO FIGURE OUT WHAT THE SUBSTANCE THAT BUBBLES UP FROM THIS BURIED CITY'S BOWELS IS.

"OIL.

"THAT'S WHY WE'RE HERE.

"AND YOU'VE GOT ONE MORE CHANCE TO TELL US WHERE IT IS."

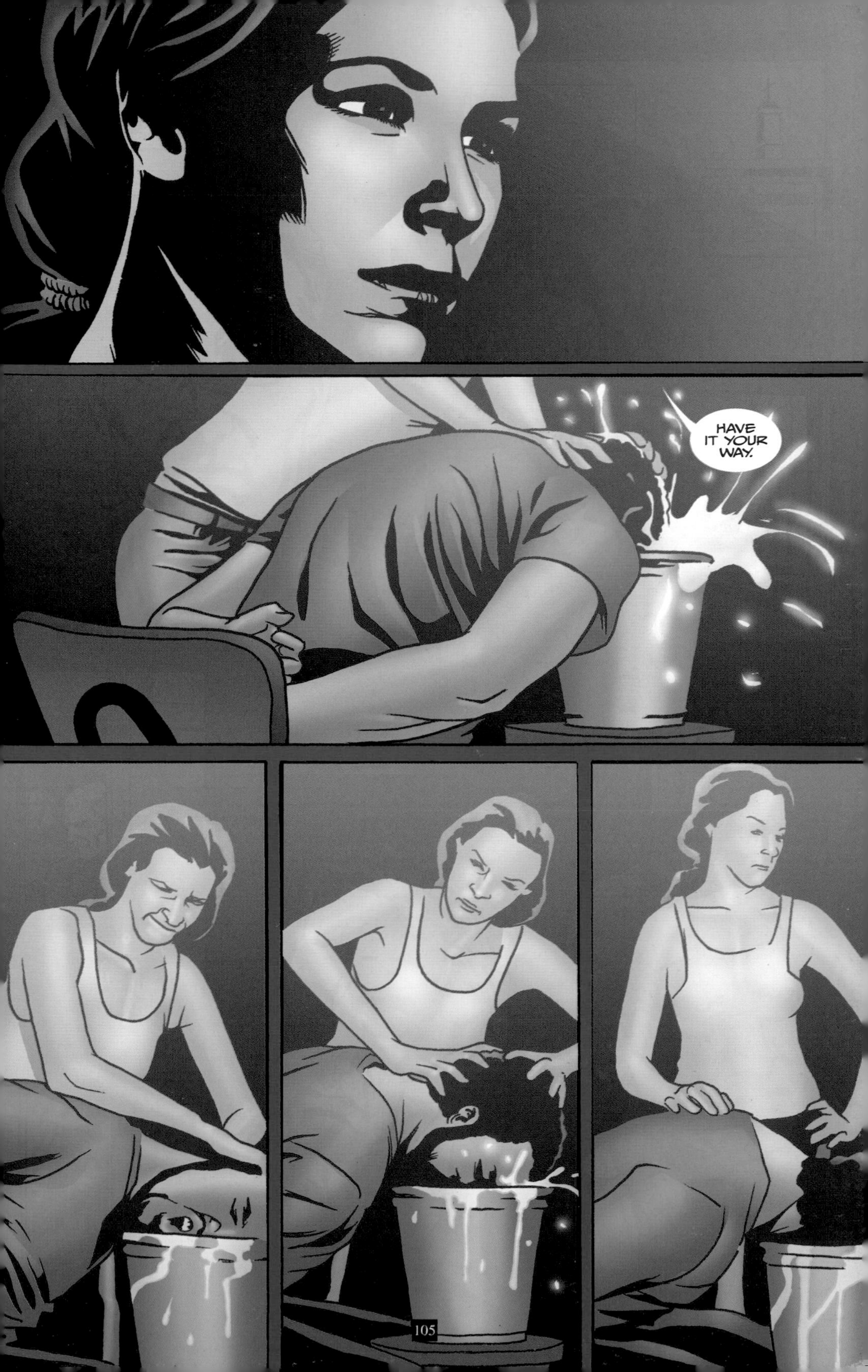
HAVE IT YOUR WAY.

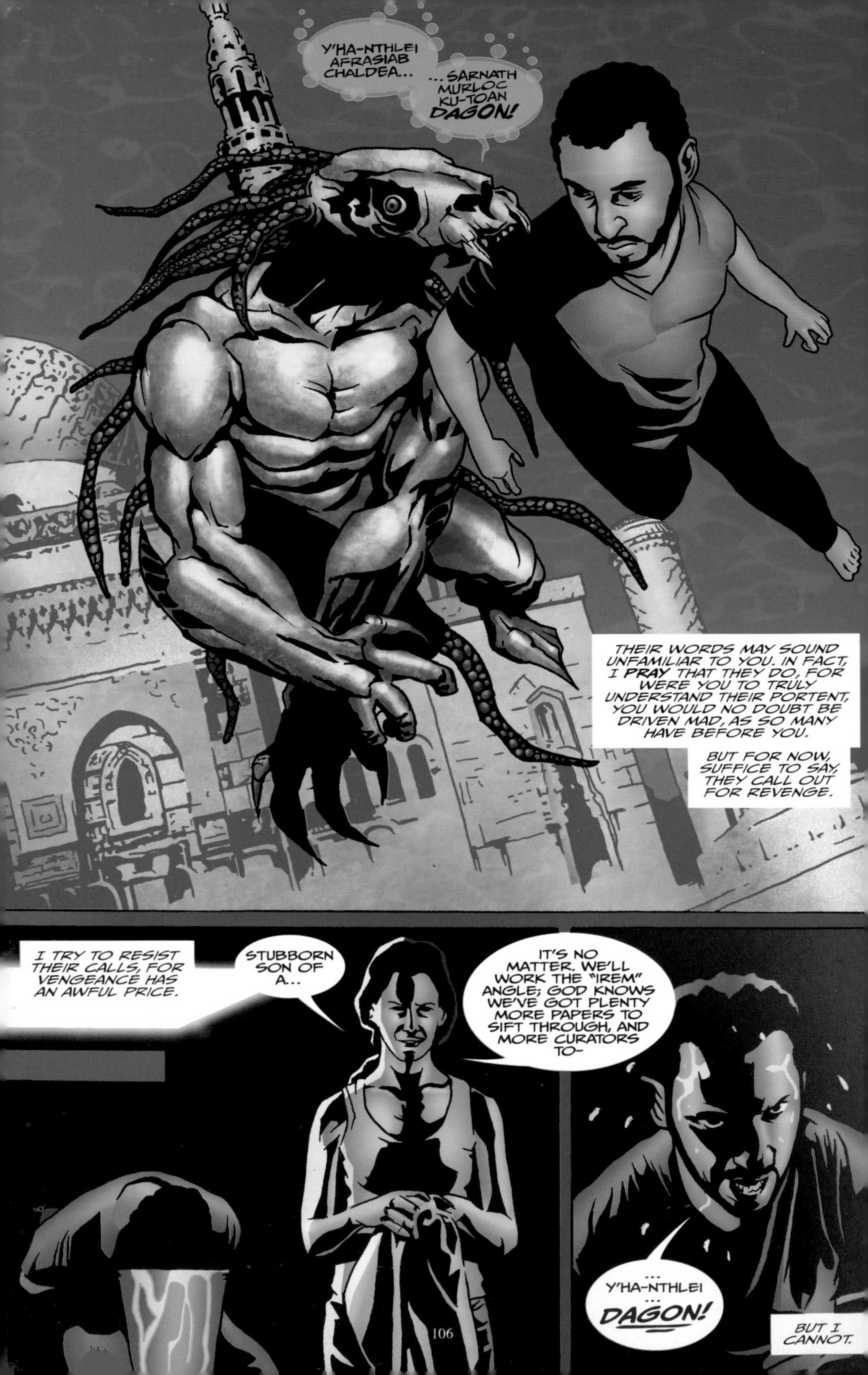
Y'HA-NTHLEI AFRASIAB CHALDEA...
...SARNATH MURLOC KU-TOAN DAGON!
THEIR WORDS MAY SOUND UNFAMILIAR TO YOU. IN FACT, I PRAY THAT THEY DO, FOR WERE YOU TO TRULY UNDERSTAND THEIR PORTENT, YOU WOULD NO DOUBT BE DRIVEN MAD, AS SO MANY HAVE BEFORE YOU.
BUT FOR NOW, SUFFICE TO SAY, THEY CALL OUT FOR REVENGE.
I TRY TO RESIST THEIR CALLS, FOR VENGEANCE HAS AN AWFUL PRICE.
STUBBORN SON OF A...
IT'S NO MATTER. WE'LL WORK THE "IREM" ANGLE; GOD KNOWS WE'VE GOT PLENTY MORE PAPERS TO SIFT THROUGH, AND MORE CURATORS TO-
... Y'HA-NTHLEI ... DAGON!
BUT I CANNOT.

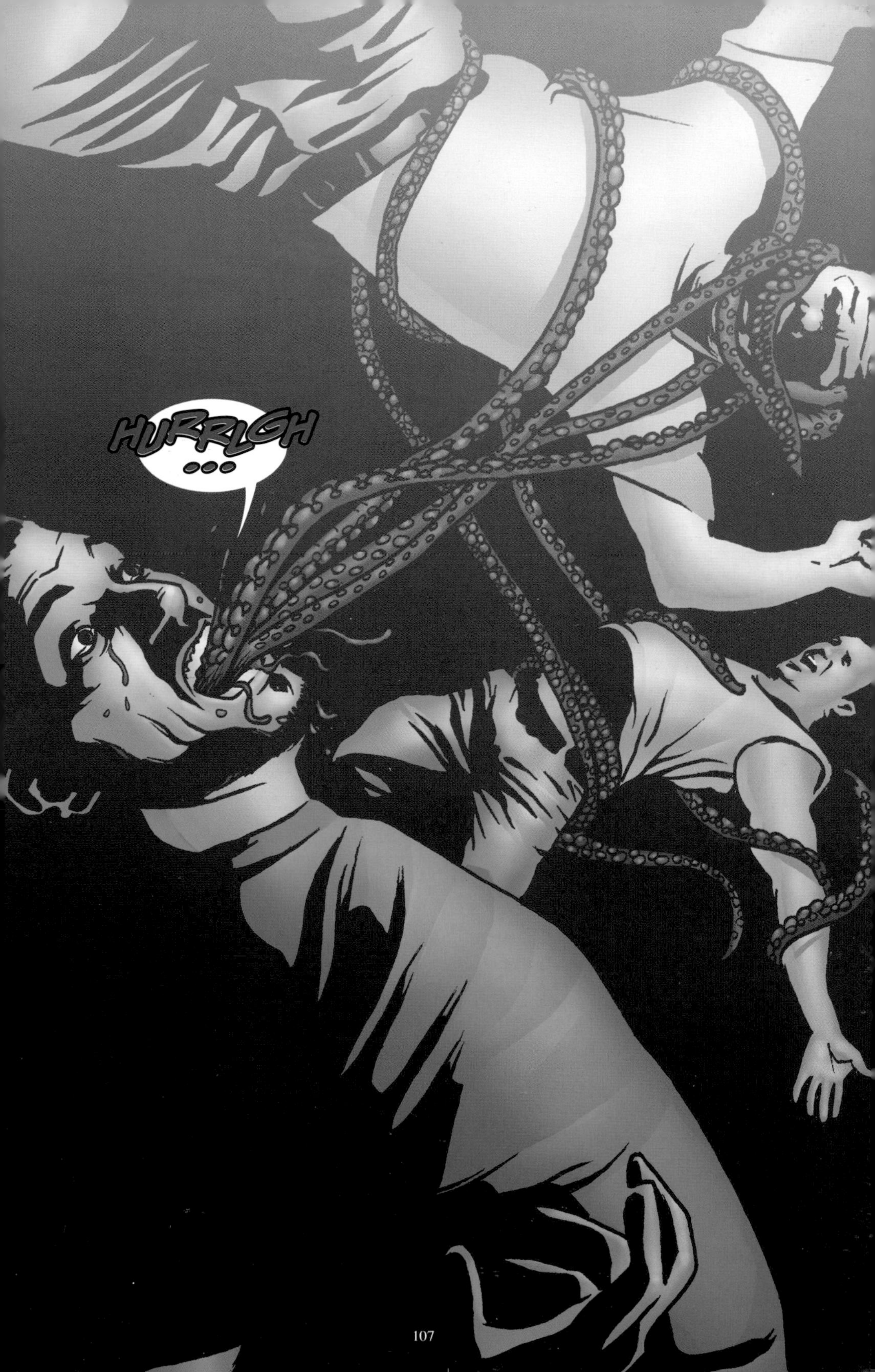
HURRLGH
...

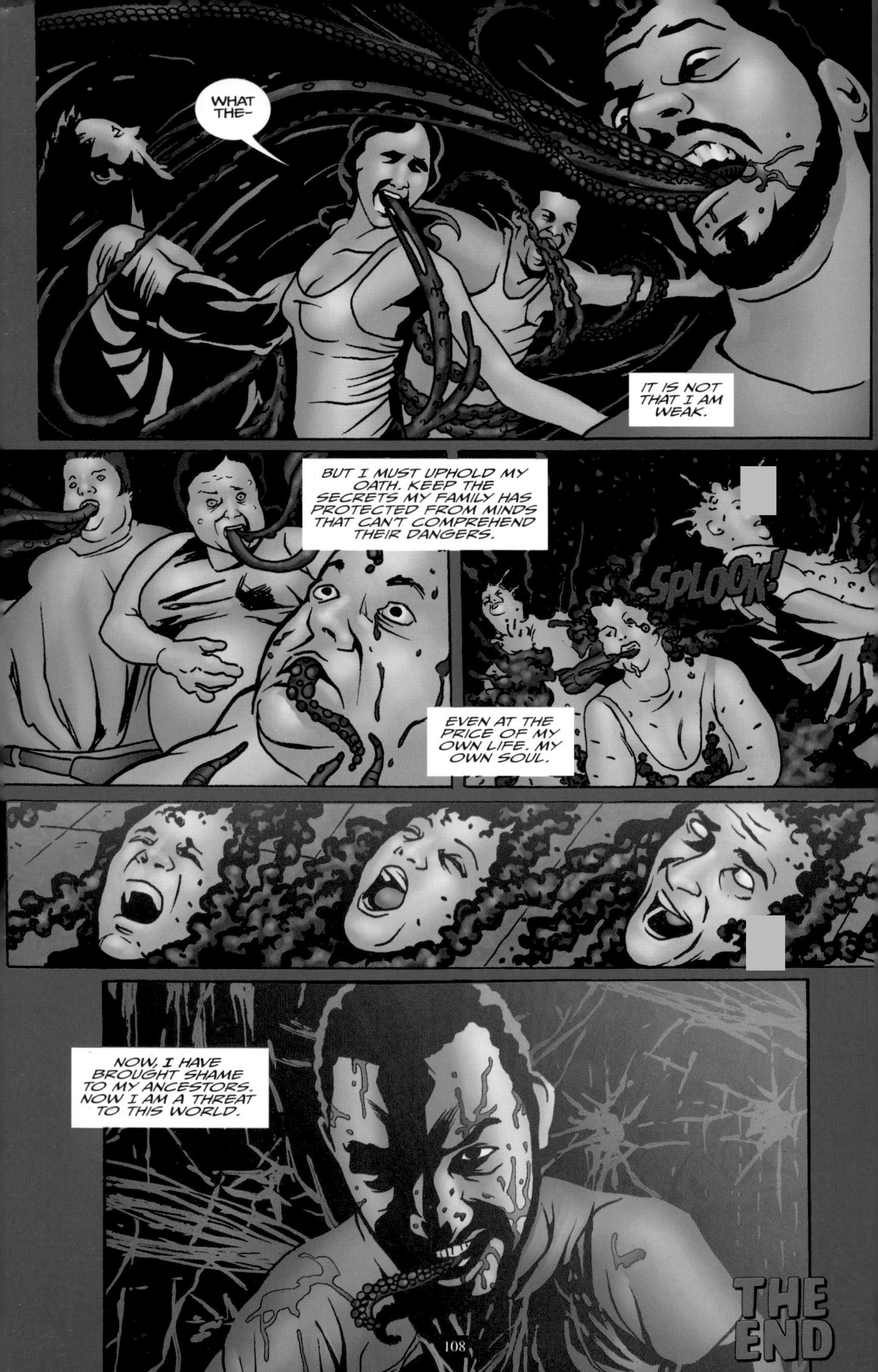
WHAT THE-
IT IS NOT THAT I AM WEAK.
BUT I MUST UPHOLD MY OATH. KEEP THE SECRETS MY FAMILY HAS PROTECTED FROM MINDS THAT CAN'T COMPREHEND THEIR DANGERS.
SPLOOK!
EVEN AT THE PRICE OF MY OWN LIFE. MY OWN SOUL.
NOW, I HAVE BROUGHT SHAME TO MY ANCESTORS. NOW I AM A THREAT TO THIS WORLD.
THE END

TRADE PAPERBACKS

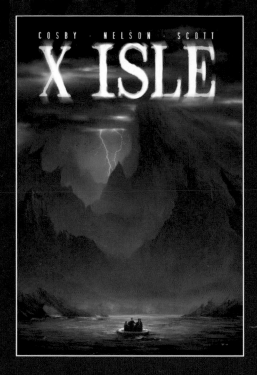

X ISLE

written by Andrew Cosby
and Michael Alan Nelson
drawn by Greg Scott
$14.99, full color, 128 pages

ISBN13: 978-1-934506-09-7

From EUREKA TV show creator Andrew Cosby and Michael Alan Nelson (Fall of Cthulhu, Second Wave) comes this tale of survival horror! A team of researchers drift on the ocean, lost, in their quest for an enigmatic island that's never been explored. Washing on its shores, they find a dense, terrifying jungle populated with animal and plant life that has evolved along a completely different path. What secret does this isle hold? Why are the life forms there so dangerous —and so alien? In the tradition of Alien and the recent horror-hit The Descent! Featuring art from Greg Scott (Gotham Central, Sword of Dracula).

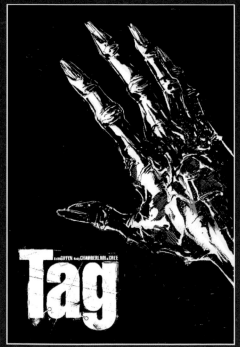

TAG
VOLUME 1

written Keith Giffen
drawn by Kody Chamberlain
and Chee
$14.99, full color, 128 pages

ISBN13: 978-1-934506-03-5

An average joe strolls down the street after a fight with his girlfriend when a random stranger TAGS him, handing off an ancient curse! He literally begins to die – and rot – seeing his body begin to decompose every day before his very eyes. Cursed, he must either surrender, or find the next victim to TAG... BONUS: Included in TPB form for the first time as an "extra" is Keith Giffen's "10" one-shot -- ten innocent people become unwilling contestants in a game of death. Given 10 bullets and a gun, it's kill or be killed as they're forced to hunt the other 10 contestants!

TRADE PAPERBACKS

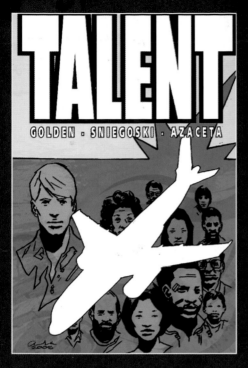

TALENT

written by Christopher Golden
and Tom Sniegoski
drawn by Paul Azaceta
$14.99, full color, 128 pages

ISBN13: 978-1-934506-05-9

The sold-out sensation is finally collected! Optioned in a five way studio bidding war by Universal Pictures, Talent tracks Nicholas Dane, miraculous sole survior of a plane crash. As mysterious men arrive to kill Dane, he discovers he can channel the talents of the victims of the crash! Discover why Ain't It Cool News said "Since the company's inception, Boom! has been creating quite a rumble in the comics world, but with Talent, they're definitely living up to their name. Highly recommended."

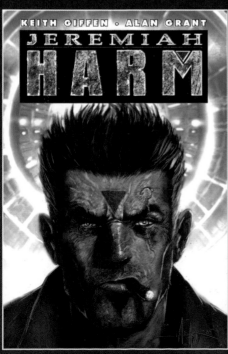

JEREMIAH HARM

written by Keith Giffen
and Alan Grant
drawn by Rael Lyra
and Rafael Albuquerque
$14.99, full color, 128 pages

ISBN13: 978-1-934506-12-7

From Keith Giffen (52, Annihilation) and Alan Grant (Batman, Lobo) comes this hard-hitting sci- fi series with a gritty tone and a brutal anti-hero as the lead! When three of the galaxy's most fearsome criminals escape confinement on a prison planet and wind up on Earth, the authorities have no choice but to free the most wanted man in the universe - Jeremiah Harm - to track these fugitives down and stop them. He doesn't love you, he doesn't want to be your friend, he isn't your super-hero - and God help you if you find yourself in Harm's way! Featuring art from Rael Lyra (Dragonlance: Legend of Huma) and Rafael Albuquerque (Blue Beetle).

BOOM! STUDIOS

WHAT'S THE BIG IDEA?
www.BOOM-STUDIOS.com

TRADE PAPERBACKS

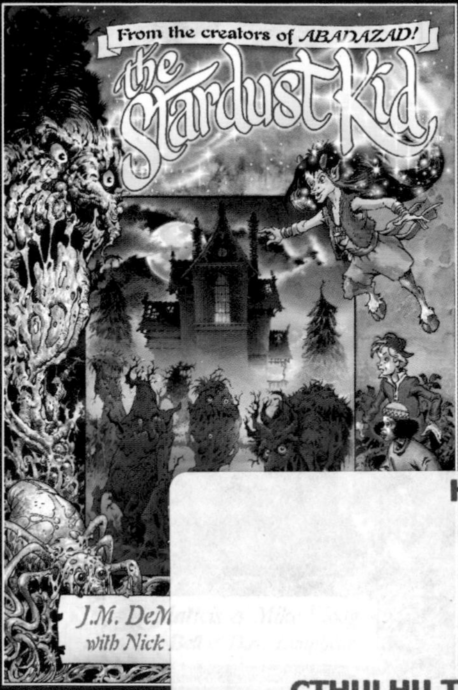
From the creators of ABADAZAD!
the Stardust Kid

STARDUST KID

written by J.M. DeMatteis
drawn by Mike Ploog
$14.99, full color, 128 pages

ISBN13: 978-1-934506-04-2

From the best-selling creative team behind Abadazad comes the collection of their conceptual sequel! Last night, when Cody DiMarco went to bed, life was the same as it's always been. This morning, when he woke up, the world he knew...was gone. A Magic older than Time. An ancient evil. And four children whose only chance to restore their families, and their world, is to solve the mystery of...The Stardust Kid. [illegible] old Cody DiMaro's best friend [illegible] Brightfield and Paul [illegible] human: He's the last of [illegible] t elemental beings [illegible] Time Before.

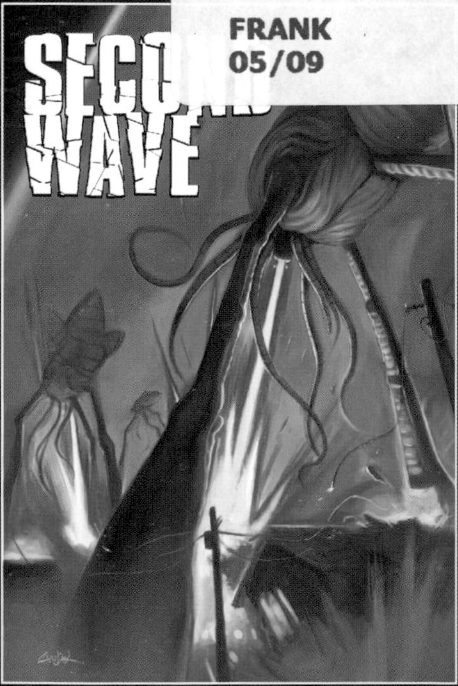
WAVE

SECOND WAVE

written by Michael Alan Nelson
drawn by Chee
$14.99, full color, 144 pages

ISBN13: 978-1-934506-06-6

Mankind held the first invasion back. But then the second wave came... Mitch was an ordinary man living an ordinary suburban life, but alien invaders took his home and his wife away. Now that they're back, how have they grown immune to mankind's defenses? And what key role does Mitch play in the invasion? What's his link to this extra-terrestrial threat? This edition collects issues 1 to 6 of the critically acclaimed series.